the great
potato
COOKBOOK

the great potato COOKBOOK

250 sensational recipes for
the world's favourite vegetable

Reader's Digest

The Great Potato Cookbook

Project Editor Janine Flew

Designer Melanie Young

Translator Christiane Myers

Nutritional analysis Jess Cox and Toni Gumley

Additional photography for this edition Andre Martin, stylist Gabrielle Wheatley

Proofreader Emma Hutchinson

Indexer Jo Rudd

Production Manager – Books Susan Maffucci

Senior Production Controller Monique Tesoriero

Editorial Project Manager General Books Deborah Nixon

READER'S DIGEST GENERAL BOOKS

Editorial Director Elaine Russell

Managing Editor Rosemary McDonald

Art Director Carole Orbell

We are interested in receiving your comments on the contents of this book. Write to: The Editor, General Books Editorial, Reader's Digest (Australia) Pty Limited, GPO Box 4353, Sydney, NSW 2001, or email us at bookeditors.au@readersdigest.com

PHOTOGRAPHY

All images are owned by Reader's Digest except for those on the following pages: 8 Stockfood; 10 Grossmann/Laif; 11 istockphoto; 13 Shutterstock; 14, 15, 16, 19 (bottom), 20 (top left) istockphoto; 21 (top right), 21, 21 (right), 21 (bottom left) Photo Alto; 22, 23 (top left), 23 (bottom right) istockphoto; 24, 25, 26, 27, 28, 29 Michael Brauner.

The Great Potato Cookbook is published by
Reader's Digest (Australia) Pty Limited
80 Bay Street, Ultimo NSW 2007
www.readersdigest.com.au, www.readersdigest.co.nz
www.readersdigest.co.za, www.rd.com, www.rd.ca,
www.readersdigest.co.uk

First published 2009
Copyright © Reader's Digest (Australia) Pty Limited 2009
Copyright © Reader's Digest Association Far East
Limited 2009 Philippines
Copyright © Reader's Digest Association Far East
Limited 2009
This book was adapted from *Köstliche Kartoffeln*
published by Reader's Digest, Germany, 2007

National Library of Australia Cataloguing-in-Publication data:

The great potato cookbook: 250 sensational recipes for the world's favourite vegetable.
Includes index.
ISBN 978 1 921569 13 5 (hbk.)
ISBN 978 1 921569 35 7 (pbk.)
1. Cookery (Potatoes). I. Reader's Digest (Australia)
641.6521

Prepress by Sinnott Bros, Sydney
Printed and bound by Leo Paper Products, China

The world's favourite vegetable

Long maligned as a fattening food, the potato has made a full comeback as a tasty source of essential nutrients. Originating in the Andes, it has spread around the globe and been so enthusiastically adopted by nearly every cuisine that it's hard to imagine our diet without it.

This book includes the most scrumptious recipes from all over the world as well as classic favourites such as gnocchi, roast potatoes and mashed potatoes in all their delicious variety. Delve into the history of the spud, learn more about its numerous varieties and use our handy tips and tricks to make preparation easier.

Contents

all about potatoes 8

The history of the potato 10 * A closer look at potatoes 14

Types of potatoes 16 * Choosing and storing potatoes 22

Basic cooking methods 24

snacks and starters 30

soups 54

salads 78

meat and poultry 110

fish and seafood 194

vegetarian 234

side dishes 268

baking and desserts 296

index 314

All about potatoes

Potatoes have a fascinating history. The food of peasants, royalty and just about everyone in between, they are plentiful, inexpensive and easy to prepare. This section tells you about the types and varieties of potatoes and demonstrates the basic ways of cooking them.

The history of the potato

South America is the home of the potato. It took until the 16th century to make its way to other parts of the world and even longer to establish itself there as a staple food. It was initially regarded with suspicion (with some justification; it is related to deadly nightshade) and considered unwholesome, if not downright poisonous.

Ten thousand years of potatoes

Originating in the Andes, the potato is a highland plant by nature. As long ago as 8000 BC, Andean people were already growing and cultivating potatoes in elevations of up to 4000 metres (13,000 feet). The harsh conditions in the high, rugged mountains promoted communities based on, among other things, mutual assistance and support in agriculture. These settlements eventually developed into the powerful Inca empire.

The Inca quickly became experts in plant cultivation and grew more than forty agricultural crops. The altitudes at which they lived were too high to allow corn – a traditional South American staple – to be planted, so they began intensive cultivation of potatoes, which became their primary food.

By using elaborate irrigation systems, the Inca converted dry terraces into fertile potato fields, where they grew about 250 different varieties of potato. To compensate for crop failures, they developed a form of dry potatoes, *chuños* (see box opposite), which can be regarded as the very first potato product.

Potatoes are still cultivated at great elevations and remain the primary staple of Andean people today.

The people of the Andes still rely heavily on the potato. Dozens of varieties are often grown in the same valley.

The potato leaves home

Various legends surround the arrival of potatoes in Europe, but the historical record is unclear. One fact is certain: the Inca empire, centre of potato cultivation, was conquered by Francisco Pizarro between 1531 and 1533. Gold and silver were Pizarro's targets, and the value of the potato plant went unrecognised – it was nothing more than an exotic souvenir.

There are two likely routes for the potato's spread. The first led from Peru to Spain via the Colombian port of Cartagena in the mid-16th century. It is said that in 1566, Philip II of Spain sent a small packet of potatoes to the ailing Pope Pius IV, along with best wishes for his recovery. After that, the potato is believed to have reached the French court and Belgium.

Arrival in the British Isles The second route could have led from South America to the British Isles. The English have always regarded Sir Francis Drake as the first importer of potatoes, although there is no proof of this. Drake writes of potatoes in his journal in November 1578, but potatoes had already been mentioned in a 1573 list of purchases by the Hospital de la Sangre in Seville, Spain, and were supposedly already growing all around the city in Drake's day. There is no way of knowing whether the 'potatoes' that Drake served to Queen Elizabeth I during the legendary banquet aboard his ship on 4 April 1581 were only sweet potatoes, or whether potatoes were part of the plunder from one of the Spanish ships he captured during his circumnavigation of the globe.

In England, the explorer Sir Francis Drake has always been regarded as the first importer of potatoes, but this is almost certainly a myth.

Legend says that Drake presented a sack of potatoes to Sir Walter Raleigh, who planted them on his country estate in Ireland. Once again, there is no proof for this. It is more likely that an unknown Spanish sailor was responsible for introducing the potato to the country that was the first to embrace it. Another theory is that potatoes washed ashore from wrecked Spanish Armada ships in 1588, and then began growing there.

Chuños: freeze-dried potatoes

The process for making *chuños* was developed centuries ago by the Incas, who bartered *chuños* for other foodstuffs, such as corn and manioc, as well as crockery. Storehouses were built everywhere to stockpile *chuños* supplies for times of need.

To this day, traditional methods are used to dehydrate and preserve a large part of the Andean potato harvest. The potatoes are washed after collection, spread over the fields and left overnight. The cell walls are ruptured by frost, and, on thawing in the sun the next day, the potatoes become as soft as rubber. Whole families stomp barefoot over the potatoes until they have expressed about 70 per cent of the water, which then evaporates in the dry air.

After about five days and nights, the potatoes can be peeled. They are then dried in the sun again for several more days. During that time, they are turned regularly. Altogether, the production of *chuños* takes about two weeks.

Chuños last for years and are far more nutritious than cooked potatoes. Freeze-drying gives them a particularly high level of starch, about 70 per cent. Their protein content is more concentrated and they possess higher levels of calcium, phosphorus and iron.

Myth and superstition

In Europe, from the Middle Ages up to the 17th century, it was widely believed that there was a link – mostly beneficial, but sometimes harmful – between certain medical conditions or parts of the body and plants that somehow resembled them.

Walnuts, for example, were considered to be linked to the human head; the hard outer shell resembled the skull and the wrinkled nut the brain, therefore eating walnuts was thought to be good for the brain. Similarly, because of the potato's shape and habits of growth, people assumed that it had certain qualities. Suspicion first attached to the way that potatoes grew – from tubers rather than seeds, like every other edible plant. Also, unlike today's potatoes, the first to arrive in Europe were often misshaped, with finger-like protruberances. They also displayed various colours; black, purple, red and even a ghostly white. People saw a resemblance between potatoes and the deformed limbs of lepers and concluded that eating potatoes could cause leprosy (Hansen's disease). Also, until the late 19th century, eating potatoes was thought to cause idleness.

The potato was also damned by association. It belongs to the *Solanaceae* family, edible members of which include the capsicum (bell pepper), eggplant (aubergine) and tomato. More sinister relatives include deadly nightshade (a poison), henbane (a hallucinogen that is toxic to animals and which was used in 'magic potions') and mandrake, one of the most potent plants of folklore and myth. The potato plant looked similar to the mandrake; rather than mistake one for the other, people tended to avoid both.

Difficult beginnings

It is likely that Spanish seamen first realised what a valuable food potatoes are, since eating potatoes prevented them from falling ill with scurvy during the long journey from the New World to the Old World. Scurvy, a disease long dreaded by seafarers, is caused by an extreme lack of vitamin C that leads to various illnesses, poor wound healing and, in extreme cases, death. For a long time, these sailors were among the few who thought potatoes of any nutritional value.

A slow spread The potato's progress throughout Europe cannot be traced any more exactly than its migration from South America. One problem is that writers of the time used the word 'potato' for both the common potato and the sweet potato, so it is often unclear which is being referred to in accounts from the time. What is certain is that potatoes caught the interest of curious botanists and royal courts, and from there found their way into various European university and pleasure gardens. At first, they were grown only as decorative plants, for their pretty star-shaped flowers.

Disadvantages There were various reasons for the potato's slow adoption into the European diet. The potatoes grown in those days still had high levels of the poisonous compound solanine; when eaten, they often caused nausea and diarrhoea. Also, yields during the early days of potato cultivation were small, because the plants imported from South America were used to less than fourteen hours of light per day. Growing under European conditions, they developed masses of leaves and flowers but did not produce tubers – and then only very small ones – until very late in the season, once the short days to which they were adapted arrived.

Harvesting and storage also had a significant impact. Both the young plants and the tubers are susceptible to frost, which made cultivation and storage difficult. In addition, compared with grain-cutting, harvesting the tubers was hard work. There was also the simple fact that people generally prefer to eat what they are used to, and in Europe, that was grain; a diet in which potatoes replaced grain was unthinkable.

Finally, the church had a significant influence. Since the potato was reputed to have an aphrodisiac effect, and moreover was not mentioned in the Bible, clergymen considered it a devil's fruit.

Gradual acceptance

The fact that potatoes had been eaten for millennia in the Andes initially did nothing to persuade Europeans to consume them. It took the desperation caused by famines to turn potatoes into an important staple.

Famines were a constant threat in Europe for many centuries. As well as those caused by drought and flood, ongoing wars played a part; marauding armies stripped the land of food, leaving nothing for the locals. In addition, crop yields then were much lower than those from today's scientifically modified food plants.

Agricultural factors Changes in farming practices also contributed. Over the years, land formerly used to produce food was used to provide raw materials for manufacturing industries. Many grain fields became sheep pastures for the production of wool − a more lucrative crop than grain. Tenant farmers were forced off their lands and no longer had the means to feed themselves. The price of wheat rose beyond the reach of many people. The results were widespread famines − and the eventual acceptance of the potato.

Once they came to be grown and eaten, however, the advantages of potatoes as a crop soon became apparent. Compared with grain, potatoes contibuted about four times as many calories for the same amount of land. Half a hectare (just over an acre) of potatoes

plus the milk of one cow could feed a whole family for a year. And, although potatoes were more laborious to plant and harvest than grain, they were otherwise easy to grow, and required little equipment; in the worst circumstances, the crop could be harvested using bare hands. Potatoes would also grow in wet and cold conditions that grain could not tolerate.

At first the potato found favour only with the poor, but eventually the middle classes and the aristocracy adopted it too, and the potato's popularity was assured.

The Great Hunger

Potatoes and famine had a tragic association in 19th century Europe. Monoculture, potato blight (a fungal disease) and bad weather caused potato-crop failures and resulting famines. Of all the countries affected, none suffered as badly as Ireland.

Potatoes seemed a blessing for the Irish, since grain growing was difficult on the wet island and people frequently went hungry. Potato cultivation changed their lives fundamentally. The brown tubers thrived in the moist Irish climate, and the nation in turn thrived on potatoes; no other people consumed as many. From the 17th to the 19th century, Ireland's population grew from 3 million to 9 million.

Ireland's population increase suddenly became a disadvantage, however, when the potato blight spread through Europe in 1845-46. This was not Ireland's first potato famine − there had been others in the 18th and earlier 19th century − but it was certainly the worst. The potatoes rotted in the ground, and as this was the only crop that most families grew, the results were devastating. There was not enough food for everyone, and within a short time, an estimated one million Irish died of starvation or disease. Those who could afford to do so emigrated, and the population plummeted from 6.5 million in 1841 to 4.4 million twenty years later. It continued to fall until the late 1960s. The most recent figure, from the 2006 census, was 4.2 million − still well short of pre-famine levels.

A closer look at potatoes

Potatoes are tubers, or swollen plant stems, from which the plant reproduces. They belong to a curious family of plants with edible, narcotic and poisonous members. Once considered a botanical curiosity but shunned as a food, the potato is now valued for its nutritional qualities as well as its flavour.

A botanical view

Like tomatoes, eggplant (aubergines), capsicums (bell peppers) and tobacco, the potato belongs to the *Solanaceae*, or nightshade family. Only the tubers are edible. The plant's above-ground parts contain various toxic alkaloids, including solanine. Solanine also develops in the tubers if they are exposed to sunlight. Any green parts of potatoes should be cut away and discarded, as it is these that contain solanine. It is thought that this compound, being bitter as well as poisonous, is the potato's natural defence against predation.

Potatoes are usually grown from seed potatoes; these chunks of potato, each bearing an 'eye', are placed in the soil in spring. The eyes then sprout and produce potato plants. Runners develop below ground, swell at the tips and grow into tubers. Depending on the variety, five to sixty new potatoes are generated. (Some varieties also produce tomato-like fruits, which are inedible.) This is an asexual form of reproduction; the young potatoes are clones of the seed potatoes from which they grow.

Nutritional value

On their own, potatoes are an extremely healthful and well-balanced food. They are a valuable source of carbohydrates, protein, vitamin C and minerals.

A medium-sized boiled potato (about 150 g/5 oz), with or without skin, contains just 440 kilojoules (105 calories). Per 100 g (3½ oz), a potato provides 15 grams (½ oz) of carbohydrates in the form of starch, almost half the body's daily requirement of vitamin C, and practically no fat. Although the potato's protein content is low by weight, it is a very

high-quality protein, containing essential amino acids that the body cannot produce itself but must get through food. On top of that, potatoes contain B-group vitamins and minerals such as potassium, phosphorus and magnesium. They also provide small amounts of the trace elements copper and fluorine.

The potato's reputation as a fattening food is an unfair one, based more on the fats in which it is often cooked than on the potato alone. Cooked without oil, potatoes are a far healthier source of kilojoules (calories) than the sugars and fats with which many modern diets are saturated.

A microscopic threat

The fungal disease *Phytophthora infestans*, cause of the late blight that has devastasted potato plantings throughout history, is still a threat; blight ruined the crop in Papua New Guinea in 2003. New strains develop constantly. Due to the plant's susceptibility to this and other diseases and pests, resilient new varieties have to be bred continually to suit respective climates and uses. There are about 5000 different varieties of potato worldwide, including a genetically modified version developed by the Monsanto Corporation.

Potato blight is spread via airborne spores. Since the late 19th century, Bordeaux Mixture (a preparation of copper sulphate, quicklime and water) has been used to treat fungal diseases in various plants, including grapevines and potatoes. In the early 1980s, however, a whole new population of blight emerged – not just a new strain. This was resistant to both Bordeaux Mixture and other, more modern, fungicides. Globally, more than US$2 billion is spent annually in controlling blight; the disease has turned potatoes into the world's most chemically dependent crop.

Breeding a better potato

Like all modern crops, the potato is subject to constant research and modification. This has two basic aims: to promote the potato among people in developing countries who might otherwise face starvation, and to exploit its commercial potential in wealthier countries.

Selective breeding aims to enhance a plant's advantageous qualities, such as yield, and minimise its undesirable features, such as proneness to disease. In addition, agronomists try to improve potato crops through more effective crop management. The 19th century saw much interest in potato breeding. In the United States, an amateur botanist called Luther Burbank conducted experiments that eventually resulted in the most famous of all American potatoes, the russet burbank – better known as the Idaho potato, after the state in which most of the crop is grown.

New frontiers

Journeying from South America to Europe and then back again to North America, Africa, Australasia and Asia, the potato has now established itself across the planet. Potatoes today are big business. They are the world's fourth most important food crop (after corn, wheat and rice) and the global crop is worth about US$100 billion per year.

Europe and North America are no longer the potato's stronghold. In 2005, potato production in the developing world exceeded that of the developed world for the first time. In 2007, the word's largest producer of potatoes was China, with 72 million tonnes (80 million tons), followed by Russia, India and the USA. Also in the top ten were Ukraine, Poland, Germany, Belarus, The Netherlands and France. Between 2002 and 2007, potato consumption in China rose by more than 40 per cent, compared with 2.5 per cent for the rest of the world. China is the world's leading consumer of potatoes overall, but not per capita: that honour belongs to Eastern European nations, with Belarus at 180 kg (397 lb) per capita, Kyrgyzstan (143 kg/ 315 lb) and Ukraine (136 kg/300 lb).

Types of potatoes

Potatoes can be new or old, waxy, floury or all-purpose. It's important to choose the right type of potato for the cooking method you intend to use. Of the many varieties of potatoes, only a comparatively small number are grown commercially.

New or old?

Whether a potato is 'new' or 'old' has nothing to do with its variety, but depends simply on when it is harvested. New potatoes are harvested when they are still a little immature. They have an intense, fresh potato flavour, and delicate, waxy skins. The label 'new' may sometimes be misleadingly given to small washed potatoes from a regular crop. True new potatoes are dug while the top of the plant is still green. They are small, varying from about the size of plums down to that of marbles.

Unlike other potatoes, new potatoes do not store well and should be eaten within a week of purchase. To emphasise their fresh flavour, they are best cooked simply. They are particularly good boiled or steamed, perhaps with a little butter or sour cream and some snipped chives or other herbs.

'Old' potatoes are those left in the ground to mature before harvesting. They keep well – for up to three months in the right conditions. During storage, the starch in potatoes slowly converts to sugar, so old potatoes will be sweeter than new.

Waxy or floury?

The range of potatoes on offer at even a small supermarket can be quite bewildering to the consumer. Basically, potatoes are either waxy or floury, and it is these qualities that determine their suitability for different cooking methods. Different types may have either white, cream, yellow or blue/purple flesh, and cream, brown, pink, red or purple skins.

Waxy potatoes are also called salad potatoes; they comprise new potatoes and most red or fingerling varieties. They have a low starch content and tend to hold their shape when boiled and fried, so they are great for chips (fries), salads and boiling or steaming whole. They can also be roasted, although they won't be as light and fluffy inside as old potatoes. Waxy potatoes are not suitable for mashing as they will produce a wet, gluey mash.

Floury potatoes have a particularly high starch content, which makes them appear 'dry' after cooking. These tend to fall apart if boiled; they are excellent for mashing, roasting and baking in their jackets, but not for boiling or steaming whole, or for chips (fries).

There are also various varieties of 'all-purpose' potatoes, which, as the name suggests, will give good results with all cooking methods.

The older potatoes are, the drier and more floury they become. Such potatoes are excellent for baking, and have a lovely fluffy interior once cooked.

The best varieties for...

Baking Atlantic, coliban, goldrush, king edward, long white, maris piper, norgold, russet (Idaho)

Boiling Atlantic, bintje, king edward, kipfler, nicola, pink fir apple, russet (Idaho), sebago

Chips (fries) Atlantic, estima, kennebec, norland, maris peer, maris piper, russet (Idaho), santé

Mashing Caribe, coliban, congo, estima, king edward, norkotah, pontiac, sebago

Potato salads Bintje, charlotte, international kidney, kipfler, nicola, patrone, pink fir apple, pontiac

Roasting Bintje, charlotte, coliban, king edward, kipfler, maris piper, nicola, pontiac

All-rounders Coliban, desiree, katahdin, kennebec, king edward, maris piper

Waxy varieties

Waxy potatoes (also known as boiling potatoes) have a lower starch content than floury (baking) potatoes and tend to keep their shape when cooked. They are good for boiling, frying and salads, but do not mash as well as floury potatoes. Some also bake and roast well. Most new potatoes, or those with yellow flesh or red skins, are waxy.

Bintje
Shape Oval
Skin Pale yellow
Flesh Pale yellow
Uses Excellent for salads, boiling, microwaving and roasting; good for frying; can be mashed and roasted

Kipfler
Shape Finger
Skin Golden
Flesh Yellow
Uses Excellent for salads, boiling and roasting; good for microwaving; can be mashed
Not recommended for Frying

Kipfler

Maris bard
Shape Oval to oblong
Skin Smooth, white
Flesh White
Uses Excellent for boiling, steaming, chips (fries), and as new potatoes
Not recommended for Roasting

Nicola

Nicola
Shape Long oval
Skin Yellow
Flesh Pale yellow
Uses Excellent for salads and gnocchi; good for boiling and roasting; can be fried
Not recommended for Mashing and microwaving

Pink fir apple
Shape Elongated
Skin Pink to red
Flesh Pale yellow
Uses Excellent for boiling and salads
Not recommended for Mashing

Pontiac
Shape Round to oval
Skin Smooth, pink to red
Flesh White, waxy
Uses Excellent for boiling, mashing and microwaving; good for salads and roasting. Red Pontiac is a related variety and can be cooked in the same ways
Not recommended for Frying

Other waxy types

Charlotte Long oval shape; white skin, pale yellow flesh; good for roasting, boiling and salads

Fingerling salad Finger-shaped heirloom variety with buff-yellow skin and yellow flesh. Good in salads and for boiling and steaming

International kidney Sometimes known as Jersey royal. Kidney shaped; pale yellow skin and flesh; excellent boiled or in salads

La ratte Finger-shaped; yellow skin, deep yellow flesh; nutty flavour; excellent for salads, boiling and steaming

Maris peer Oval shape; cream skin and flesh; good for salads, wedges, chips (fries) and boiling

Nadine Oval shape; cream skin and flesh; good for wedges, roasting, boiling, mashing

Patrone Oval shape; pale yellow skin and flesh; excellent for salads, steaming and boiling; can be fried; not recommended for mashing or microwaving

Pentland javelin Round to oval shape; white skin; cream flesh; good for salads, mashing, boiling and roasting

Rocket Round to oval shape; white skin and flesh; good for boiling, baking, new potatoes

Yellow finn Round shape; deep yellow skin; yellow flesh; good for boiling, salads and jacket potatoes. Yukon Gold is a good substitute

Floury varieties

Floury potatoes (also called baking or roasting potatoes) have a higher starch content than waxy (boiling) potatoes. They are the best type to use for jacket potatoes and for light, fluffy mashed potatoes. Some varieties can also be fried. Many floury types tend to break up if boiled, so they are not the best choice for salads.

Atlantic
Shape Round to oval
Skin White
Flesh White
Uses The best variety for chips (fries) and crisps (potato chips), it is used by commercial crisp producers; good for boiling and jacket potatoes
Not recommended for Salads and roasting

Coliban

Coliban
Shape Round
Skin Cream
Flesh White
Uses Good for microwaving, mashing, jacket potatoes, steaming and roasting
Not recommended for Frying, boiling, salads

Golden wonder
Shape Long oval
Skin Cream
Flesh Pale yellow
Uses Excellent for jacket potatoes; good for boiling and roasting

King edward
Shape Oval to long
Skin White and pink
Flesh Cream
Uses A British classic. Excellent for jacket potatoes, roasting and gnocchi; good for boiling and mashing; can be fried
Not recommended for Microwaving

Romano
Shape Round
Skin Red
Flesh Cream
Uses Excellent for boiling, mashing, roasting and jacket potatoes; has a dry, firm texture when cooked

Russet (Idaho)
Shape Long oval to slightly flattened
Skin Brown
Flesh White
Uses North America's favourite potato. Excellent for jacket potatoes and chips (fries); good for boiling

Russet (Idaho)

Other floury types

Agria Oval shape; yellow skin and flesh; good for jacket potatoes, boiling and frying

Estima Oval shape; cream skin; yellow flesh; good for jacket potatoes, mashing, chips (fries)

Goldrush Oblong shape; dark brown russeted skin; white flesh; excellent for baking, boiling and mashing, good for chips (fries)

Marfona Oval shape; cream skin; pale yellow flesh; excellent for jacket potatoes; good for wedges and boiling

Nooksack Oblong to long shape, flattened; brown skin, white flesh; good for boiling, baking, chips (fries), crisps (potato chips); used for commercial frozen chips (fries)

Norgold Oblong shape; brown skin; white flesh; good for baking and boiling; not suited to frying

Norkotah Oblong to long shape; brown skin; white flesh; good for mashing and jacket potatoes; good for frying only when newly harvested

Ranger Long, slightly flattened; brown skin, white flesh; good for jacket potatoes and chips (fries)

Red rascal Round to flat shape; red skin, white flesh; a New Zealand variety, excellent for jacket potatoes, roasting and mashing; good for chips (fries)

Santé Round shape; light yellow flesh and skin; excellent for chips (fries) and wedges; good for boiling, roasting and mashing

All-purpose varieties

Many of the potatoes sold in supermarkets are all-purpose varieties. If you're in doubt about what potatoes to buy, these all-rounders are a safe bet. They come in all flesh and skin colours from white to purple. Their texture tends to be halfway between waxy and floury, and they give good results with most cooking methods.

Desiree

Desiree
Shape Oval to long
Skin Pink to red
Flesh Pale yellow
Uses The world's favourite red potato, and probably the best all-rounder. Good for boiling, salads, roasting, jacket potatoes, mashing, chips (fries), sliced potato dishes

Katahdin
Shape Round to oval
Skin Buff
Flesh White
Uses Boiling, jacket potatoes, chips (fries) and crisps (potato chips)

Kennebec
Shape Round to slightly oval
Skin Creamy buff
Flesh White
Uses Excellent for chips (fries) and crisps (potato chips); good for boiling, mashing, jacket potatoes and roasting; can be used for salads and microwaving

Long white
Shape Long oval
Skin Buff
Flesh White
Uses Excellent for jacket potatoes and chips (fries). Also known as California long white

Sebago
Shape Round to oval
Skin Ivory-yellow
Flesh White
Uses Excellent for boiling, mashing, microwaving; good for salads, jacket potatoes, roasting, chips (fries) and crisps (potato chips)

Sebago

Toolangi delight
Shape Round
Skin Purple
Flesh White
Uses Excellent for salads, boiling, mashing, jacket potatoes, roasting and gnocchi; can also be used for chips (fries)
Not recommended for Microwaving

Other all-purpose types

Aldo Round to oval; white skin, cream flesh; a good all-rounder

Caribe Oblong shape; smooth red-purple skin, sometimes with tan patches; excellent for mashing and chips (fries); good for boiling, fair for baking

Congo Finger-shaped; dark purple skin and flesh; excellent for mashing; colour fades when boiled. Also known by other names, including British Columbia Blue and McIntosh Black

Maris piper Oval shape; white to yellow skin; cream flesh; very reliable, and good for jacket potatoes, wedges, chips (fries), boiling, roasting and mashing

Mondial Oblong shape; smooth, buff skin; pale yellow flesh; excellent for mashing

Nadine Oval shape; cream skin and flesh; good for mashing, wedges, boiling and roasting

Norland Oval shape; red skin, white flesh; excellent for boiling, chips (fries) and jacket potatoes

Pentland dell Long oval shape; white skin, white flesh; a versatile variety, but particularly good for chips (fries), especially long or large chips

Rooster Oval shape; red skin, white flesh; excellent for mashed potatoes, chips (fries); good for roasting and jacket potatoes

Superior Oval to oblong shape; buff skin, white flesh; excellent for chips (fries); good for boiling, baking and crisps (potato chips)

Sweet potatoes

Sweet potatoes belong to the *Convulvulaceae* family and are not true potatoes at all. They are available all year round but are most abundant, and at their best, from early autumn through winter. They can be cooked in the same ways as potatoes, although some varieties cook to a dryish texture, while others are more moist.

Sweet potato

When the sweet potato plant is one year old, some of its roots begin to store starch and sugar, swell and eventually grow into tubers. Sweet potatoes can be white, orange, red, gold or purple. White-skinned sweet potatoes have white flesh, while purple sweet potatoes have creamy-white flesh. The pink-skinned type with moist, deep orange flesh is also known as kumera or kumara.

Sweet potatoes can be baked, mashed, cooked as crisps (potato chips) or patties, or used in salads. Baking or grilling (broiling) enhances their sweetness.

Choose firm tubers with smooth, dry skin and no cracks or blemishes. Check the tips; this is where decay usually begins. They will last for up to a week at room temperature, or up to a month in a cool, dark place. They should not be refrigerated, but can be frozen for longer storage.

Other tubers

The following tubers are not related to the potato, but they caused a lot of confusion on their discovery due to their very similar flavour and sometimes striking resemblance to the 'original' from South America.

Jerusalem artichoke

Yam

Manioc

Jerusalem artichoke

This tuber is a member of the sunflower family and got its name because the scaliness of its skin resembles the leaves of artichokes. To avoid confusion with globe artichokes, it is sometimes called the sunchoke or sunroot.

The tubers are harvested after the first frost – the longer they are exposed to the cold, the stronger their flavour (which is similar to that of potatoes). They are good baked or puréed for soups, but tend to become mushy if boiled. It's best to steam them if you want to preserve their texture.

Yam

There are about 600 different types of yam, all members of the *Dioscoreaceae* family of vines. The tubers can be up to 2.5 metres (8 feet) long and weigh 70 kg (150 lb). Yams are mealy and have a high starch content and a neutral to pleasantly sweetish flavour. Some types of sweet potato are often erroneously called 'yams'.

Manioc

A member of the spurge family, manioc can only be eaten after cooking. Tubers may reach 50 cm (20 inches) and 5 kg (11 lb).

Choosing and storing potatoes

The range of potatoes on offer can be quite bewildering to the consumer. To get the most out of your potatoes, it's a good idea to become familiar with the three basic types and what cooking methods they are best suited to. Also, whether you are buying potatoes to use right away or to keep, they need to be stored correctly.

The right potato for every purpose

Before you start shopping, you should decide how you are going to prepare the potatoes, since not all varieties are suitable for every cooking method.

Boiling (waxy) varieties such as bintje, kipfler and nicola are great for potato salads, gratins and potato röstis as well as for pan-frying, boiling and boiling in their jackets. If you want to use the potatoes for a soup or stew, you should choose waxy potatoes or all-purpose varieties such as desiree or sebago. Mashed potatoes, dumplings, gnocchi and oven-baked potatoes require a roasting (floury) variety such as king edward, coliban or russet. If you're buying an unfamiliar variety, it's best to buy a small quantity at first to see if they are suited to the intended cooking method.

Since most mature potatoes store well, they are available all year. The variety of potato will not always be stated on the packaging or on signage in the store.

What to look for when buying

Only buy undamaged, clean and dry potatoes. The tubers should be firm and well formed, still hold a slightly earthy scent and have an even colour. They should have no cuts, cracks, bruises or sprouted eyes. Reject any soft potatoes or those that are oozing liquid. Packaged potatoes in plastic bags that are already sweating or even sprouting should be rejected. Avoid potatoes with green spots, as this indicates the presence of a toxin called solanine, which develops when potatoes are exposed to light.

Varieties differ quite widely from country to country, but if you are buying from a supermarket, most of the potatoes are likely to be general-purpose types. If in doubt as to which variety to choose, these are the type to opt for. Some potatoes are sold already scrubbed; these do not store as well as potatoes that have a light coating of earth still on them.

Put to the test

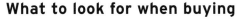

If you are buying potatoes in bulk for storage, you should first test a small sample for its quality. If you can, cut through two or three potatoes to examine if they are also flawless on the inside. In addition, do the following quality checks, if possible:
- Rubbing test: halve a potato and rub the cut faces against each other. They should stick together and a light froth should appear around the rim.
- Pressure test: halve a potato and squeeze it tightly in your hand. No liquid should emerge from it.
- Cooking test: boil a potato. It should cook evenly throughout.
- Visual test: check that none of the potatoes have any green areas or signs of sprouting.

Correct storage

If storing a small quantity of potatoes, wrap them in paper or netting, or store them in baskets or hessian bags (burlap sacks). Keep them in a cool, dry place with good air circulation. Potatoes should never be refrigerated. Under ideal conditions, potatoes will keep for several months. New potatoes are the exception; they should be eaten within a week of purchase.

Larger quantities of potatoes should be stored in a dry, well-aired, dark room with a temperature of 4-8°C (39-46°F). Potatoes are best placed in slatted crates to allow air to circulate. As potatoes are sensitive to pressure and impact, avoid simply pouring them into the crate; instead, let them roll in gently. Each layer of potatoes should not exceed 40 cm (16 inches) in height.

Averting storage problems

In poor storage conditions, the following can occur:
- If the storage room's temperature is too low, the potato starch transforms into sugar and the potatoes will develop a sweetish flavour.
- If the temperature is too high, the potatoes' water content evaporates. They will shrivel and lose weight. They will also start to sprout, which depletes their valuable nutrients.
- Light causes potatoes both to sprout and to produce the toxin solanine, which causes the potatoes to become green. Any green spots must be cut out before cooking.
- Potatoes also sprout when apples are stored near them. This is because the apples release ethylene, a gas that promotes sprouting.
- Potatoes grow mouldy in damp conditions.

Organic potatoes: natural and tasty

Over the last years, demand for organic produce – including organic potatoes – has increased. Now there is quite a wide range of organic potato varieties available.

Organically grown potatoes are popular for various reasons. They have a more intense flavour due to their slower growth, they contain less water, and they have a lower nitrogen content because they have not been exposed to synthetic nitrogen fertilisers. Weeds are kept in check by mechanical, not chemical means, and only natural substances are allowed to be used for insect control. This means that organic potatoes are largely free of toxins.

Another reason for the high demand is the wide range of varieties. Old or 'heirloom' varieties have great appeal for their spectrum of flavours and often unusual appearance. Haute cuisine has also discovered organic potatoes; many restaurants make a feature of them in various dishes, and chefs like to seek out varieties to experiment with.

Local farmers' markets are a good place to look for organic potatoes. Ask the stall-holder for advice about the best cooking methods to use for the different varieties.

Organic potatoes are free of the pesticides that are used in conventionally farmed potato crops.

Basic cooking methods
From the pot

Steaming and boiling are the best ways to preserve the fresh taste of new potatoes, and are also ideal methods for waxy potatoes, whether served on their own or used in salads. For mashed potatoes and dumplings, floury potatoes are recommended.

Potatoes **steamed** in their **jackets**

serves 4

1 kg (2 lb) small new potatoes, unpeeled
1-2 teaspoons caraway seeds (optional)

Cook's tip
New potatoes are sold scrubbed, but should be brushed under cold running water before cooking to get rid of any specks of dirt.

1 Brush potatoes clean under cold running water, place in a steamer basket and sprinkle with caraway seeds if you like.

2 Pour cold water into a saucepan to come 1 cm ($\frac{1}{2}$ inch) below the steamer basket. Insert the steamer basket and bring the water to a boil. Cover pan when water starts to boil, reduce heat to low and steam for 20-25 minutes or until tender when pierced with a skewer or the point of a knife. Serve immediately.

Boiled potatoes

serves 4

1 kg (2 lb) boiling (waxy) potatoes
1-2 tablespoons finely chopped parsley (optional)

1 Peel potatoes and remove any eyes. Wash and cut into even-sized pieces.

2 Place potatoes in saucepan, add cold water to just cover and sprinkle with 1 teaspoon salt. Bring water to a boil. Cover pan when water starts to boil, reduce heat to low and simmer for 15-20 minutes or until potatoes are tender when pierced with a skewer or the point of a knife.

3 Drain, return potatoes to the saucepan and let them steam briefly on the switched-off hotplate, shaking the pan repeatedly. Serve immediately.

4 For parsley potatoes, sprinkle potatoes with chopped parsley before serving. Alternatively, melt 100 g ($3\frac{1}{2}$ oz) butter in a small pan, stir in parsley and briefly heat with the butter. Drizzle potatoes with butter and serve immediately.

Mashed potatoes

serves 4

1 kg (2 lb) baking (floury) potatoes
1 teaspoon salt
200 ml (7 fl oz) milk
40 g (1½ oz) butter
freshly ground nutmeg (optional)

1 Cook as for boiled potatoes (opposite) in a covered saucepan on low heat for 15-20 minutes or until soft, then let them steam briefly. In the meantime, heat the milk and butter in a small saucepan over low heat until the butter is melted.

2 Mash the hot potatoes well with a potato masher, or pass them through a potato ricer. (They should never be mashed in a food processor, or they will be gluey.)

3 Add milk and whisk until the mixture is nice and fluffy. Add a little more hot milk if you prefer a softer texture. Season to taste with salt and nutmeg, if you like, and serve immediately.

Potato dumplings

serves 4

400 g (14 oz) baking (floury)
    potatoes
¼ cup (60 ml/2 fl oz) milk
60 g (2 oz) butter
30 g (1 oz) semolina

1 Peel potatoes, wash and coarsely grate into a bowl of cold water. Pour off water and squeeze potatoes in a tea towel (dish towel).

2 Bring milk, butter and a pinch of salt to a boil in a saucepan. Gradually stir in the semolina; boil briefly. Add to the potatoes, mix well and season with salt.

3 Bring lightly salted water to a boil in a large saucepan. With moistened hands, shape dough into 4 dumplings. Simmer dumplings on low heat for about 20 minutes, then remove from water using a slotted spoon. Drain briefly, then serve immediately with soups, stews or casseroles.

Cook's tips

Grating the potatoes into a bowl of cold water prevents them from discolouring. Squeeze all the water out before cooking the dumplings.

The semolina mixture helps bind the dumpling dough together.

From the deep-fryer and frying pan

When frying potatoes, use a vegetable oil, such as sunflower, canola (rapeseed) or a blended vegetable oil. Such oils have a higher smoke point than, for example, olive oil, so can withstand high temperatures without burning.

Chips (fries)

serves 4

750 g (1½ lb) baking (floury) or
    all-purpose potatoes
vegetable oil for deep-frying

1   Peel and wash the potatoes. Slice lengthwise about 1 cm (½ inch) thick, then cut into strips of the same width. Dry thoroughly with paper towels.

2   Heat a generous amount of oil to 180°C (350°F) in a large saucepan or deep-fryer. If you don't have a thermometer, put the handle of a wooden spoon into the oil; if small bubbles form on the handle, the oil is hot enough. Fry potatoes in four batches for about 5 minutes, or until golden. Remove using a slotted spoon, drain well on paper towel and keep warm. Allow the oil to return to the correct temperature before frying the next batch. Season with salt just before serving.

Pan-fried potatoes

serves 4

1 kg (2 lb) small boiling (waxy)
    potatoes, unpeeled
½ cup (125 ml/4 fl oz)
    vegetable oil
2 onions, finely chopped
salt and freshly ground black
    pepper

1   Place potatoes in a saucepan and just cover with water. Bring to a boil, cover and cook on low heat for 20-25 minutes, until just softening. Drain, let potatoes steam briefly on the stovetop, then peel and allow to cool (leave overnight if possible).

2   Cut potatoes into slices. Heat oil in a large frying pan. Fry potatoes on medium heat for about 15 minutes, turning them over occasionally. Push to one side of the pan.

3   In other half of pan, sweat the onions for about 5 minutes. Combine potatoes and onions with a spatula and fry for 5 minutes more, or until the potatoes are crunchy and golden brown. Season to taste and serve.

Potato **pancakes**

serves 4

750 g (1½ lb) boiling (waxy) or
    all-purpose potatoes, peeled,
    coarsely grated, excess moisture
    squeezed out (see Cook's tip)
1 onion, coarsely grated
2 eggs
30 g (1 oz) plain (all-purpose) flour
½ teaspoon salt
150 ml (5 fl oz) vegetable oil

1 Combine potatoes, onions, eggs, flour and salt in a large bowl and mix well.

2 In a large frying pan, heat about half the oil until very hot. Add 1 heaped tablespoon potato dough and flatten. Repeat to make three more pancakes. Fry on medium heat for 4–5 minutes. Remove, drain on paper towel and keep warm.

3 Heat remaining oil in the pan until very hot. Fry the rest of the potato dough in the same way until golden brown and crunchy.

Cook's tip
Put the grated potato in a clean tea towel (dish towel) and squeeze out as much moisture as you can. This will help to make the pancakes nice and crisp.

Potato **rösti**

serves 4

750 g (1½ lb) boiling (waxy)
    potatoes, peeled, coarsely grated
1 onion, finely chopped
salt and freshly ground black pepper
2 tablespoons vegetable oil

1 Place potatoes in a bowl. Cover with ice-cold water and let stand for 10 minutes. Drain; squeeze potatoes well in a tea towel (dish towel).

2 Combine onion and potatoes. Season with salt and black pepper and mix well. Heat oil in a frying pan over medium heat, add all of the potato mixture and flatten into a large pancake using a spatula.

3 Fry underside of rösti for about 15 minutes or until golden brown. Turn out onto a plate, then slide the rösti back into the pan and fry the other side for about 10 minutes, or until golden. Quarter before serving.

From the oven

Jacket potatoes (with butter, sour cream or one of the toppings on pages 290–91) make an ideal light meal. Crunchy roast potatoes or creamy gratins are delicious accompaniments for meat, fish and vegetable dishes.

Baked potatoes

serves 4

4 large baking (floury) potatoes, unpeeled
2 tablespoons vegetable oil

1 Preheat the oven to 200°C (400°F/gas 6). Wash potatoes and dry thoroughly with paper towel.

2 Brush eight large pieces of aluminium foil with some oil and use to loosely wrap the potatoes. Put the potatoes on a baking tray. Bake in the oven for about 1 hour, then remove from the oven.

3 Open the foil. Using a sharp knife, cut a deep cross in each potato. Gently push the flesh outward with two forks. Serve the potatoes with butter, sour cream and chives, or the topping of your choice (see pages 290–91).

Cook's tip

Potatoes can also be baked in foil in the coals of a barbecue or an open fire, or baked without foil in a hot oven.

Roast potatoes

serves 4

1 kg (2 lb) new potatoes, unpeeled
2 tablespoons vegetable oil
coarse sea salt
1–2 tablespoons thyme leaves
1 tablespoon rosemary leaves

Cook's tip
To ensure that the potatoes will be crisp when cooked, it is essential to dry them thoroughly.

1 Preheat the oven to 200°C (400°F/gas 6). Wash the potatoes under running cold water, dry thoroughly with paper towel, then cut in halves lengthwise.

2 Brush a baking tray with oil and sprinkle with the herbs and some sea salt. Place potatoes cut side down on the tray. Bake in hot oven for about 30 minutes. Serve with sour cream or crème fraîche.

Fan potatoes

serves 4

8 boiling (waxy) potatoes
40 g (1½ oz) butter, melted, plus
   extra for greasing
salt and freshly ground black
   pepper

1 Preheat the oven to 200°C (400°F/gas 6). Grease an ovenproof dish with butter. Peel and wash potatoes and dry with paper towel. Use a sharp knife to slice potatoes at 3 mm (⅛ inch) intervals, but do not cut all the way through them.

2 Place potatoes in dish with the sliced sides facing upwards. Brush with melted butter and season with salt and pepper. Bake in hot oven for about 50 minutes until golden, occasionally basting with butter from the bottom of the dish. Accompany with a mixed-leaf salad with vinaigrette or yogurt dressing.

3 For fan potatoes with parmesan, sprinkle potatoes with 3 tablespoons finely grated parmesan 15 minutes before the end of the cooking time, and drizzle with the butter from the bottom of the dish.

Potato **gratin**

serves 4

750 g (1½ lb) all-purpose potatoes
salt and freshly ground black pepper
freshly grated nutmeg
200 ml (7 fl oz) pure (light/single)
   cream
50 ml (1¾ fl oz) milk
2 tablespoons grated emmenthal
   or Swiss cheese

1 Preheat the oven to 200°C (400°F/gas 6). Grease an ovenproof dish with butter. Peel and wash potatoes, thoroughly dry with paper towel and cut into thin slices using a sharp knife or a mandoline.

2 Layer potatoes in the dish, overlapping the slices, and season them with some salt, pepper and nutmeg. Combine cream and milk and pour over the potatoes, then sprinkle with cheese. Bake in hot oven for about 45 minutes, until golden. Serve hot. This gratin goes well with meat dishes or a salad, such as a tomato salad with basil or chives.

Snacks and starters

This chapter presents recipes for tasty snacks,
including potato pancakes, crisps (potato chips)
and wedges, as well as elegant starters such
as soufflés, tortillas and frittatas.

Baked potato quarters with smoked salmon

8 small baking (floury) potatoes
2 tablespoons extra virgin olive oil
salt and freshly ground black pepper
1 tablespoon butter
125 g (4½ oz) smoked salmon
1 tablespoon lemon juice
⅔ cup (170 g/6 oz) low-fat natural
   (plain) yogurt
1 tablespoon capers, drained and chopped
2 tablespoons chopped fresh dill
small sprigs of fresh dill, to garnish

serves 4 as a starter, 8 as a snack
preparation 25 minutes
cooking 1 hour 30 minutes

per serving 1190 kJ (284 calories), 14 g protein,
15 g total fat, 4 g saturated fat, 23 g carbohydrate

Cook's tip

Instead of making potato skins,
bake 12 small potatoes for about
50 minutes, or until tender. Halve
the potatoes and scoop out most of
the flesh, then fill with the smoked
salmon and yogurt mixture or one
of the toppings on pages 290-91.

1 Preheat the oven to 200°C (400°F/gas 6). Scrub the potatoes and dry them with paper towel. Thread them onto metal skewers, brush with 1 tablespoon oil, then sprinkle with a little salt. Arrange on a baking tray and bake for 1-1¼ hours, or until tender.

2 Remove the potatoes from the skewers and cut them in half lengthwise. Scoop out some of the flesh, leaving a layer of potato next to the skin about 1 cm (½ inch) thick. (Use the scooped-out flesh for fish cakes, or mash it to make a savoury pie topping.) Cut each piece in half lengthwise again and place, flesh side up, on a large, clean baking tray.

3 Melt the butter with the remaining oil and season with salt and black pepper. Lightly brush this mixture over the flesh side of the potatoes. Return to the oven and bake for a further 12-15 minutes, or until golden and crisp.

4 Meanwhile, cut the smoked salmon into thin strips and sprinkle with the lemon juice. In a bowl, mix together the yogurt, capers and chopped dill, then stir in the salmon.

5 Allow the potato quarters to cool for 1-2 minutes, then top each with a little of the salmon and yogurt mixture and garnish with a dill sprig. Serve warm.

Salmon

Salmon is an oily fish and a rich source of omega-3 fatty acids, a type of polyunsaturated fat that is thought to help protect against heart disease. The process of smoking the fish to make smoked salmon doesn't destroy these beneficial oils or any other nutrients.

Baked potato quarters with smoked salmon

Baked potatoes with caviar

1 Preheat the oven to 180°C (350°F/gas 4). Line a baking tray with baking (parchment) paper. Wash 12 small unpeeled baking (floury) potatoes, dry them with paper towel and cut each in half lengthwise. Place face down on the baking tray, brush with 1 tablespoon olive oil and season with salt. Bake for 45 minutes, or until soft.

2 Top the hot potato halves with a large dollop of crème fraîche or sour cream and some caviar. Garnish with fresh dill sprigs and serve. Accompany the dish with a rocket (arugula) salad with Italian dressing. For the dressing, combine 3 tablespoons extra virgin olive oil, 1 tablespoon balsamic vinegar, salt and freshly ground black pepper. Sprinkle the salad with shaved parmesan or 2 tablespoons pine nuts.

Layered Spanish tortilla

200 g (7 oz) peas
150 g (5 oz) green beans, trimmed and
    cut into 2 cm ($^3/_4$ inch) lengths
4 tablespoons extra virgin olive oil
150 g (5 oz) small button mushrooms,
    thinly sliced
salt and freshly ground black pepper
12 eggs
250 g (8 oz) boiling (waxy) potatoes,
    peeled and thinly sliced
1 onion, finely chopped
410 g (14$^1/_2$ oz) can chopped tomatoes
2 teaspoons fresh oregano,
    or 1 teaspoon dried

serves 6
preparation 20 minutes
cooking 1 hour 15 minutes

per serving *1349 kJ (322 calories), 18 g protein,*
23 g total fat, 5 g saturated fat, 12 g carbohydrate

1 Cook the peas in a saucepan of salted boiling water for 10 minutes. Scoop the peas out using a slotted spoon, return the water to a boil, then cook the beans in the same water for 10 minutes. Drain well and set aside.

2 Heat 1 tablespoon oil in a frying pan. Add the mushrooms and sauté for 10 minutes, then season with salt and black pepper. Beat 3 of the eggs in a bowl and pour over the mushrooms. Let the mixture set over medium heat, then turn (see Cook's tip) and fry the other side until golden. Remove from the pan and keep warm.

3 Heat another tablespoon of oil in the pan, then add the potatoes and onion and sauté for 10 minutes. Beat another 3 eggs, pour over the vegetable mixture and cook in the same way as before. Place the potato tortilla on top of the mushroom tortilla and keep warm.

4 Proceed in the same manner to make a pea tortilla from the peas, and a bean tortilla from the beans. Place each on top of the previous tortillas and keep warm.

5 Meanwhile, heat the tomatoes and oregano in a saucepan over medium heat. Season with salt and black pepper.

6 Cut the tortilla stack into six wedges and serve with the sauce drizzled over the top.

Tortillas

Usually made with potatoes, onions and eggs, tortillas are an integral part of Spanish cuisine. Served warm with a side salad, they make a small individual meal, but they are also often found among the lavish tapas displays in Spanish bars and restaurants, where they are generally washed down with a glass of red wine.

Cook's tip

To turn a tortilla, slide the set tortilla out of the pan onto a plate, put another plate on top, then flip the two plates. Remove the top plate and slide the tortilla back into the pan.

Roasted potato salad with cumin and yogurt dressing

3 teaspoons olive oil
salt and freshly ground black pepper
5 small baking (floury) potatoes,
    scrubbed
6 cups (125 g/4½ oz) mixed salad leaves

cumin and yogurt dressing

½ teaspoon ground cumin
juice of ½ lemon
½ cup (125 g/4½ oz) low-fat
    Greek-style yogurt

serves 4
preparation 15 minutes
cooking 55 minutes

per serving *597 kJ (143 calories), 4 g protein, 7 g total fat,*
3 g saturated fat, 16 g carbohydrate

1 Preheat the oven to 200°C (400°F/gas 6). In a bowl, mix the oil with ½ teaspoon salt, add the potatoes then use your hands to turn and coat the potatoes in the mixture. Place the potatoes on a baking tray and roast for 50–55 minutes, or until crisp on the outside but soft when squeezed.

2 Meanwhile, to make the dressing, place the cumin in a small ovenproof dish, such as a ramekin, and toast in the hot oven for no more than 2 minutes while the potatoes are baking. Do not let it burn. Remove from the oven and leave to cool.

3 In a small bowl, stir together the cooled cumin, lemon juice and yogurt, then add salt and black pepper to taste. Cover and chill, or put aside at a cool room temperature.

4 Arrange the salad leaves on serving plates. When the potatoes are done, remove them from the oven and, using an oven mitt for protection, quarter them lengthwise into wedges.

5 Put five potato wedges on each plate. Drizzle with the dressing and serve immediately.

Cook's tip

Any kind of lettuce or mixture of salad leaves can be used for this recipe. If your salad leaves are a little wilted, but otherwise fine to eat, soak them in cold water for 15 minutes or so to refresh them, then whiz them in a salad spinner.

Potato soufflés with parmesan and pancetta

Potato soufflés with parmesan and pancetta

500 g (1 lb) all-purpose potatoes, peeled, cooked and mashed
50 g (1¾ oz) butter, plus extra for greasing
½ cup (125 ml/4 fl oz) thick (heavy/double) cream
¼ teaspoon freshly grated nutmeg
salt and freshly ground black pepper
2 tablespoons dry breadcrumbs
3 eggs, separated
100 g (3½ oz) pancetta, cooked until crisp and broken into small pieces
4 tablespoons grated parmesan, plus extra to serve

serves 4
preparation 40 minutes
cooking 35 minutes

per serving *1868 kJ (446 calories), 17 g protein, 33 g total fat, 19 g saturated fat, 21 g carbohydrate*

1 Preheat the oven to 200°C (400°F/gas 6). Place the mashed potatoes, butter and cream in a saucepan and stir over a low heat for 10 minutes, or until well combined and coming away from the side of the pan. Add the nutmeg and season with salt and black pepper.

2 Grease four individual 1 cup (250 ml/8 fl oz) soufflé dishes with butter and sprinkle the base and sides with breadcrumbs, tipping out any excess. Put the soufflé dishes on a baking tray.

3 Beat the egg yolks one by one into the potato mixture, then stir the pancetta and parmesan through. Whisk the egg whites until stiff. Using a large metal spoon, fold one-third of the egg whites through the potato mixture, then gently fold the rest through. Take care not to deflate the mixture.

4 Spoon into the soufflé dishes and bake for 25 minutes, or until puffed and golden. Do not open the oven door until the end of the cooking time.

5 Serve immediately, with some extra parmesan sprinkled over the top.

Potato and spinach cakes

1 Preheat the oven to 220°C (425°F/gas 7). Cook 750 g (1½ lb) unpeeled baking (floury) potatoes in boiling water for 8 minutes, then drain and leave to cool. Meanwhile, sauté 1 chopped onion in 1 tablespoon vegetable oil for 2 minutes. Stir in 1 tablespoon chopped fresh ginger, 1 tablespoon cumin seeds and 1 tablespoon medium-hot curry paste and gently cook for 1 minute more, stirring constantly.

2 Add 5 cups (250 g/8 oz) baby spinach leaves and 3 tablespoons water and gently cook for 3 minutes, or until the spinach has wilted. Tip the mixture into a large bowl. Peel the cooled potatoes and grate them into the bowl. Add 3 tablespoons chopped fresh coriander (cilantro), season to taste with salt and freshly ground black pepper and mix together using two forks.

3 Make 8 mounds of mixture on lightly oiled baking trays and flatten them slightly. Bake for 15 minutes, then turn the cakes over and bake for a further 10 minutes. Serve with a minty yogurt raita, made by mixing ⅔ cup (150 g/5 oz) low-fat natural (plain) yogurt with ⅓ cucumber, finely diced, and 2 tablespoons chopped fresh mint.

Five ways...

with potato patties

Potato patties are perfect for starters or light meals. For best results, squeeze as much liquid as you can out of the grated potatoes before combining them with other ingredients.

Potato patties with smoked salmon

serves **4** · prep **25** mins · cook **20** mins

Preheat the oven to 140°C (275°F/gas 1). Peel, wash and coarsely grate 500 g (1 lb) baking (floury) potatoes, place in a tea towel (dish towel) and squeeze well. Place in a large bowl, add 1 finely chopped onion, 1 egg, 2 tablespoons plain (all-purpose) flour, salt and freshly ground black pepper; mix well. Pour vegetable oil into a frying pan to a depth of about 1 cm (½ inch) and heat. Add heaped tablespoonfuls of mixture to the pan and flatten into 5 cm (2 inch) patties. Fry for 2 minutes per side, or until golden brown and crunchy. Remove, drain briefly on paper towel and keep warm while cooking the remaining patties. Top patties with a large dollop of sour cream and 200 g (7 oz) smoked salmon, sliced into strips. Garnish with fresh dill sprigs and serve immediately.

per serving *1646 kJ (393 calories), 17 g protein, 26 g total fat, 5 g saturated fat, 22 g carbohydrate*

Potato and carrot patties

serves **4** · prep **25** mins · cook **20** mins

Preheat the oven to 140°C (275°F/gas 1). Peel and wash 400 g (14 oz) baking (floury) potatoes, grate coarsely, place in a tea towel (dish towel) and squeeze well. Combine in a large bowl with 2 coarsely grated carrots, 1 finely chopped onion, 1 beaten egg, salt and freshly ground black pepper and mix well. Heat 1 tablespoon vegetable oil in a non-stick frying pan. Add heaped tablespoonfuls of potato mixture and spread into small patties. Fry for 2-3 minutes per side until golden brown, drain briefly on paper towel and keep warm in the oven. Heat another tablespoon of oil in the pan to make more patties. Serve hot, with parsley cream. For parsley cream, whip ⅔ cup (150 ml/5 fl oz) cream until stiff. Stir in 2-3 tablespoons finely grated parmesan and 1 tablespoon finely chopped fresh parsley. Season with salt and freshly ground black pepper.

per serving *1279 kJ (305 calories), 7 g protein, 23 g total fat, 12 g saturated fat, 17 g carbohydrate*

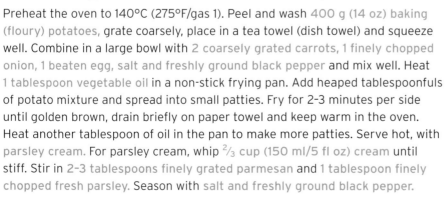

Sweet potato hash browns

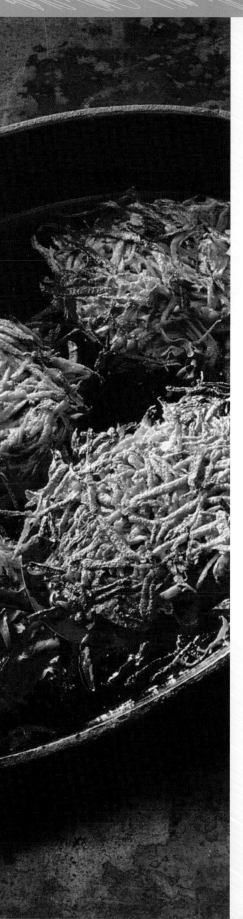

Sweet potato, carrot and celeriac patties

serves **4** | prep **40** mins | cook **50** mins

Preheat the oven to 140°C (275°F/gas 1). Grate 200 g (7 oz) peeled celeriac (celery root), 300 g (10½ oz) orange sweet potato and 2 carrots into a bowl. Add 4 tablespoons plain (all-purpose) flour, 2 eggs, 2 tablespoons sour cream and 1 cup finely chopped parsley. Season to taste with salt, freshly ground black pepper and nutmeg; mix well. Heat 2 tablespoons olive oil in a large frying pan. Add 2 tablespoonfuls of mixture per patty to the pan and flatten with a spatula. Fry over low-medium heat for 10-12 minutes per side, or until golden and crunchy. Remove, drain briefly on paper towel and keep warm in the oven while cooking the remaining patties. Serve immediately.

per serving *1089 kJ (260 calories), 7 g protein, 15 g total fat, 4 g saturated fat, 25 g carbohydrate*

Sweet potato hash browns

serves **4** | prep **20** mins | cook **25** mins

Preheat the oven to 140°C (275°F/gas 1). Peel and coarsely grate 650 g (1 lb 7 oz) orange sweet potatoes. Place in a bowl with salt and freshly ground black pepper; mix well. Heat 1 tablespoon vegetable oil and 2 teaspoons butter in a large, non-stick frying pan until sizzling. Shape the sweet potato mixture into eight patties, each about 1 cm (½ inch) thick, pressing firmly. Cook four patties over medium heat for 5 minutes, or until crisp and golden brown underneath, then turn carefully with a spatula and cook for 5 minutes more (if the patties break up, simply pat them back into shape). Drain briefly on paper towel and keep warm in the oven while cooking the remaining four patties, using another 1 tablespoon vegetable oil and 2 teaspoons butter. Serve hot.

per serving *930 kJ (222 calories), 3 g protein, 13 g total fat, 4 g saturated fat, 23 g carbohydrate*

Potato and zucchini patties

serves **4** | prep **30** mins | cook **35** mins

Preheat the oven to 140°C (275°F/gas 1). Coarsely grate 500 g (1 lb) zucchini (courgettes), pat dry with paper towel and place in a large bowl. Peel and grate 500 g (1 lb) boiling (waxy) potatoes, place in a clean tea towel (dish towel) and squeeze well. Add to the bowl with 1 finely chopped onion, 3 tablespoons chopped chives, 1 egg, 3 tablespoons plain (all-purpose) flour, salt, freshly ground black pepper and freshly grated nutmeg; mix well. Heat 3 tablespoons olive oil in a large frying pan. Place tablespoonfuls of mixture in the pan and flatten with a spatula. Cook in batches over low-medium heat for 10-12 minutes on each side, until golden and crunchy, adding more oil as needed. Serve hot.

per serving *1217 kJ (291 calories), 8 g protein, 16 g total fat, 2 g saturated fat, 29 g carbohydrate*

Potato and spinach frittata

500 g (1 lb) boiling (waxy) potatoes, peeled
and diced
250 g (8 oz) baby spinach leaves
1 tablespoon extra virgin olive oil
1 red capsicum (bell pepper), quartered
lengthwise, then thinly sliced
5-6 spring onions (scallions), thinly sliced
5 eggs
salt and freshly ground black pepper
2 tablespoons grated parmesan

serves 4
preparation 10 minutes
cooking 30 minutes

per serving *1033 kJ (247 calories), 15 g protein,*
12 g total fat, 3 g saturated fat, 19 g carbohydrate

1 Cook the potatoes in a saucepan of boiling water for 5-6 minutes, or until almost tender. Place the spinach in a steamer or colander over the potatoes and cook for another 5 minutes, or until the potatoes are tender and the spinach has wilted. Drain the potatoes. Press the spinach firmly with the back of a spoon to extract as much excess moisture as possible, then chop the leaves.

2 Heat the oil in a non-stick frying pan that is about 25 cm (10 inches) in diameter. Add the capsicum and sauté over medium heat for 2 minutes. Stir in the spring onions and drained potatoes and continue cooking for 2 minutes.

3 Beat the eggs in a large bowl, season with salt and black pepper and mix in the spinach. With a slotted spoon, remove about half of the vegetables from the pan and add to the egg mixture, leaving the oil in the pan. Briefly mix the egg and vegetables, then pour into the frying pan. Cover and cook, without stirring, for 6 minutes, or until the omelette is almost set but still a little soft on top.

4 Meanwhile, preheat the grill (broiler) to medium-high. Sprinkle the top of the frittata with parmesan and place under the grill. Cook for 3-4 minutes, or until browned and puffed around the edges. Cut into quarters or wedges and serve.

Spinach

Baby spinach is available ready washed in packets, but it is more economical to buy loose leaves. If buying mature leaves in bunches, wash them well, whiz in a salad spinner and remove any tough stalks. Choose spinach with fresh, bright green leaves. Avoid yellowing, wilting or crushed leaves. Store in the refrigerator and use within 2 days.

Potato and beetroot chips with peanut dip

2 baking (floury) potatoes, scrubbed
3 beetroot (beets), scrubbed
2 tablespoons vegetable oil

spicy peanut dip

2 teaspoons vegetable oil
1 large French shallot, finely chopped
1 clove garlic, crushed
1/2 teaspoon ground cumin
1/2 teaspoon ground coriander
3 tablespoons crunchy peanut butter
1 teaspoon salt-reduced soy sauce
1 tablespoon honey
1 tablespoon lemon juice

serves 4
preparation 15 minutes
cooking 45 minutes

per serving *1299 kJ (310 calories), 7 g protein,*
22 g total fat, 3 g saturated fat, 23 g carbohydrate

1 To make the dip, heat the oil in a small saucepan over medium heat, then fry the shallot and garlic, stirring, for 3–4 minutes. Stir in the cumin and coriander and cook for a few more seconds, then add the peanut butter, soy sauce, honey and 1/3 cup (80 ml/2 1/2 fl oz) water. Stir over low heat until combined. Remove from the heat and mix in the lemon juice. Spoon into a small bowl, cover and set aside.

2 Preheat the oven to 220ºC (425ºF/gas 7). Cut the potatoes and beetroot into very thin slices using a mandoline or the fine slicing blade in a food processor, or slice as thinly as possible using a sharp knife.

3 Place the potato and beetroot slices in two separate bowls and add 1 tablespoon oil to each bowl. Toss until lightly coated with oil, then spread the slices out in a single layer on three large non-stick baking trays. Bake for 35 minutes, turning the slices frequently and swapping the position of the trays each time you turn the vegetables – the potatoes should be crisp and golden, and the beetroot firm but slightly moist. Keep a close eye on them to make sure they do not burn. Transfer to a wire rack to cool.

4 To serve, place the bowl of peanut dip on a large serving platter and pile the cooled vegetable chips around it.

Beetroot

Beetroot was originally grown for its edible spinach-like leaves rather than its now more familiar dark red root. It is related to the sugar beet and has a sugar content similar to that of an apple. Beetroot is a good source of folate, a B vitamin essential for healthy blood. The baby leaves make a colourful addition to salads, and are often used in salad mixes.

Potato and beetroot chips with peanut dip

Some more ideas...

For something different, serve the potato and beetroot chips opposite with
a refreshing radish and yogurt dip or a tomato, garlic and basil dip.

✳ To make the radish and yogurt dip, wash and finely grate 5 red radishes.
Mix together 1 cup (250 g/8 oz) natural (plain) yogurt and 1 teaspoon mustard
and season with salt and freshly ground black pepper to taste. Stir in the radishes
and 1 tablespoon snipped fresh chives.

✳ To make the tomato, garlic and basil dip, halve, seed and finely dice 2 firm,
ripe tomatoes. Combine with 1 tablespoon extra virgin olive oil, 1 finely chopped
clove garlic, salt and freshly ground black pepper. Finally, mix in 1 tablespoon
roughly torn fresh basil leaves.

Spicy filo triangles

Curried vegetable triangles

1 Preheat the oven to 220°C (425°F/gas 7). In a bowl, combine 2½ cups (350 g/12 oz) plain (all-purpose) flour, 1 egg, 3 tablespoons vegetable oil and 1 tablespoon vinegar. Knead on a floured work surface for 10 minutes and shape into a ball. Heat a large ceramic bowl, invert it over the dough and leave for 30 minutes.

2 Heat 2 tablespoons vegetable oil in a large saucepan. Add 1 cup (150 g/5 oz) coarsely grated peeled all-purpose potato, 1¼ cups (150 g/5 oz) coarsely grated pumpkin (winter squash), 1½ cups (100 g/3½ oz) chopped broccoli, 2 chopped cloves garlic and 4 chopped spring onions (scallions). Sauté for 5 minutes, then mix in 1 tablespoon mild curry powder, 2 teaspoons lemon juice, 1 egg yolk, 3 tablespoons pure (light/single) cream and salt and freshly ground black pepper to taste.

3 Divide the pastry into 12 portions. Stretch each piece into an 8 x 30 cm (3¼ x 12 inch) rectangle. Brush with oil. Place 1 tablespoon filling along one narrow end; fold over the opposite end and wrap the pastry a few times diagonally around the filling to make a triangle, sealing the edges. Repeat to make 12 triangles. Brush triangles generously with oil, place on a baking tray lined with baking (parchment) paper and bake for 20 minutes. Brush with 1 beaten egg white, sprinkle with sesame seeds and bake for 5 minutes more. Serve hot or warm.

Spicy filo triangles

2 sheets filo pastry, each 30 x 50 cm
   (12 x 20 inches)
1 tablespoon vegetable oil
½ teaspoon coriander seeds, coarsely crushed

filling

1 all-purpose potato, peeled and diced
1 small carrot, diced
½ cup (65 g/2½ oz) frozen peas
1 tablespoon mild curry powder
1 tablespoon chopped fresh coriander
   (cilantro)
1 pinch salt

mango and ginger salsa

1 large ripe but firm mango
½ teaspoon grated fresh ginger
1 teaspoon lemon juice
1 teaspoon caster (superfine) sugar
¼ teaspoon dried red chilli flakes
1 teaspoon vegetable oil

makes 12
preparation 35 minutes
cooking 20 minutes

----

per serving *199 kJ (48 calories), 1 g protein, 2 g total fat,*
1 g saturated fat, 6 g carbohydrate

1 Preheat the oven to 200°C (400°F/gas 6). To make the filling, cook the potato and carrot in a saucepan of boiling water for 5 minutes. Add the peas and cook for a further 2 minutes. Drain well, then tip the vegetables into a bowl. Stir in the curry powder, fresh coriander and salt, and mash very slightly to combine. Leave to cool.

2 Cover one sheet of pastry so it doesn't dry out. Cut the other sheet crosswise into six strips, each 30 cm (12 inches) long. Brush them with a little oil.

3 Lay a pastry strip lengthwise in front of you on the work surface. Place 1 rounded tablespoon of filling in the middle of the end nearest to you. Lift the corner of that end and fold it diagonally over the filling to make a triangular shape, flattening the filling slightly. Continue folding the strip over in a triangular shape until you come almost to the end. Trim off any excess pastry. Repeat with the remaining filo pastry and filling to make 12 triangles.

4 Place the filo triangles on two non-stick baking trays, brush with the remaining oil and scatter the coriander seeds over the top. Bake for 10-15 minutes, or until golden.

5 To make the salsa, cut the mango cheeks from both sides of the stone (see Cook's tip), then finely dice the flesh. Gently mix in a serving bowl with the ginger, lemon juice, sugar, chilli flakes and oil. Serve with the hot filo triangles.

Cook's tip

To prepare a mango, slice down either side of the stone. Cut a lattice pattern in the flesh of each outside piece (without piercing the skin). Press against the skin to turn the piece inside out; the cubes of mango flesh will pop up. Cut these off. Repeat with the other cheek. Remove the skin from the piece surrounding the stone, then cut away the flesh as neatly as you can.

Sweet potato risotto with crisp sage

5 cups (1.25 litres/44 fl oz) chicken
    or vegetable stock
5 tablespoons extra virgin olive oil
1 small onion, finely diced
1¾ cups (400 g/14 oz) risotto rice,
    such as arborio or carnaroli
400 g (14 oz) orange sweet potato,
    peeled and cut into large dice
1 cup (250 ml/8 fl oz) white wine
¼ teaspoon saffron threads
50 g (1¾ oz) butter
⅔ cup (60 g/2¼ oz) grated parmesan,
    plus extra to serve
2 tablespoons fresh sage leaves

serves 4
preparation 15 minutes
cooking 30 minutes

per serving *3586 kJ (857 calories), 20 g protein,*
39 g total fat, 14 g saturated fat, 97 g carbohydrate

1 Heat the stock and keep it at a low simmer while you cook the risotto. Heat 2 tablespoons oil in a large saucepan and sauté the onion over medium heat for 2–3 minutes, or until translucent. Add the rice and sweet potato and stir until coated with the oil. Stir in the wine and saffron and cook, stirring, until the liquid has been absorbed. Add the hot stock ½ cup (125 ml/4 fl oz) at a time, stirring constantly and ensuring all the stock is absorbed before adding more. Once all the stock has been absorbed, the rice should be soft and creamy.

2 Stir in the butter and parmesan.

3 Heat the remaining olive oil in a small frying pan until hot, then add the sage leaves and fry until crisp.

4 Serve the risotto topped with the sage leaves and extra parmesan for sprinkling.

Cook's tip

When making risotto, always use a special risotto rice such as arborio. Keep the stock hot, so that the temperature of the risotto remains constant during cooking. Add the stock gradually, stirring until each batch is almost completely absorbed before adding any more. Finally, stir the risotto constantly. Stirring releases the starch in the grains and absorbs the liquid, giving the risotto its characteristic creamy consistency.

Potato and zucchini tortilla

600 g (1 lb 5 oz) boiling (waxy) potatoes,
    peeled and diced
2 tablespoons extra virgin olive oil
1 red onion, finely chopped
1 zucchini (courgette), diced
2 slices (strips) bacon, trimmed of fat
    and chopped
6 eggs
2 tablespoons chopped fresh parsley
freshly ground black pepper

serves 8
preparation 15 minutes
cooking 20 minutes

per serving *694 kJ (166 calories), 9 g protein, 9 g total fat,*
2 g saturated fat, 11 g carbohydrate

1 Add the potatoes to a saucepan of boiling water. Return to a boil, then lower the heat slightly and cook for 3 minutes. Drain thoroughly.

2 Heat the oil in a heavy-based non-stick frying pan that is about 25 cm (10 inches) in diameter. Add the potatoes, onion, zucchini and bacon and cook over medium heat for 10 minutes, turning and stirring from time to time, until the potatoes are tender and lightly golden.

3 Meanwhile, preheat the grill (broiler) to high. In a bowl, beat the eggs with 1 tablespoon cold water. Add the parsley and some black pepper. Pour the egg mixture over the vegetables in the pan and cook for 3–4 minutes, or until the egg has set on the bottom, lifting the edges to allow the uncooked egg mixture to run onto the pan.

4 When there is just a little uncooked egg on top, place the pan under the hot grill and cook for a further 2 minutes to set the top. Slide the tortilla out onto a plate or board and allow to cool for 2–3 minutes. Cut into small wedges and serve warm, or leave to cool completely before cutting and serving.

Zucchini

Zucchini are available all year, but are at their best in summer. Choose smallish zucchini, no more than 15 cm (6 inches) long; larger specimens tend to be watery and tough. Choose zucchini with bright, shiny skins and a firm texture. A few surface scratches are normal. Store zucchini in a perforated plastic bag in the refrigerator for up to 4 days.

Potato and zucchini tortilla

Potato and asparagus tortilla

1 Peel, dice and boil 600 g (1 lb 5 oz) boiling (waxy) potatoes, then drain well. Trim 250 g (8 oz) green asparagus stalks (preferably thin ones), discarding the woody bases, then cut into 2 cm (¾ inch) lengths.

2 Heat 1 tablespoon olive oil in a non-stick frying pan and sauté the potatoes, asparagus and 2 finely diced slices (strips) bacon for about 10 minutes.

3 Whisk 5 eggs with 1 tablespoon water, season with salt and freshly ground black pepper and stir in 2 tablespoons grated parmesan. Pour over the vegetables and cook as described in the recipe opposite.

Oven-baked spicy potato wedges

Oven-baked spicy potato wedges

1 kg (2 lb) large baking (floury) potatoes
2 teaspoons vegetable oil
2 tablespoons fresh wholemeal (whole grain)
   breadcrumbs
1 teaspoon paprika
1 pinch cayenne pepper
½ teaspoon ground cumin
1 teaspoon garlic salt
1 teaspoon freshly ground black pepper
1 teaspoon dried thyme
garlic mayonnaise (page 213) or Greek-style
   yogurt, for dipping (optional)

serves 4-6
preparation 5 minutes
cooking 40 minutes

*per serving (4 serves) 823 kJ (197 calories), 7 g protein,
3 g total fat, 0 g saturated fat, 36 g carbohydrate*

1 Preheat the oven to 220°C (425°F/gas 7). Scrub the potatoes, leaving the skins on, and cut each one lengthwise into eight wedges. Place in a large mixing bowl, add the oil and toss to coat the wedges.

2 In a large bowl, mix together the breadcrumbs, paprika, cayenne pepper, cumin, garlic salt, black pepper and thyme. Add the potatoes and toss until evenly coated.

3 Spread the wedges in a single layer on a large non-stick baking tray and bake for 35-40 minutes, or until golden brown and crisp. Serve hot, with garlic mayonnaise or Greek-style yogurt, for dipping into, if you like.

Cook's tip
Make sure the potatoes are of a similar size so they cook through evenly.

Potato and sage patties

1 Cook 750 g (1½ lb) baking (floury) potatoes in boiling water for 25 minutes, or until soft. Meanwhile, heat 2 tablespoons olive oil in a large saucepan and sauté 2 finely chopped red onions and 3 finely diced red capsicums (bell peppers) for 5 minutes. Stir in 2 tablespoons tomato passata (puréed tomatoes) and 100 ml (3½ fl oz) pure (light/single) cream, cover and bring to a boil. Season with salt, some cayenne pepper and sweet paprika to taste. Remove the lid and simmer over low heat for 10 minutes, stirring occasionally. Purée, then strain through a sieve and set aside.

2 Drain the potatoes and cool briefly under cold running water. Peel, then mash while still hot, or press through a potato ricer (potato press). Place in a bowl and mix in 1 egg yolk, 2 tablespoons plain (all-purpose) flour and 3-4 tablespoons chopped fresh sage. Season with salt, freshly ground black pepper and freshly grated nutmeg. With flour-dusted hands, shape mixture into 12 patties. Set aside for several minutes.

3 Heat 1 tablespoon butter in a non-stick frying pan. In two or three batches, fry the patties for about 5 minutes per side until golden brown, adding a little more butter each time. Just before serving, whip 100 ml (3½ fl oz) cream and stir into the capsicum sauce. Serve separately, with the patties.

Soups

With their mild but delicious flavour and starchy texture, potatoes are excellent for soups. Whether they're the star ingredient or a complement to others, they make it easy to create tempting soups for all occasions.

Moroccan sweet potato soup

2 tablespoons olive oil

2 onions, chopped

2 cloves garlic, crushed

5 cm (2 inch) piece fresh ginger, finely grated

1 teaspoon ground cumin

1 teaspoon ground turmeric

½ teaspoon ground cinnamon

750 g (1½ lb) orange sweet potato, peeled and diced

250 g (8 oz) boiling (waxy) potatoes, peeled and diced

2 bay leaves

5 cups (1.25 litres/44 fl oz) chicken or vegetable stock

2 teaspoons honey

2 tablespoons lemon juice

salt and freshly ground black pepper

3 tablespoons chopped coriander (cilantro) leaves

serves 4-6

preparation 10 minutes

cooking 30 minutes

---

per serving 1109 kJ (265 calories), 9 g protein, 8 g total fat, 1 g saturated fat, 40 g carbohydrate

1 Heat the oil in a large saucepan over medium heat. Add the onions and sauté for 2-3 minutes, or until translucent. Stir in the garlic, ginger and spices and cook for 2 minutes, or until fragrant.

2 Add the sweet potato, potato, bay leaves and stock. Bring to a boil, then reduce the heat and simmer for 20 minutes, or until the potatoes are soft.

3 Allow the soup to cool a little, then purée the mixture and gently reheat. Stir in the honey, lemon juice and salt and black pepper to taste. Serve sprinkled with the coriander.

Food facts

In these days of refrigerated transport and year-round availability, it is easy to forget the importance of traditional vegetables such as potatoes and swedes (rutabagas) as a source of vitamin C. These tubers were once vital in preventing scurvy during winter months. Eaten frequently, they contribute a useful amount of vitamin C, a nutrient with anti-oxidant properties that help guard against cancer and heart disease.

Chunky vegetable soup

1 In a large saucepan, sauté 1 small chopped onion in 1 tablespoon vegetable oil for 5 minutes, or until softened but not browned. Meanwhile, wash and thinly slice 1 small leek and 1 large carrot. Slice 1 bulb fennel, reserving the fronds to garnish. Peel 1 swede (rutabaga) and 2 boiling (waxy) potatoes, then dice them. Add all the vegetables to the pan and cook for 5 minutes, or until slightly softened.

2 Tie 1 dried bay leaf and some fresh thyme and parsley sprigs together into a bouquet garni. Add to the pan with 600 ml (21 fl oz) vegetable stock and a 410 g (14½ oz) can chopped tomatoes. Season with salt and freshly ground black pepper. Bring to a boil, then cover and simmer gently for 45 minutes, or until all the vegetables are tender. Remove the bouquet garni and check the seasoning. Serve piping hot, sprinkled with snipped fennel fronds.

Some more ideas...

❋ For a hearty winter chowder-style soup, simply add more vegetables to the basic Chunky Vegetable Soup opposite. Try celeriac (celery root), turnips and parsnips. Shredded white or green cabbage is also good, added halfway through the simmering. Any leftovers will taste even more flavoursome reheated the next day.

❋ You can replace the swede with extra potato or even sweet potato.

❋ Pearl barley can also be added for a delightful nutty texture. Proceed as for the Chunky Vegetable Soup recipe but stir ¼ cup (50 g/1¾ oz) pearl barley into the softened vegetables, just before adding the stock and tomatoes. Also add 1 finely chopped clove garlic and 2 teaspoons caraway seeds when you sauté the onions.

Moroccan sweet potato soup

Corn and kipper chowder

1 tablespoon olive oil
1 leek, white part only, washed and
    thinly sliced
300 g (10½ oz) small new potatoes,
    unpeeled, quartered
1 bay leaf
1 fish stock (bouillon) cube
1¼ cups (300 ml/10½ fl oz) milk
410 g (14½ oz) can creamed corn
2 tablespoons snipped fresh chives
2 tablespoons chopped fresh parsley
200 g (7 oz) can kippers in brine or oil,
    thoroughly drained and skinned
salt and freshly ground black pepper

serves 4
preparation 10 minutes
cooking 20 minutes

---

per serving *1305 kJ (312 calories), 14 g protein,*
14 g total fat, 3 g saturated fat, 33 g carbohydrate

1 Heat the oil in a large saucepan. Add the leek and sauté over medium heat for 2 minutes, or until just softened. Add the potatoes and cook for a further 2 minutes. Stir in 2½ cups (625 ml/22 fl oz) boiling water, add the bay leaf, crumble in the stock cube and bring to a boil. Reduce the heat, cover and simmer for 15 minutes.

2 Remove and discard the bay leaf. Stir in the milk, corn and half the chives and parsley. Use a fork to break the kippers into chunks and add them to the soup. Taste the soup and season with salt and black pepper, if necessary. Return to a boil, then immediately ladle into bowls to stop the kippers overcooking.

3 Garnish with a sprinkling of the remaining chives and parsley and serve.

Cook's tips

New potatoes stay in firm pieces in the chowder, but baking (floury) or old potatoes can be used too. They will give a thicker texture, as they'll break up a little during cooking.

If kippers aren't available, substitute another kind of smoked fish fillets.

Kippers

Kippers are whole split herrings that have been hot smoked. The hot-smoking process uses high temperatures to both flavour and cook the fish. Kippers and other hot-smoked fish have a dry, firm flesh. They do not need to be cooked further, although they are usually heated through for serving. Fresh kippers can be used instead of canned in this recipe, if you prefer.

Spicy lentil dal

2 tablespoons vegetable oil
1 large onion, finely chopped
1–2 cloves garlic, finely chopped
5 cm (2 inch) piece fresh ginger,
    finely chopped
2 tablespoons mild curry paste
1 small cauliflower, cut into florets
1 red capsicum (bell pepper), seeded and diced
¾ cup (175 g/6 oz) red lentils
1 tablespoon ground cumin
1 tablespoon ground turmeric
1 teaspoon salt
400 g (14 oz) small new potatoes,
    unpeeled, cut in half
4 tomatoes
250 g (8 oz) baby English spinach leaves
4 tablespoons chopped coriander
    (cilantro) leaves

carrot chutney

3 carrots, peeled and grated
1 green chilli, seeded and finely
    chopped
juice of 1 lime
2 tablespoons finely chopped
    coriander (cilantro)

banana raita

2 firm bananas, sliced
1¼ cups (300 g/10½ oz) natural
    (plain) yogurt
⅔ cup (60 g/2¼ oz) toasted flaked almonds

serves 4
preparation 30 minutes
cooking 40 minutes

----

per serving *2449 kJ (585 calories), 28 g protein,*
25 g total fat, 4 g saturated fat, 64 g carbohydrate

1 Heat the oil in a large saucepan. Add the onion, garlic and ginger and sauté over medium heat for about 5 minutes. Stir in the curry paste and cook for another 2 minutes, then add the cauliflower, capsicum, lentils, cumin, turmeric, salt and 4 cups (1 litre/35 fl oz) water. Bring to a boil, then cover and simmer over low heat for 10 minutes. Add the potatoes and simmer for 10 minutes more.

2 Meanwhile, prepare the chutney and raita. To make the chutney, combine the carrots, chilli, lime juice and coriander in a bowl and mix well. To make the raita, place the sliced bananas in a bowl, spread the yogurt over them and sprinkle with the flaked almonds.

3 Blanch the tomatoes in boiling water for 30 seconds, then peel away the skins. Cut the flesh into quarters and discard the seeds. Add the tomatoes to the dal and simmer for another 5 minutes. Add the spinach and warm through for 2 minutes, or until the spinach has wilted. Stir in the coriander just before serving. Serve with the chutney and raita.

Cook's tip

Vary the vegetables according to the season. For example, if cauliflower isn't available, you could instead use zucchini (courgettes) or green beans.

Potato, bacon and spinach chowder

Potato, bacon and spinach chowder

4 cups (1 litre/35 fl oz) milk
1 tablespoon olive oil
2 slices (strips) lean bacon, finely chopped
1 large onion, finely chopped
2 tablespoons plain (all-purpose) flour
400 g (14 oz) boiling (waxy) potatoes,
     peeled and diced
1 parsnip, peeled and grated
salt and freshly ground black pepper
freshly grated nutmeg
150 g (5 oz) baby spinach leaves

serves 4
preparation 10 minutes
cooking 25 minutes

---

per serving *1631 kJ (390 calories), 18 g protein,*
20 g total fat, 9 g saturated fat, 34 g carbohydrate

1 In a saucepan, bring the milk just to a boil. Meanwhile, in another large saucepan, heat the oil over medium-high heat. Add the bacon and onion and cook for 2 minutes, stirring frequently. Add the flour and stir to combine, then slowly add about one-quarter of the hot milk, stirring and scraping the bottom of the pan to mix in the flour. When the mixture thickens, stir in the remaining hot milk.

2 Add the potatoes and parsnip. Season to taste with salt, black pepper and nutmeg and bring just to a boil, stirring occasionally. Reduce the heat so the soup bubbles gently. Half cover the pan and cook for a further 10 minutes, or until the vegetables are nearly tender, stirring occasionally.

3 Stir in the spinach and cook for 1-2 minutes, or until the spinach has wilted. Adjust the seasoning if necessary and serve at once.

Potato and sausage soup

1 In a saucepan, bring 4 cups (1 litre/35 fl oz) strong vegetable stock to the boil.

2 Meanwhile, in another large saucepan, heat 1 tablespoon olive oil over medium-high heat. Add 2 finely chopped slices (strips) lean bacon and 1 finely chopped large onion and cook for 2 minutes, stirring frequently.

3 Add 2 tablespoons plain (all-purpose) flour and stir to combine, then slowly add about one-quarter of the hot stock, stirring and scraping the bottom of the pan to mix in the flour. When the mixture thickens, stir in the remaining hot stock. Add 1 washed and finely sliced leek, 2 finely diced carrots and 400 g (14 oz) boiling (waxy) potatoes, peeled and diced.

4 About 5 minutes before the end of the cooking time, stir in 4 sliced cooked sausages. Taste the soup and add salt if needed and freshly ground black pepper to taste. Serve sprinkled with 2 tablespoons finely chopped fresh parsley.

Creamy potato and clam soup

1 kg (2 lb) small clams (vongole); or use
   300 g (10½ oz) drained canned clams
1 tablespoon butter
2 French shallots, finely chopped
1 clove garlic, finely chopped
8 sprigs fresh thyme
salt and freshly ground black pepper
2½ cups (625 ml/22 fl oz) vegetable stock
500 g (1 lb) boiling (waxy) potatoes, peeled
   and diced
100 ml (3½ fl oz) pure (light/single) cream
2 tablespoons finely chopped fresh parsley
2 slices (strips) bacon, chopped and fried
   until crisp (optional)

serves 4
preparation 35 minutes
cooking 25 minutes

per serving *2035 kJ (486 calories), 41 g protein,*
23 g total fat, 11 g saturated fat, 29 g carbohydrate

1 If using clams in the shell, wash them, discarding any open ones. Heat the butter in a large saucepan, then sauté the shallots and garlic for 3 minutes. Add the clams and thyme and enough water to cover the clams. Season with black pepper.

2 Cover and bring to a boil, then reduce the heat and simmer for 5 minutes, or until the clam shells open. Remove the pan from the heat. Scoop out the clams using a large slotted spoon, discarding any unopened ones. Strain the liquid into a large pan.

3 Add the stock to the cooking liquid and return to a boil. Add the potatoes and salt and black pepper to taste. Cover and simmer on low heat for 10 minutes, or until the potatoes are soft. Meanwhile, remove the clams from the shells.

4 Stir the clam flesh (or the drained canned clams) and cream into the soup and heat through thoroughly, but do not allow the mixture to boil. Serve sprinkled with the parsley and fried bacon pieces, if you like.

Clam and leek chowder

1 Wash 1 kg (2 lb) clams (vongole), discarding any open ones. In a large saucepan, place the clams, 8 sprigs fresh thyme and enough water to cover the clams. Season with freshly ground black pepper. Cover and bring to a boil, then reduce the heat and simmer for 5 minutes, or until the clam shells open. Remove the pan from the heat. Scoop out the clams using a large slotted spoon, discarding any open ones. Strain the liquid and reserve. Discard the thyme sprigs.

2 Heat 1 tablespoon butter in a large saucepan, then sauté 2 finely chopped French shallots, 1 finely chopped clove garlic and 250 g (8 oz) young leeks, washed and thinly sliced, for 3 minutes. Add 2½ cups (625 ml/22 fl oz) vegetable stock and the cooking liquid from the clams and return to the boil. Add 250 g (8 oz) boiling (waxy) potatoes, peeled and diced, and salt and black pepper. Cover and simmer for 10 minutes, or until the potatoes are soft. Meanwhile, remove the clams from the shell. Stir the clam flesh and 100 ml (3½ fl oz) pure (light/single) cream into the soup and heat for 2 minutes. Serve sprinkled with 2 tablespoons finely chopped fresh parsley.

Creamy potato and clam soup

Potato and onion soup topped with garlic prawns

2 tablespoons butter
1 large onion, peeled and finely chopped
4 cloves garlic, crushed
750 g (1½ lb) all-purpose potatoes,
    peeled and sliced
2 bay leaves
1 sprig fresh thyme
3 cups (750 ml/26 fl oz) chicken stock
150 ml (5 fl oz) pure (light/single) cream
salt and freshly ground black pepper
3 tablespoons olive oil
12 large raw prawns (uncooked shrimp), peeled
    and deveined, tails left on
4 cloves garlic, crushed
2 tablespoons snipped fresh chives

serves 4
preparation 25 minutes
cooking 35 minutes

per serving 2289 kJ (547 calories), 20 g protein,
38 g total fat, 18 g saturated fat, 32 g carbohydrate

1 Heat the butter in a large saucepan and gently sauté the onion and garlic for 3-5 minutes, or until softened. Add the potatoes, bay leaves, thyme and stock, bring to a boil, then simmer for 20 minutes or until the potatoes are soft. Remove and discard the bay leaves and thyme, and stir in the cream.

2 Allow the soup to cool a little, then purée, season to taste with salt and black pepper and reheat gently.

3 Heat the oil in a frying pan over medium heat. Add the prawns and garlic and stir constantly until the prawns turn pink and curl up, taking care not to burn the garlic.

4 Ladle the soup into four bowls and arrange three prawns in the centre of each. Top with the chopped chives and serve.

Vichyssoise

1 Wash and trim 500 g (1 lb) leeks, then cut in half lengthwise and slice thinly. Heat 1 tablespoon olive oil in a saucepan. Add the leeks, 2 peeled and sliced all-purpose potatoes and 1 finely chopped clove garlic. Cook for 10 minutes, stirring frequently, until the leeks are slightly softened but not coloured.

2 Pour in 4 cups (1 litre/35 fl oz) vegetable or chicken stock, preferably home-made, and bring to a boil. Cover, reduce the heat and simmer for 10 minutes, or until the leeks and potatoes are cooked.

3 Allow the soup to cool a little, then purée. Pour into a bowl and leave to cool, then chill well. Stir in ½ cup (125 g/4 oz) low-fat natural (plain) yogurt, season to taste, then ladle into four bowls. Float 2–3 ice cubes in each bowl, if you wish, and serve sprinkled with snipped fresh chives.

Potato and onion soup topped with garlic prawns

Potato and parmesan soup with bacon

Potato and parmesan soup with bacon

400 g (14 oz) baking (floury) potatoes,
   peeled and diced
250 g (8 oz) leeks, white part only,
   washed and thinly sliced into rings
1 tablespoon vegetable oil
1 onion, finely chopped
100 g ($3\frac{1}{2}$ oz) lean bacon, finely diced
600 ml (21 fl oz) ham or beef stock
100 ml ($3\frac{1}{2}$ fl oz) pure (light/single) cream
2–3 tablespoons grated parmesan
salt and freshly ground black pepper
1 tablespoon fresh thyme leaves

serves 4
preparation 25 minutes
cooking 30 minutes

per serving *1307 kJ (312 calories), 15 g protein,*
19 g total fat, 9 g saturated fat, 20 g carbohydrate

1 Cook the potatoes in a saucepan of boiling water for 15 minutes, or until soft. Meanwhile, cook the leeks in a separate saucepan of boiling water for 15 minutes, or until tender but still firm to the bite. Pour the water off both pans.

2 Heat the oil in a large saucepan and gently sauté the onion and bacon for 5 minutes. Pour in the stock and bring to a gentle boil. Add the potatoes and leeks, allow to heat through, then stir in the cream. Do not allow the cream to boil.

3 Mix in the parmesan and allow to melt. Season with salt and black pepper, sprinkle with the thyme and serve.

Cook's tip

Before grating parmesan, if you brush your grater with a little oil the cheese will not stick to it.

Potato soup with bacon gnocchi

1 Heat 2 tablespoons butter in a large saucepan and sauté 2 finely chopped onions for 5 minutes. Add some peeled and finely chopped vegetables, such as 600 g (1 lb 5 oz) baking (floury) potatoes, $\frac{1}{2}$ head celeriac (celery root), 2 carrots, a few sprigs fresh parsley (optional) and 2 small leeks. Sauté for 5 minutes. Pour in 4 cups (1 litre/35 fl oz) meat stock, bring to a boil, then simmer for 30 minutes, or until vegetables are soft. Allow the soup to cool a little, then purée, add salt and freshly ground black pepper to taste and gently reheat.

2 Meanwhile, soak 1 thinly sliced stale bread roll in 75 ml ($2\frac{1}{4}$ fl oz) warm milk for 15 minutes. Sauté $\frac{2}{3}$ cup (100 g/$3\frac{1}{2}$ oz) finely diced ham, 1 finely chopped onion and 1 tablespoon finely chopped fresh parsley in 1 tablespoon butter for 3 minutes. Tip into a bowl. Add the well-squeezed bread roll and 1 small egg and mix well. Season with salt, black pepper and freshly grated nutmeg. Shape into small gnocchi using two teaspoons. Simmer the gnocchi in boiling salted water for 5 minutes, or until they rise to the surface. Drain briefly, add to the soup, cover and gently heat through. Serve sprinkled with chopped parsley.

Creamy sweetcorn and potato soup

1 tablespoon vegetable oil
1 onion, finely chopped
500 g (1 lb) small boiling (waxy) potatoes,
    peeled and diced
2 cups (500 ml/16 fl oz) vegetable stock
$^2/_3$ cup (75 g/2$^1/_2$ oz) crushed crackers
400 ml (14 fl oz) milk
410 g (14$^1/_2$ oz) can sweetcorn kernels, drained
100 ml (3$^1/_2$ fl oz) pure (light/single) cream
salt and freshly ground black pepper
2 slices (strips) lean bacon, finely diced
1 tablespoon finely chopped fresh parsley

serves 4
preparation 35 minutes
cooking 45 minutes

per serving *2127 kJ (508 calories), 16 g protein,*
27 g total fat, 13 g saturated fat, 51 g carbohydrate

1 Heat the oil in a large saucepan and gently sauté the onion for 5 minutes. Add the potatoes and fry for 3 minutes, stirring well. Pour in the stock, bring to a boil, then simmer for 20 minutes, or until the potatoes are soft.

2 Meanwhile, place the crackers in a bowl, add the milk and soak for 5 minutes.

3 Scoop about half the potatoes out of the soup. Purée the soup, then return the potatoes to the soup. Stir in the sweetcorn, cream, and the milk and cracker mixture. Gently simmer for another 5 minutes, then season to taste with salt and black pepper.

4 Meanwhile, fry the bacon in a non-stick frying pan until crisp. Serve scattered over the soup, with the chopped parsley.

Creamy potato and chanterelle soup

1 Simmer 1 finely sliced leek and 500 g (1 lb) unpeeled, sliced boiling (waxy) potatoes in 4 cups (1 litre/35 fl oz) vegetable stock for 25 minutes, or until soft.

2 Meanwhile, in a non-stick frying pan, gently sauté 250 g (8 oz) chopped chanterelle mushrooms and 1 finely diced slice (strip) bacon in 1 tablespoon butter for 10 minutes. Season the potato mixture with salt and black pepper and stir in 100 ml (3½ fl oz) pure (light/single) cream and a 310 g (11 oz) can sweetcorn, drained. Gently reheat and serve sprinkled with the mushroom mixture.

Potato soup with watercress

Potato and chervil soup

1 Wash 150 g (5 oz) chervil, pat dry and chop finely (it should yield about 3 cups). Heat 1 tablespoon butter in a saucepan, add 1 finely chopped French shallot and 2 peeled and finely diced baking (floury) potatoes and sauté for 3 minutes. Add the chervil and sauté briefly.

Add 3 cups (750 ml/26 fl oz) vegetable stock, bring to a boil, then simmer for 5 minutes. Purée the soup, then add salt and freshly ground black pepper to taste. Add ½ cup (125 ml/4 fl oz) pure (light/single) cream and gently reheat.

Note This soup is delicious with poached eggs. In a wide saucepan, bring 2 cups (500 ml/16 fl oz) salted water and a dash of vinegar to a boil. Individually crack 4 eggs and lower each one into the boiling water using a soup ladle. Poach for 4 minutes, lift out with a slotted spoon and season with salt and black pepper.

Potato soup with watercress

250 g (8 oz) boiling (waxy) potatoes,
    peeled and quartered
200 g (7 oz) watercress
4 tablespoons butter
1 onion, finely chopped
1 small clove garlic, finely chopped
2 cups (500 ml/16 fl oz) chicken stock
$\frac{1}{2}$ cup (125 ml/4 fl oz) pure (light/single) cream
1 tablespoon dry white vermouth, such
    as Noilly Prat
salt and freshly ground white pepper
freshly grated nutmeg
4 tablespoons crème fraîche or sour cream
100 g (3$\frac{1}{2}$ oz) smoked salmon, cut into strips

serves 4
preparation 25 minutes
cooking 40 minutes

per serving 1888 kJ (451 calories), 12 g protein,
39 g total fat, 25 g saturated fat, 13 g carbohydrate

1 Bring 2 cups (500 ml/17 fl oz) lightly salted water to the boil in a saucepan. Add the potatoes and cook for 20 minutes, or until soft. Do not drain; you will need the cooking liquid.

2 Meanwhile, pick the leaves from the watercress, discarding the hard stalks. Wash and drain.

3 Heat the butter in a saucepan and gently sauté the onion and garlic for 2–3 minutes. Add the watercress and sauté for another 3 minutes. Pour in the stock, cream and vermouth and simmer for 10 minutes.

4 Add the watercress mixture to the cooked potatoes and their cooking liquid, allow to cool a little, then finely purée. Season to taste with salt, if needed, white pepper and nutmeg. Stir in the crème fraîche or sour cream and gently reheat. Serve scattered with the smoked salmon strips.

Cook's tip
Warm your soup bowls before serving up soup – either on the cooktop or in a warm oven.

Watercress
Watercress has a peppery flavour and is rich in iron. It is at its best when the leaves are absolutely fresh and a vivid dark green; avoid any with traces of yellowing. To keep watercress fresh, store it with the leaves submerged in a bowl of water. It can be served raw as a salad green, or briefly cooked — for example, by simply adding it to a soup at the end of the cooking time and letting the leaves wilt. If overcooked, watercress will lose its brilliant green colour.

Fish and vegetable soup

2 tablespoons olive oil

2 onions, finely chopped

3 cloves garlic, thinly sliced

1 large red capsicum (bell pepper), cut into
    matchsticks

500 g (1 lb) sweet potatoes, peeled and cut
    into 1 cm ($\frac{1}{2}$ inch) chunks

2 cups (500 ml/16 fl oz) fish or vegetable
    stock

$\frac{3}{4}$ teaspoon salt

$\frac{1}{2}$ teaspoon dried thyme

1$\frac{1}{2}$ cups (235 g/8$\frac{1}{2}$ oz) frozen peas

1 cup (150 g/5$\frac{1}{2}$ oz) frozen corn kernels

750 g (1$\frac{1}{2}$ lb) skinless, firm white fish fillets,
    boned and cut into chunks

freshly ground black pepper

fresh thyme leaves, to garnish (optional)

serves 4
preparation 20 minutes
cooking 25 minutes

per serving 1891 kJ (452 calories), 47 g protein,
14 g total fat, 3 g saturated fat, 33 g carbohydrate

1 Heat the oil in a large saucepan or flameproof casserole dish over medium heat. Add the onions and garlic and sauté for 5 minutes, stirring frequently, until the onions are light golden.

2 Add the capsicum and sweet potatoes, then cover and cook for 5 minutes, or until the sweet potatoes start to soften. Stir in the stock, salt and thyme. Bring to a boil, then reduce the heat, cover and simmer for 5 minutes, or until the sweet potatoes are just tender.

3 Stir in the peas and corn. Place the fish chunks on top of the vegetables. Cover and simmer for 8-10 minutes, or until the fish is cooked through but still tender. Season to taste with black pepper, then serve immediately, sprinkled with fresh thyme leaves, if you like.

Cook's tip

If you have a bottle of dry white wine open, use $\frac{1}{2}$ cup (125 ml/4 fl oz) to replace part of the stock.

Fish soup with spring vegetables

1 Heat 2 tablespoons olive oil in a large saucepan. Add 2 finely chopped French shallots and 3 thinly sliced cloves garlic and sauté over medium heat for 3 minutes, or until golden, stirring frequently.

2 Add 250 g (8 oz) snow peas (mangetout), trimmed and cut in half, 250 g (8 oz) baby carrots, sliced diagonally, 250 g (8 oz) green asparagus spears, trimmed and cut into short lengths, and 500 g (1 lb) small new potatoes, unpeeled and sliced, and sauté for a further 8 minutes. Stir in 2 cups (500 ml/16 fl oz) fish or vegetable stock and 1 teaspoon chopped fresh thyme and season with salt and freshly ground black pepper to taste. Bring to a boil, then reduce the heat, cover and simmer for 5 minutes.

3 Place 500 g (1 lb) skinless firm white fish fillets, cut into bite-sized pieces, on top of the vegetables. Cover and cook gently for 8–10 minutes, or until the fish is cooked through. Season to taste with black pepper and serve sprinkled with fresh thyme leaves, if you like.

Fish and vegetable soup

Borsch with mashed potatoes and vegetables

Borsch with beef

1 Make a meat stock the day before by simmering 750 g (1½ lb) beef brisket for several hours in a large saucepan with 10 cups (2.5 litres/87 fl oz) lightly salted water, 1 bay leaf, 1 chopped onion, 1 chopped carrot, 1 chopped stalk celery, a few sprigs parsley and 1 washed and chopped leek. When the meat is tender, remove it from the stock, cover and refrigerate. Strain the stock, cover and refrigerate.

2 The next day, skim any fat off the surface of the stock. Prepare the borsch as directed in the main recipe at right, replacing the vegetable stock with 4 cups (1 litre/35 fl oz) beef stock. Cut the beef into small pieces and simmer in the pureéd soup for 5 minutes to heat through. Serve the borsch as described in the main recipe, around a mound of the mashed potatoes and vegetables.

Borsch with mashed potatoes and vegetables

½ teaspoon lemon juice
1 bulb fennel
1 large carrot
1 tablespoon olive oil
1 onion, chopped
500 g (1 lb) beetroot (beets),
    peeled and diced
4 cups (1 litre/35 fl oz) vegetable stock
salt and freshly ground black pepper
750 g (1½ lb) roasting (floury) potatoes,
    peeled and finely diced
½ cup (125 ml/4 fl oz) low-fat milk
4 tablespoons Greek-style yogurt
2 spring onions (scallions), finely chopped

serves 4
preparation 15 minutes
cooking 40 minutes

per serving *1308 kJ (313 calories), 11 g protein,*
8 g total fat, 2 g saturated fat, 49 g carbohydrate

1 Place the lemon juice in a small bowl. Cut the fennel bulb into quarters, reserving the fronds to garnish. Finely grate one quarter of the fennel into the lemon juice and toss well. Finely grate half the carrot and mix it into the grated fennel. Cover and set aside.

2 Chop the remaining carrot. Heat the oil in a large saucepan and add the carrot and onion. Mix well, then cover and cook over medium heat for 5 minutes.

3 Chop the remaining fennel and add it to the pan with the beetroot. Pour in the stock and bring to a boil. Reduce the heat, cover and simmer for 30 minutes, or until the vegetables are tender. Allow the soup to cool a little, then purée it until smooth, add salt and black pepper to taste and gently reheat.

4 Meanwhile, cook the potatoes in another pan of boiling water for 10 minutes, or until very tender. Drain well, return to the pan and place over low heat for about 1 minute to dry, shaking the pan occasionally so the potatoes don't stick. Increase the heat to medium and mash until completely smooth, gradually working in the milk. Stir in the yogurt, grated fennel and carrot mixture and spring onions, and season to taste with salt and black pepper.

5 Divide the mashed potatoes among four bowls, piling up the mixture in the centre. Ladle the soup around the mashed potatoes, sprinkle with chopped fennel fronds and serve.

Salads

Hearty and filling, potatoes turn salad into a substantial and satisfying meal. Whether you eat salads all the time or just occasionally, you're sure to be tempted by the interesting recipes in this section.

Gado gado

peanut sauce

2 tablespoons red curry paste
1 cup (250 ml/8 fl oz) coconut cream
½ cup (125 g/4½ oz) crunchy peanut butter
1 tablespoon soy sauce
1 tablespoon lime juice
1 tablespoon soft brown sugar

salad

2 large boiling (waxy) potatoes, peeled,
    boiled until just tender and sliced
100 g (3½ oz) green beans, trimmed
    and blanched
2 carrots, peeled, sliced and blanched
2 eggs, hard-boiled and quartered
2 tomatoes, cut into wedges
1 cucumber, sliced
1 cup (90 g/3½ oz) bean sprouts, trimmed
150 g (5 oz) fried tofu, sliced

serves 4
preparation 15 minutes
cooking 10 minutes

per serving *2110 kJ (504 calories), 19 g protein,*
36 g total fat, 16 g saturated fat, 27 g carbohydrate

1 To make the peanut sauce, fry the curry paste with half the coconut cream in a small saucepan for 2–3 minutes, until sizzling. Add the remaining coconut cream and peanut butter and stir until the mixture is smooth and comes back to a boil. Simmer gently for a few minutes, stirring constantly. Add the remaining sauce ingredients and stir to combine.

2 Arrange the salad ingredients on a plate, drizzle with the peanut sauce and serve cold or at room temperature.

Mix and match

❋ Use halved cherry tomatoes or whole grape tomatoes instead of tomato wedges.

❋ A mixture of red and yellow tomatoes looks attractive.

Recipe note

'Gado' means 'mixed'. This traditional Indonesian salad combines raw and lightly cooked vegetables with a spicy peanut sauce. The ingredients used vary from region to region; other additions are spinach, snow peas (mangetout) or cauliflower. Firm vegetables can be used raw, blanched or steamed in this dish, depending on your preference, but they should remain crunchy.

Potato salad with bresaola

Warm new potato salad with beetroot and pastrami

1 Cook 3 scrubbed unpeeled beetroot (beets) in a saucepan of boiling water until tender. In a separate saucepan of boiling water, cook 750 g (1½ lb) unpeeled whole small new potatoes for 15 minutes, or until tender, adding ¾ cup (125 g/4½ oz) frozen peas in the last 2–3 minutes. Drain all the vegetables well.

2 Thickly slice the potatoes and combine in a serving bowl with the peas, 3 thinly sliced spring onions (scallions) and 85 g (3 oz) shredded pastrami. To make a dressing, mix together ⅓ cup (85 g/3 oz) low-fat natural (plain) yogurt, 1 tablespoon mayonnaise, 2 teaspoons wholegrain mustard, 2 tablespoons chopped fresh dill and 1 tablespoon rinsed and chopped capers. Peel the beetroot, cut into thin matchsticks, add to the salad and gently fold in the dressing. Scatter with 3 thinly sliced spring onions and 6 thinly sliced radishes. Serve warm.

Potato salad with bresaola

600 g (1 lb 5 oz) small unpeeled new
    potatoes, thickly sliced
1¼ cups (115 g/4 oz) thinly sliced button
    mushrooms
1 red onion, halved and thinly sliced
150 g (5 oz) endive and radicchio salad,
    or mixed salad leaves
2½ cups (75 g/2½ oz) watercress sprigs
8 slices bresaola or pastrami, about 90 g
    (3¼ oz) in total, cut in half
paprika, to garnish
thin slices of rye or pumpernickel bread,
    to serve (optional)

dressing

½ cup (125 g/4½ oz) fromage frais
    or light sour cream
½ cup (125 g/4½ oz) low-fat natural
    (plain) yogurt
1 tablespoon horseradish cream, from a jar
salt and freshly ground black pepper

serves 4
preparation 15 minutes
cooking 10 minutes

---

*per serving 923 kJ (221 calories), 17 g protein,
3 g total fat, 1 g saturated fat, 31 g carbohydrate*

1 Cook the potatoes in a saucepan of boiling water for 7-8 minutes, or until just tender.

2 Meanwhile, make the dressing by mixing together the fromage frais, yogurt and horseradish in a large bowl, adding salt and black pepper to taste.

3 When the potatoes are cooked, drain them and add them to the dressing while they are still warm. Add the mushrooms and most of the onion and toss together gently.

4 Tear any large salad leaves into bite-sized pieces. Divide the leaves and watercress among four serving plates and spoon the potato salad on top. Arrange the bresaola slices over the potatoes, then the remaining onion slices and sprinkle with a little paprika. Serve warm, with slices of rye or pumpernickel bread, if you like.

Health tip

Everyone loves potato salad, but it can be high in kilojoules (calories) and fat. This lower-fat version is made with a light fromage frais and yogurt dressing flavoured with horseradish to give a creamy finish with plenty of zing.

Bresaola

Bresaola is a type of air-dried Italian beef. Lean beef is rubbed with a mixture of coarse salt and spices, left to cure for a few days, then dried for 1–3 months. The resulting meat is a dark red colour and is served very thinly sliced, on its own or as part of a salad or antipasto plate.

Potato and tuna salad

6 small red or boiling (waxy) potatoes,
    peeled if you like
1²⁄₃ cups (250 g/9 oz) frozen peas
425 g (15 oz) can tuna in olive oil
2 carrots, grated
Juice of 1 lemon
salt and freshly ground black pepper
1¼ cups (300 g/10½ oz) mayonnaise
4 hard-boiled eggs, quartered
snipped fresh chives or chopped flat-leaf
    parsley, to sprinkle

serves 4
preparation 15 minutes + 30 minutes chilling
cooking 15 minutes

----

*per serving 3237 kJ (773 calories), 36 g protein,
54 g total fat, 8 g saturated fat, 36 g carbohydrate*

1 Cook the potatoes in a saucepan of boiling water for 15 minutes, or until just tender. Remove with a slotted spoon and drain. Cook the peas in the same saucepan for 3 minutes, then drain and rinse under cold running water.

2 Slice the potatoes and place in a serving bowl. Drain the oil from the tuna into a measuring cup, then flake the tuna onto the potatoes. Add the carrots and peas.

3 Add the lemon juice to the tuna oil. Season with salt and black pepper and add enough mayonnaise to make 350 ml (12 fl oz). Whisk the dressing and stir it through the salad. Arrange the eggs on top and sprinkle with the herbs. Cover and refrigerate for 30 minutes before serving.

Cook's tip

*Chives are best cut with a pair
of scissors to avoid squashing
and bruising the tender stalks.*

Tuna salad with green beans

1 Follow the recipe above, but substitute 200 g (7 oz) frozen green beans for the peas, adding them to the potatoes about 10 minutes before the end of cooking. Drain the potatoes, let them steam briefly, then peel and cut into slices. Drain the beans well, cut into halves or thirds, then place in a bowl with the potatoes.

2 Instead of carrots, use 2 firm tomatoes blanched in boiling water for 30 seconds. Peel, remove the seeds, dice the flesh and add to the salad. Lightly stir through the mayonnaise mixture. Cover and chill for 30 minutes. Season again with salt and freshly ground black pepper and arrange on four plates. Garnish with the hard-boiled eggs and some pitted and chopped black olives instead of the herbs.

Potato and tuna salad

Root vegetable salad with spicy vinaigrette

Potato salad with caramelised carrots

1 Boil 500 g (1 lb) boiling (waxy) potatoes for 15–20 minutes, or until tender. Peel, then cut into slices. Peel and slice 4 carrots. Heat 2 tablespoons olive oil in a frying pan, add the carrots and 1 teaspoon soft brown sugar and caramelise for about 2 minutes, turning the slices over. Add 1 finely chopped clove garlic and sauté briefly. Pour in 50 ml (1½ fl oz) dry Marsala and 50 ml (1½ fl oz) beef stock and cook for 8 minutes more, or until the carrots are tender but still firm. Season with salt and freshly ground black pepper and cool briefly.

2 Gradually mix 2 tablespoons extra virgin olive oil into 4 tablespoons sherry vinegar then season with salt and black pepper. Add two-thirds of this dressing to the potatoes and stir in carefully. Mix the remaining dressing into the carrots. Arrange the vegetables on a platter or individual serving plates, garnish with 2 tablespoons finely chopped fresh parsley and serve warm.

Root vegetable salad
with spicy vinaigrette

500 g (1 lb) beetroot (beets)
500 g (1 lb) boiling (waxy) potatoes
3 tomatoes
2 spring onions (scallions), finely chopped
2 cloves garlic, finely chopped
$\frac{1}{2}$ cup (20 g/$\frac{3}{4}$ oz) finely chopped fresh
    flat-leaf parsley
3 sprigs coriander (cilantro), leaves finely
    chopped
$\frac{3}{4}$ cup (100 g/3$\frac{1}{2}$) pitted black olives,
    to garnish

spicy vinaigrette

100 ml (3$\frac{1}{2}$ fl oz) white wine vinegar
$\frac{1}{2}$ cup (125 ml/4 fl oz) extra virgin olive oil
$\frac{1}{2}$ teaspoon salt
1 pinch freshly ground black pepper
1 pinch cayenne pepper

serves 4
preparation 30 minutes + 30 minutes chilling
cooking 1 hour 30 minutes

----
per serving *1959 kJ (468 calories), 7 g protein,*
34 g total fat, 5 g saturated fat, 33 g carbohydrate

1   Place the unpeeled beetroot in a large saucepan, cover with water and bring to a boil. Cook for 1$\frac{1}{2}$ hours, or until tender when pierced with a knife. Drain, reserving 4 tablespoons of the cooking water. Refresh under cold running water and leave to cool.

2   Meanwhile, cook the unpeeled potatoes in a saucepan of boiling water for 15-20 minutes, or until just tender. Drain, refresh under cold running water and leave to cool. Peel the beetroot and potatoes, cut in half and slice thinly. Place in separate bowls.

3   Blanch the tomatoes in boiling water for 30 seconds. Peel away the skins, then cut in half, remove the seeds and dice the flesh. Add to the beetroot with the spring onions, garlic, parsley, coriander and reserved cooking water.

4   To make the vinaigrette, whisk the vinegar, oil, salt, black pepper and cayenne pepper until combined. Stir two-thirds of the vinaigrette into the beetroot mixture and the remainder through the potatoes. Cover and refrigerate for 30 minutes.

5   Just before serving, add salt, black pepper and more vinegar to taste. Spoon the beetroot salad onto a platter and arrange the potato salad around it. Garnish with the olives.

Cook's tips

Beetroot tastes sweet because it is richer in natural sugar than any other vegetable. Small beetroot with their greens still attached have the most flavour.

You can find cooked, peeled vacuum-packed beetroot in the vegetable section of well-stocked supermarkets. If you cook the beetroot yourself, wear disposable gloves when peeling the skin off, as the juice stains are hard to remove.

Russian potato salad

1 cup (250 ml/8 fl oz) vegetable stock
500 g (1 lb) boiling (waxy) potatoes,
    peeled and diced
2 carrots, peeled and diced
150 g (5 oz) green beans, trimmed
1 large red capsicum (bell pepper), diced
1 cup (150 g/5 oz) frozen peas
2 tablespoons small capers, plus
    2-3 tablespoons brine from the jar
2 hard-boiled eggs
3 tablespoons chopped fresh parsley

mayonnaise

1 egg yolk
1 pinch mustard powder
1 large pinch salt
½ cup (125 ml/4 fl oz) vegetable oil
1-2 tablespoons lemon juice
1 pinch freshly ground black pepper

serves 4
preparation 30 minutes + 1 hour chilling
cooking 15 minutes

per serving *1837 kJ (439 calories), 11 g protein,*
33 g total fat, 5 g saturated fat, 24 g carbohydrate

1 Bring the stock to a boil in a large saucepan. Add the potatoes, carrots and beans. Cover and cook over medium heat for 5 minutes. Add the capsicum and peas, then cover and cook for another 5 minutes. Transfer the vegetables to a sieve and leave to cool.

2 Before making the mayonnaise, bring all the ingredients and the mixing bowl to room temperature to prevent the mayonnaise from separating. Whisk the egg yolk, mustard powder and salt until creamy. Add the oil in a thin stream, whisking until the mixture thickens. Add 1 tablespoon lemon juice, and salt and black pepper to taste. Add 2 tablespoons caper brine, or more if you think it needs it.

3 Place the vegetables and capers in a serving bowl. Spoon on the mayonnaise, stirring to coat. Cover and chill for 1 hour.

4 Just before serving, add more salt, pepper and lemon juice to taste. Peel the eggs, slice into wedges and add to the salad. Sprinkle with parsley and serve.

Cook's tip

It's worth doubling the quantity of this salad because it keeps very well and the flavours intensify on sitting. Cover and store in the refrigerator for up to 3 days.

Potato and asparagus salad

For a Russian salad with asparagus, cook the potatoes and vegetables as for step 1 of the recipe above, but substitute 250 g (8 oz) asparagus spears, trimmed and cut into thirds, for the capsicum and peas. Omit the capers from the salad and the caper brine from the mayonnaise.

Russian potato salad

Potato and lentil salad

Potato and lentil salad

1 kg (2 lb) boiling (waxy) potatoes, peeled
and cut into large chunks
3 tablespoons olive oil
2 tablespoons red wine vinegar
410 g (14½ oz) can brown lentils, rinsed
and drained well
1¼ cups (150 g/5 oz) pitted black olives
1 tablespoon capers, rinsed and chopped
2 cloves garlic, chopped
1 tablespoon lemon juice
3 tablespoons roughly chopped fresh
flat-leaf parsley
6 spring onions (scallions), sliced diagonally
salt and freshly ground black pepper

serves 6
preparation 15 minutes
cooking 20 minutes

per serving 1157 kJ (276 calories), 7 g protein,
14 g total fat, 2 g saturated fat, 29 g carbohydrate

1 Cook the potatoes in a saucepan of boiling water for 15-20 minutes, or until tender. Drain; transfer to a large bowl.

2 While the potatoes are still hot, add the olive oil and vinegar and stir through. Then add the lentils, olives, capers, garlic, lemon juice, parsley and spring onions. Season with a pinch of salt and a good grind of black pepper and toss well to combine. Serve warm.

Potato and lentil salad with fried onions

1 Place 2 cups (400 g/14 oz) French-style green (puy) lentils, 1 small sprig fresh rosemary and 1 small dried bay leaf in a saucepan. Add water to cover and bring to a boil. Cook on medium heat for about 40 minutes or until the lentils are tender. Leave to cool in the cooking liquid. Drain, reserving liquid. Discard rosemary and bay leaf.

2 Peel and dice 3 just-cooked small boiling (waxy) potatoes and place in a large bowl with the lentils and 2 large tomatoes, cored and diced. Whisk together 2 tablespoons olive oil, 2 tablespoons red wine or herb vinegar, 1 tablespoon lemon juice, 1 teaspoon grated lemon zest, ½ teaspoon ground cumin, 1 crushed clove garlic and 3 tablespoons reserved cooking liquid. Add salt and freshly ground black pepper to taste. Stir into the salad. Refrigerate the salad, covered, for 1 hour.

3 Close to serving time, sauté 2 large white onions, sliced into rings, in 2 tablespooons olive oil over moderate heat until golden brown. Taste the salad, then add more salt, pepper and vinegar, if needed. Stir in ½ cup (40 g/1½ oz) finely chopped fresh flat-leaf parsley. Divide the salad among four serving bowls and top with warm onions.

Cajun-style potato salad

1 kg (2 lb) small new potatoes, preferably
    red-skinned
2 red onions, roughly chopped
3-4 spring onions (scallions), finely chopped
2 tablespoons finely chopped fresh parsley
½ cup (125 ml/4 fl oz) apple vinegar
½ cup (125 ml/4 fl oz) olive oil
250 g (8 oz) chorizo (Spanish spicy pork
    sausage), thinly sliced
1 tablespoon dijon mustard
½ teaspoon sweet paprika
1 pinch cayenne pepper

serves 6
preparation 10 minutes
cooking 35 minutes

per serving 1663 kJ (397 calories), 10 g protein,
27 g total fat, 6 g saturated fat, 27 g carbohydrate

1 Cook the unpeeled potatoes in boiling salted water for 15-20 minutes, or until just tender. Drain, allow the potatoes to cool briefly, then slice and place in a bowl. Add the onions, spring onions, parsley and half the vinegar.

2 Heat the oil in a frying pan and gently brown the chorizo on both sides for about 8 minutes. Add the chorizo, olive oil and pan juices to the potatoes, and mix gently.

3 Briefly heat the remaining vinegar in a pan with the mustard, paprika and cayenne pepper, stirring constantly. Drizzle the mixture over the potato salad and stir in lightly. This salad is best served warm.

Cook's tip

Any new potatoes can be used, but red-skinned ones look particularly attractive in this dish. Desiree, pontiac, red pontiac, kerr's pink and pink eye are a few of the commonly available red varieties.

Potato and cucumber salad

1 Peel 750 g (1½ lb) just-cooked small boiling (waxy) potatoes and cut into slices, not too thinly. Place in a large bowl and leave to cool. Add 1 chopped onion and 1 small cucumber, peeled and shaved into thin slices.

2 Combine 3 tablespoons white wine vinegar, 4 tablespoons extra virgin olive oil, ½ teaspoon red wine vinegar, 50 ml (1¾ fl oz) beef stock and salt and freshly ground black pepper to taste. Add to the potatoes and stir in carefully. Cover and chill for 30 minutes. If the salad is too dry, add some more stock and vinegar. Serve sprinkled with 1 tablespoon snipped fresh chives.

Cajun-style potato salad

Five ways...

with potato salads

Potato salads are a great way to enjoy new potatoes or specialty salad potatoes. Be sure to use a waxy variety so the potatoes keep their shape when cooked and combined with other ingredients.

serves	prep	cook
6	15 mins	15 mins

Potato and turkey salad with mustard dressing

Cut 2 kg (2 lb) red potatoes into 1 cm (½ inch) chunks. Cook in a large saucepan of boiling water for 10 minutes, or until tender. Drain well.

Heat 1 tablespoon olive oil in a large frying pan. Sauté 1 large diced onion, 1 diced red capsicum (bell pepper) and 1 diced green capsicum over medium heat for 5 minutes, or until the capsicums are crisp-tender. Place in a large serving bowl and whisk in 1 cup (250 ml/8 fl oz) chicken stock, 3 tablespoons distilled white vinegar, 1 tablespoon dijon mustard and ½ teaspoon salt. Add the potatoes and 60 g (2 oz) smoked turkey, cut into 1 cm (½ inch) cubes. Toss well and serve warm or chilled.

per serving 1200 kJ (287 calories), 13 g protein, 4 g total fat, 1 g saturated fat, 48 g carbohydrate

serves	prep	cook
4	15 mins	10 mins

New potato salad with herb cream

Cook 1 kg (2 lb) small new potatoes in a saucepan of boiling water for 15 minutes, or until just tender. Drain, return to the pan and shake over low heat for a few minutes to evaporate any moisture. Place in a mixing bowl and leave to cool for 5 minutes. Sprinkle with 1 teaspoon white wine vinegar and 2 tablespoons dry white vermouth or dry white wine. Season with salt and freshly ground black pepper, toss gently and leave to cool completely.

Dice ½ large firm cucumber and add to the potatoes with 4 thinly sliced spring onions (scallions), 3 tablespoons chopped fresh dill and 1½ tablespoons chopped fresh tarragon. In a small bowl, mix together 1 finely chopped clove garlic, 3 tablespoons low-fat mayonnaise and 100 g (3½ oz) low-fat natural (plain) yogurt. Spoon over the potatoes and mix gently. Serve at room temperature or chilled, garnished with dill and tarragon leaves.

per serving 951 kJ (227 calories), 8 g protein, 3 g total fat, 1 g saturated fat, 39 g carbohydrate

New potato salad with herb cream

Potato and ham salad

serves 4 · prep 25 mins · cook 15 mins

Peel and dice 750 g (1½ lb) boiling (waxy) potatoes and cook until just soft. Drain and let steam briefly. Meanwhile, finely chop 5 cornichons or small gherkins (pickled cucumbers) and 1 tablespoon capers, then combine with ¾ cup (200 g/7 oz) mayonnaise and 2 teaspoons mustard. Mix together thoroughly, adding some cornichon liquid if necessary. Season with salt and freshly ground black pepper. Add the potatoes. Finely chop or slice 4 celery stalks, 1 green capsicum (bell pepper) and 1 onion and add to the bowl with 200 g (7 oz) finely diced ham. Add 3 chopped hard-boiled eggs and 12 pitted black olives and stir lightly. Line a bowl with cos (romaine) lettuce leaves and arrange the salad on top. Garnish with slices from 1 hard-boiled egg and serve.

per serving 1935 kJ (462 calories), 20 g protein, 25 g total fat, 4 g saturated fat, 40 g carbohydrate

Potato and bacon salad

serves 4 · prep 10 mins · cook 15 mins

Cook 5 chopped slices (strips) lean bacon in a lightly oiled frying pan over high heat until crisp, then drain on paper towels. Cook 1 kg (2 lb) small new potatoes in a saucepan of boiling water for 15 minutes, or until just tender. Drain, cut in half, and place in a large serving bowl while still warm. Add 4 quartered hard-boiled eggs, ½ cup (50 g/1¾ oz) chopped pickled cucumbers and 3 tablespoons chopped fresh flat-leaf parsley. Combine ⅔ cup (150 g/5 oz) mayonnaise, 4 tablespoons sour cream, 1 tablespoon lemon juice and 1 teaspoon paprika, then add to the salad and toss gently. Sprinkle with the bacon and 2 tablespoons chopped fresh dill.

per serving 2539 kJ (607 calories), 25 g protein, 36 g total fat, 11 g saturated fat, 45 g carbohydrate

Potato salad with spring onions

serves 4 · prep 20 mins · cook 15 mins

Peel 750 g (1½ lb) boiling (waxy) potatoes, cut into 2 cm (¾ inch) dice and boil until just soft. Drain and let steam briefly over low heat. In a large bowl, mix together ¾ cup (200 g/7 oz) mayonnaise, 2 tablespoons natural (plain) yogurt, 2 teaspoons mustard and 1 tablespoon finely chopped capers. Season with salt and freshly ground black pepper. Add the potatoes, 4–5 finely chopped spring onions (scallions), 1 sliced green capsicum (bell pepper) and 200 g (7 oz) finely diced ham. Add 3 chopped hard-boiled eggs and 12 pitted black olives and stir lightly. Line a bowl with cos (romaine) lettuce leaves and arrange the salad on top. Garnish with slices from 1 hard-boiled egg and serve.

NOTE You can also use canned tuna instead of ham. Drain 2 x 185 g (6½ oz) cans tuna, then flake the flesh apart with a fork. Stir into the mayonnaise together with the other ingredients.

per serving 1943 kJ (464 calories), 20 g protein, 25 g total fat, 4 g saturated fat, 39 g carbohydrate

Warm potato salad with artichokes

Potato, artichoke and pancetta salad

1   To make a potato salad using fresh artichokes instead of canned, trim the stalks and leaf tips from 500 g (1 lb) small globe artichokes. Cut into quarters and simmer in boiling water with some lemon juice and a good pinch of salt for about 20 minutes. Drain well, then fry as directed in the recipe opposite.

2   Replace the bacon with finely diced pancetta (an Italian dry-cured streaky bacon), sautéed in the olive oil with the onion for about 3 minutes. Then add the capsicum and fry for another 5 minutes. Add to the artichokes and potatoes as for the main recipe and finish preparing the salad as described in step 4 opposite.

Warm potato salad with artichokes

750 g (1½ lb) small new potatoes
400 g (14 oz) jar or can artichoke hearts,
    drained and rinsed
2 tablespoons olive oil
2 slices (strips) lean bacon, finely chopped
1 red onion, cut in half and thinly sliced
1 red or yellow capsicum (bell pepper),
    cut into thin strips
75 g (2½ oz) rocket (arugula) leaves
1 tablespoon balsamic vinegar
1 tablespoon dry white wine
salt and freshly ground black pepper
2 tablespoons pine nuts, toasted

serves 4
preparation 10 minutes
cooking 25 minutes

per serving 1547 kJ (370 calories), 12 g protein,
22 g total fat, 4 g saturated fat, 29 g carbohydrate

1 Cook the unpeeled potatoes in a saucepan of boiling water for 15 minutes, or until just tender. Drain well, then cut the potatoes in half, or into quarters if they are large.

2 While the potatoes are cooking, cut the artichoke hearts in half lengthwise and pat dry with paper towel. Heat half the oil in a non-stick frying pan over medium-high heat. Place the artichoke hearts in the pan in a single layer, cut side down, and cook for 2-3 minutes or until golden brown underneath. Turn them over and cook for a further minute or so to brown the other side. Transfer the artichokes to a serving bowl. Add the potatoes and keep warm.

3 Heat the remaining oil in the frying pan. Sauté the bacon and onion over medium-high heat for 1-2 minutes, then add the capsicum and cook for a further 1 minute. Using a slotted spoon, transfer the bacon, onion and capsicum to the bowl with the potatoes and artichokes. Scatter the rocket on top.

4 Return the pan to the heat and add the vinegar and wine. Tilt the pan to swirl and mix the vinegar and wine with the cooking juices. Pour over the salad, season to taste with salt and black pepper and toss gently until well combined. Sprinkle with the toasted pine nuts and serve.

Serving tip

This piquant salad is a perfect partner for lamb or chicken, or can be served as a starter before a light main course.

Globe artichokes

A member of the daisy family, the globe artichoke is an edible thistle native to the Mediterranean region. It was considered a delicacy as far back as Roman times. The edible parts are the bases of the leaves and the fleshy heart. Artichoke hearts are available in jars and cans, preserved in oil, vinegar or brine. Buy the ones in oil if you can, as these have a more refined flavour. The oil can be reserved and used in salad dressings.

Warm potato and spring vegetable salad

1 tablespoon butter
1 tablespoon olive oil
½ small onion, finely chopped
2 cloves garlic, crushed
500 g (1 lb) baking (floury) potatoes,
    peeled and diced
12 asparagus spears, trimmed and
    cut into 1 cm (½ inch) lengths
1 zucchini (courgette), diced
⅔ cup (100 g/3½ oz) fresh or frozen peas
2 tablespoons lemon juice
½ teaspoon dijon mustard
½ cup (10 g/¼ oz) fresh mint leaves, chopped
salt and freshly ground black pepper
grated parmesan, to serve (optional)

serves 4
preparation 10 minutes
cooking 10 minutes

per serving 787 kJ (188 calories), 6 g protein,
9 g total fat, 3 g saturated fat, 20 g carbohydrate

1 Heat the butter and oil in a small frying pan over medium heat. Add the onion and garlic and sauté for 3 minutes, or until softened.

2 Meanwhile, add the potatoes to a large saucepan of boiling water and cook for 3–4 minutes, or until just tender. Add the asparagus, zucchini and peas and cook for 1 minute more, then drain well.

3 Tip the vegetables into a serving bowl and add the onion mixture, lemon juice, mustard and mint. Season well with salt and black pepper and serve warm, topped with grated parmesan, if you like.

Potato and brussels sprout salad

1 Cook 500 g (1 lb) unpeeled whole small new potatoes in boiling water for 15 minutes, or until just tender. Drain thoroughly, then slice.

2 In a frying pan, sauté 400 g (14 oz) young brussels sprouts in 1 tablespoon butter for 5 minutes. Add a little water and cook for another 10 minutes, then remove from the pan, drain and season with salt, freshly ground black pepper and freshly grated nutmeg.

3 To make a dressing, combine 3 tablespoons white wine vinegar, ¼ teaspoon dijon mustard and some salt and black pepper. Gradually stir in ½ cup (125 ml/4 fl oz) extra virgin olive oil, then add 1 finely chopped French shallot and 1 tablespoon each finely chopped fresh parsley and chives. Wash 2 heads of chicory, separate the leaves and chop. Arrange on four plates with the potatoes and brussels sprouts. Drizzle with the dressing and leave for a short while before serving.

Note If you wish to use frozen brussels sprouts, add them to the boiling potatoes 10 minutes before the end of cooking time. Drain and cut in half, if you like.

Warm potato and spring vegetable salad

Potato and avocado salad with prawns

500 g (1 lb) unpeeled small new potatoes, diced
2 tablespoons vegetable oil
1 small red onion, thinly sliced
1 clove garlic, crushed
1 large mild red chilli, seeded and finely chopped
1 teaspoon coriander seeds, roughly crushed
1 teaspoon cumin seeds, roughly crushed
1 large ripe avocado
400 g (14 oz) peeled cooked prawns (shrimp)
juice of 2 limes
freshly ground black pepper
$\frac{1}{2}$ cup (125 g/$4\frac{1}{2}$ oz) low-fat natural (plain) yogurt
3 tablespoons chopped fresh coriander (cilantro)
8 large lettuce leaves

serves 4
preparation 20 minutes
cooking 20 minutes

per serving *1780 kJ (425 calories), 28 g protein,*
25 g total fat, 4 g saturated fat, 22 g carbohydrate

1 Cook the potatoes in a saucepan of boiling water for about 10 minutes, or until just tender. Drain and rinse under cold running water, then dry in a clean tea towel (dish towel).

2 Heat the oil in a frying pan. Add the onion and sauté over medium heat for 5 minutes, or until softened and lightly browned. Add the garlic, chilli and the crushed coriander and cumin seeds and cook for 1 minute more, stirring. Stir in the potatoes and fry over high heat for 3 minutes. Remove from the heat and leave to cool.

3 Peel the avocado (see Cook's tip), remove the stone and dice the flesh. Add to the potatoes with the prawns and lime juice. Season with black pepper and toss gently.

4 Mix together the yogurt, coriander and black pepper to taste. Line four serving bowls with the lettuce leaves, spoon the salad into them, top with the coriander yogurt and serve.

Cook's tip

To peel an avocado easily, cut it in half lengthwise, running the knife around the stone. Twist the halves to separate. Scoop out the stone with a spoon. With a knife, make several slices through the flesh (but not the skin), run a knife around the inside of the skin to loosen the slices, then scoop them out.

Salad niçoise

500 g (1 lb) new or boiling (waxy) potatoes
350 g (12 oz) thin green beans, trimmed
    and halved
1 red or yellow capsicum (bell pepper),
    thinly sliced
1 small bulb fennel, thinly sliced
4 tuna steaks, about 400 g (14 oz) in total
1 teaspoon olive oil
salt and freshly ground black pepper
8–12 crisp lettuce leaves
16 baby roma (plum) tomatoes, halved
3 hard-boiled eggs, quartered
12–16 black olives, pitted
1 cup (30 g/1 oz) fresh basil leaves,
    torn if large
crusty French bread, to serve

anchovy dressing

45 g (1½ oz) can anchovy fillets, drained
1 small clove garlic, peeled
2 teaspoons dijon mustard
1 tablespoon lemon juice
4 tablespoons extra virgin olive oil

serves 4
preparation 20 minutes
cooking 25 minutes

per serving *2341 kJ (559 calories), 39 g protein,*
33 g total fat, 7 g saturated fat, 26 g carbohydrate

1 Cook the unpeeled potatoes in a saucepan of boiling water for 15–20 minutes, or until tender, adding the beans for the last 5 minutes of cooking. Drain and refresh under cold running water. Cut the potatoes in half, then transfer the potatoes and beans to a mixing bowl. Add the capsicum and fennel.

2 To make the dressing, put three of the anchovy fillets and the garlic clove in a food processor and blend to a purée. Add the mustard, lemon juice and olive oil and process until smooth. Alternatively, use a pestle and mortar, pounding the anchovies and garlic to a paste before whisking in the remaining ingredients. Pour the dressing over the vegetables and toss to coat.

3 Brush the tuna steaks with the oil and season with black pepper. Heat a non-stick frying pan or ridged cast-iron grill pan. Add the tuna steaks and cook over medium-high heat for about 4 minutes on each side, or until lightly browned. Do not overcook or the tuna will be dry.

4 Make a layer of lettuce leaves on four serving plates and divide the potato mixture among them. Top with the tuna steaks. Arrange the tomatoes and egg quarters around the edge and scatter with the olives and basil leaves. Arrange the remaining anchovies over the top and serve with crusty French bread.

Health tips

Fennel provides useful amounts of beta-carotene, folate and potassium, as well as cancer-fighting phytochemicals.

Green beans are a good source of folate and dietary fibre.

Recipe note

For a quicker and more economical version of this salad, use a 425 g (15 oz) can tuna, drained well and flaked, instead of the tuna steaks.

Pork and pear salad with pecans

Pork and pear salad with pecans

½ cup (55 g/2 oz) pecans
1 kg (2 lb) new potatoes
1 small daikon (Japanese radish), about
    170 g (6 oz), or other mild radishes
6 red radishes
2 ripe but firm pears
1 oakleaf lettuce
100 g (3½ oz) watercress, tough stalks
    discarded
350 g (12 oz) lean roast pork, thinly sliced

mustard and ginger dressing

5 cm (2 inch) piece fresh ginger, peeled
    and finely chopped
2 teaspoons wholegrain mustard
2 teaspoons white wine vinegar
3 tablespoons peanut oil
1 tablespoon hazelnut oil
salt and freshly ground black pepper

serves 6
preparation 20 minutes
cooking 20 minutes

- -

per serving *1677 kJ (401 calories), 22 g protein,*
23 g total fat, 4 g saturated fat, 33 g carbohydrate

1 Heat a frying pan and toast the pecans over low-medium heat for 6-7 minutes, turning often. Transfer to a small bowl, allow to cool, then chop roughly. Set aside.

2 Meanwhile, cook the unpeeled potatoes in a large saucepan of boiling water for about 15 minutes, or until tender. Drain well. When cool enough to handle, cut the potatoes into quarters and place in a mixing bowl.

3 To make the dressing, first put the ginger in a garlic press and squeeze out the juice (you will need to do this in several batches). Pour 2 teaspoons of the ginger juice into a screwtop jar. Add the mustard, vinegar, peanut and hazelnut oils and some salt and black pepper and shake well to mix. Pour about one-third of the dressing over the warm potatoes and toss gently to coat. Leave to cool.

4 Peel and thinly slice the daikon and place in another bowl. Toss half the remaining dressing through to stop it browning. Cut the red radishes into quarters and toss with the daikon. Halve the pears lengthwise, scoop out the cores, cut into long wedges and toss with the radishes.

5 Arrange the lettuce leaves and watercress in a shallow salad bowl. Add the radish mixture to the potatoes and gently mix together. Pile onto the middle of the salad leaves and arrange the pork slices on top.

6 Stir the toasted pecans into the remaining dressing, drizzle over the salad and serve.

Pork and apple salad with hazelnuts

Substitute 2 apples for the pears in the above recipe. Wash the apples, cut them in half, remove the core and seeds and cut into wedges. Instead of the daikon and red radishes, use 2 finely sliced celery stalks and 2 small carrots, peeled and cut into thin matchsticks. Add the apples, celery and carrots to the dressed potatoes and combine carefully. Arrange the salad as described in the main recipe, using roasted hazelnuts instead of pecans to sprinkle over the salad.

Spinach, sweet potato and shiitake salad

500 g (1 lb) sweet potatoes, peeled, halved lengthwise, then cut crosswise into 1 cm (1/2 inch) slices
1/3 cup (35 g/1 1/4 oz) walnuts
2 tablespoons olive oil
2 cloves garlic, slivered
350 g (12 oz) fresh shiitake mushrooms, stems discarded and caps thickly sliced
1/2 teaspoon salt
350 g (12 oz) baby spinach leaves
1/2 cup (125 ml/4 fl oz) red wine vinegar
1 tablespoon dijon mustard

serves 4
preparation 20 minutes
cooking 20 minutes

---

per serving *1104 kJ (264 calories), 8 g protein,
16 g total fat, 2 g saturated fat, 21 g carbohydrate*

Cook's tip

*To save time, instead of baking the
sweet potatoes, you can microwave
whole, unpeeled potatoes and then
peel and slice them after cooking.*

1 Preheat the oven to 200°C (400°F/gas 6). Place the sweet potatoes on a lightly oiled baking tray and bake for 15-20 minutes, or until tender. Meanwhile, toast the walnuts in a frying pan for 5-7 minutes, or until crisp. Remove from the pan, leave until cool enough to handle, then coarsely chop.

2 In a large frying pan, heat half the oil over medium heat. Add the garlic and cook for 30 seconds, or until fragrant.

3 Add half the mushrooms, sprinkle them with 1/4 teaspoon salt and sauté for 4 minutes, or until they begin to soften. Remove from the pan using a slotted spoon, and repeat with the remaining mushrooms and salt.

4 Place the spinach in a large bowl. Add the sweet potatoes, walnuts and mushrooms.

5 Add the vinegar, mustard and remaining oil to the pan and stir over high heat until warm. Pour the dressing over the salad and toss to combine.

Sweet potato salad with mushrooms

1 Prepare the sweet potatoes as described above. Omit the walnuts, and replace the shiitake mushrooms with 400 g (14 oz) small button mushrooms, sliced. Heat 1 tablespoon olive oil in a non-stick frying pan. Briefly sauté the garlic, then add the mushrooms and fry for 10 minutes, turning them over occasionally.

2 Season the mushrooms with salt and freshly ground black pepper. Place in a bowl with the spinach and cooked sweet potatoes. Pour 1/2 cup (125 ml/4 fl oz) dry white wine into the frying pan and briefly bring to a boil. Stir in 100 ml (3 1/2 fl oz) pure (light/single) cream, pour over the salad and gently mix. Drizzle with a few drops of truffle oil (optional) or extra virgin olive oil and serve warm.

Spinach, sweet potato and shiitake salad

Potato, celery and capsicum salad

Potato, celery and capsicum salad

500 g (1 lb) boiling (waxy) potatoes
salt and freshly ground black pepper
1 small green capsicum (bell pepper),
    sliced into strips
2 stalks celery, finely sliced (reserve
    the leaves to garnish, if you like)
1 small red onion, cut into crescents
²/₃ cup (150 g/5 oz) mayonnaise
2 teaspoons dijon mustard
Tabasco sauce, to taste
freshly ground black pepper

serves 4
preparation 10 minutes
cooking 20 minutes

per serving 961 kJ (230 calories), 4 g protein,
12 g total fat, 1 g saturated fat, 25 g carbohydrate

1 Cook the unpeeled potatoes in a saucepan of salted boiling water for 15-20 minutes, or until tender.

2 Meanwhile, put the capsicum, celery and onion in a salad bowl. Mix the mayonnaise and mustard in a small bowl and add a splash of Tabasco.

3 Drain the potatoes, cool under cold running water, drain again thoroughly, then peel if you like. Add to the salad. Spoon the dressing over, grind some black pepper over the top and mix well. Garnish with celery leaves, if you like.

Potato salad with radicchio

1 Cook 500 g (1 lb) unpeeled whole small new potatoes in a saucepan of boiling water for 20–25 minutes, or until just tender. Drain, allow to steam briefly over low heat, then slice.

2 In a non-stick frying pan, melt 1 tablespoon butter. Cut 150 g (5 oz) ham into thin strips and fry in the butter until crisp. Remove with a slotted spoon and set aside. Melt another 1 tablespoon butter in the same pan and sauté 400 g (14 oz) young brussels sprouts with 2 teaspoons finely chopped fresh thyme leaves for 5 minutes. Add a little water and cook for another 10 minutes, then remove from the pan, drain and season with salt, freshly ground black pepper and freshly grated nutmeg.

3 To make a dressing, combine 3 tablespoons white wine vinegar, ¼ teaspoon dijon mustard and salt and black pepper to taste. Gradually stir in ½ cup (125 ml/4 fl oz) extra virgin olive oil, then add 1 finely chopped French shallot. Wash 1 head of radicchio and 2 heads of chicory, separate the leaves and tear into bite-sized pieces. Arrange on four plates with the potatoes and brussels sprouts. Drizzle with the dressing and leave for a short while before serving. Garnish with the fried ham strips.

Meat and poultry

Meat and potatoes are a classic combination. Roasts, braises, curries and casseroles are among the main meals in this chapter that pair succulent meat and tender poultry with potatoes cooked in many tempting ways.

Seared pork fillet with cumquats and mashed potatoes

750 g (1½ lb) baking (floury) potatoes,
    peeled and cut into chunks
350 g (12 oz) green beans, trimmed
1 tablespoon olive oil
400 g (14 oz) pork fillet (tenderloin),
    thinly sliced
1 small onion, finely sliced
115 g (4 oz) cumquats
1 tablespoon honey
1 tablespoon dijon mustard
150 ml (5 fl oz) dry white wine
150 ml (5 fl oz) vegetable stock
salt and freshly ground black pepper
3 tablespoons milk
freshly grated nutmeg
snipped fresh chives, to garnish (optional)

serves 4
preparation 15 minutes
cooking 20 minutes

per serving 1565 kJ (374 calories), 31 g protein,
8 g total fat, 2 g saturated fat, 38 g carbohydrate

1 Cook the potatoes in a saucepan of boiling water for about 10 minutes, or until tender. During the last 5 minutes of cooking, steam the beans in a steamer basket or colander over the potatoes.

2 Meanwhile, heat the oil in a large ridged cast-iron grill pan. Add the pork slices in batches and fry over a very high heat for 1 minute on each side, or until browned. Lift the slices out of the pan and set aside.

3 Add the onion to the pan and sauté over high heat for 3 minutes. Reduce the heat slightly, then return the pork to the pan and fry for an additional 5 minutes.

4 Thinly slice the cumquats, skin and all. Add to the pan with the honey and cook for 1 minute. Mix the mustard, wine and stock together, then pour the mixture into the pan. Season with salt and black pepper to taste and simmer for 3 minutes.

5 Drain the potatoes and mash them with the milk. Season to taste with salt, black pepper and nutmeg. Spoon the mashed potato into the middle of four serving plates. Arrange the pork slices around the mashed potato and pour over a little of the sauce. Add the cumquats and beans and pour the remaining sauce over. Garnish with chives, if using.

Duck breast with mashed potatoes

1 Prepare the potato mash and green beans as described in step 1 of the recipe above. Substitute 2 duck breasts for the pork fillet. Remove the skin and fat from the duck breasts, cut the flesh in half horizontally and cut each half into four thin slices. Fry the duck breast in the same way as the pork slices in step 2, and add the onion as in step 3 above.

2 Replace the mustard with a 2 cm (¾ inch) piece of fresh ginger, peeled and finely chopped. Add to the pan with the cumquats in step 4, adding the seared duck slices right at the end to moisten them. Finally, finish and serve the dish as instructed in step 5 above.

Seared pork fillet with cumquats and mashed potatoes

Meat and potato turnovers

Meat and potato turnovers

2 cups (250 g/8 oz) plain (all-purpose) flour,
plus extra for rolling
$\frac{1}{2}$ teaspoon salt
$\frac{1}{2}$ teaspoon dried thyme
$\frac{1}{2}$ cup (125 g/4$\frac{1}{2}$ oz) cold butter, diced
90 ml (3 fl oz) iced water, or as needed
1 beaten egg

filling

2 tablespoons vegetable oil
2 onions, finely chopped
400 g (14 oz) rump (sirloin) steak, diced
salt and freshly ground black pepper
200 ml (7 fl oz) beef stock
250 g (8 oz) boiling (waxy) potatoes,
peeled and finely diced
2 carrots, peeled and finely diced

serves 4
preparation 35 minutes + 30 minutes chilling
cooking 1 hour

---

per serving 3127 kJ (747 calories), 34 g protein,
42 g total fat, 21 g saturated fat, 58 g carbohydrate

1 Sift the flour into a bowl with the salt and thyme. Using your fingertips, rub the butter into the flour until the mixture is crumbly. Gradually work in enough iced water to form a smooth dough. Shape into a ball, cover with plastic wrap and allow to rest in the refrigerator for 30 minutes.

2 Meanwhile, make the filling. Heat the oil in a heavy-based saucepan and sauté the onions over medium heat for about 5 minutes. Add the beef in batches and brown for 2-3 minutes each time, then remove as each batch is done. Return all the browned meat to the pan and fry for another 5 minutes, stirring constantly.

3 Season the beef with salt and black pepper, pour in the stock and briefly bring to a boil. Add the potatoes and carrots, then cover and simmer over low heat for 15 minutes.

4 Preheat the oven to 210°C (415°F/gas 6-7). Line two baking trays with baking (parchment) paper. Divide the dough into four portions. On a lightly floured surface, roll each portion out to a 20 cm (8 inch) circle. Spread one-quarter of the filling on one side of each circle, leaving a rim. Brush the rims with water, then fold the other pastry half over the filling. Firmly press the pastry rims together using the prongs of a fork. Place the turnovers on the baking trays, brush with the beaten egg and bake for 30 minutes, or until golden. Serve hot.

Potato and zucchini turnovers

1 Prepare the dough as described in the recipe above and allow to rest in the refrigerator for 30 minutes. Substitute 2 firm zucchini (courgettes) for the carrots. Fry the onions and beef as directed in step 2 above, then season and sprinkle with 1 teaspoon chopped fresh rosemary and 1 teaspoon chopped fresh thyme.

2 Pour in the stock as in step 3 and briefly bring to a boil. Add the potatoes and cook for 5 minutes, then add the sliced zucchinis and cook for 10 minutes more. Roll out the pastry, then fill and cook the turnovers as instructed in step 4.

Barbecued potato and sausage packet

500 g (1 lb) boiling (waxy) potatoes, peeled
and sliced
500 g (1 lb) carrots, peeled and sliced
1 red onion, sliced into thick rings
1 red capsicum (bell pepper), cut into strips
1 green capsicum (bell pepper), cut into strips
1 yellow capsicum (bell pepper), cut into strips
2 firm tomatoes, such as roma (plum)
tomatoes, cut into large dice
500 g (1 lb) Polish sausage (firm sausage
made from pork and beef), sliced
4 tablespoons butter
salt and freshly ground black pepper

serves 6
preparation 20 minutes
cooking 1 hour

per serving *879 kJ (210 calories), 15 g protein,*
24 g total fat, 13 g saturated fat, 23 g carbohydrate

1   Spread the potatoes, carrots, onion, capsicums, tomatoes and sausage on a large piece of extra-strength foil, shaping the edges of the foil into a high rim.

2   Top the mixture with dots of butter and season with salt and freshly ground black pepper.

3   Cover with a matching sheet of foil to make a parcel. Place on a moderately hot charcoal barbecue grill for 30 minutes. Turn the potatoes, vegetables and sausage over and cook for another 30 minutes. Serve hot.

Cook's tip

This dish can also be cooked in the oven. Preheat the oven to 180°C (350°F/gas 4). Line a baking tray with baking (parchment) paper and spread the potatoes, vegetables and sausage over it. Drizzle with 2–3 tablespoons vegetable oil and season with salt and freshly ground black pepper to taste. Bake for about 45 minutes, turning the ingredients over occasionally.

Capsicums

Capsicums (bell peppers) are members of the chilli family. They have mild-flavoured, crisp flesh and may be yellow, orange, red, green, purple or even black. Red capsicums are an excellent source of vitamin C; weight for weight, they contain more than twice as much as oranges. Buy glossy, firm and unwrinkled capsicums and store in the refrigerator for up to 10 days. Remove the stem, seeds and white inner membranes before cooking. Capsicums grow well under indoor cultivation, so are available all year round, but they are at their best in late summer.

Thai chicken curry

Thai chicken curry

400 ml (14 fl oz) light coconut milk

200 ml (7 fl oz) chicken stock

2 tablespoons Thai green curry paste

4 boneless, skinless chicken breasts, about
    600 g (1 lb 5 oz) in total, cut into thin strips

350 g (12 oz) unpeeled new potatoes, cut
    into chunks

6 spring onions (scallions), sliced on the
    diagonal

2 tablespoons lime juice

$\frac{3}{4}$ cup (125 g/4$\frac{1}{2}$ oz) shelled fresh or frozen
    peas, thawed if necessary

8 grape or cherry tomatoes, halved

4 tablespoons chopped fresh coriander
    (cilantro)

salt and freshly ground black pepper

serves 4

preparation 10 minutes

cooking 25 minutes

*per serving 1908 kJ (456 calories), 39 g protein,
22 g total fat, 14 g saturated fat, 24 g carbohydrate*

1 Put the coconut milk, stock and curry paste in a wok, stir together and heat until boiling. Stir in the chicken strips and potatoes, then bring back to a boil.

2 Reduce the heat and simmer, uncovered, for 15 minutes, or until the potatoes are just tender and the chicken is cooked.

3 Stir in the spring onions, lime juice, peas and tomatoes and simmer for a further 3-4 minutes. Stir in the coriander and season to taste with salt and black pepper. This dish is good served with jasmine rice (Thai fragrant rice).

Cook's tips

If you find it hard to squeeze the juice out of limes, put them in the microwave for a few seconds – the heat will make them easier to juice. Alternatively, roll them around on the work surface a few times. This breaks the cell membranes inside.

If you don't have a wok, you can prepare this dish in a large frying pan or a wide saucepan.

Chicken curry with eggplant

Replace the spring onions and peas in the recipe above with 1 small eggplant (aubergine), cut into bite-sized pieces. Add the chicken strips, potatoes and eggplant to the hot coconut milk mixture as in step 1 and simmer over low heat for about 15 minutes as in step 2. Add the tomatoes and lime juice as in step 3 and briefly heat with the other ingredients. Season with salt and freshly ground black pepper. Finally, stir in the coriander and serve hot with rice, if you like.

Chicken and blue cheese gratin

750 g (1½ lb) boiling (waxy) potatoes,
    peeled and thinly sliced
300 g (10½ oz) celeriac (celery root),
    peeled and thinly sliced
350 g (12 oz) leeks, white part only,
    washed and sliced
250 g (8 oz) boneless, skinless chicken
    breasts, cut widthwise into thin strips
1 tablespoon chopped fresh thyme or
    ½ teaspoon dried thyme
freshly ground black pepper
1 cup (250 ml/8 fl oz) chicken stock, hot
75 g (2½ oz) firm blue cheese, crumbled
1 tablespoon butter, cut into small dice

serves 4
preparation 20 minutes
cooking 50 minutes

*per serving 1572 kJ (376 calories), 26 g protein,
14 g total fat, 8 g saturated fat, 36 g carbohydrate*

1 Preheat the oven to 200°C (400°F/gas 6). Place the potatoes and celeriac in a saucepan of lightly salted water, then cover and bring to a boil over medium heat. Remove the lid and simmer for 3 minutes, or until starting to soften. Remove from the heat and drain well.

2 Neatly spread about one-third of the potato and celeriac slices in an 8 cup (2 litre/70 fl oz) baking dish, overlapping the slices. Scatter about half the leeks, chicken strips and thyme over the vegetable layer. Season with plenty of black pepper.

3 Continue layering the potatoes and celeriac with the remaining leeks, chicken and thyme. Finish with a layer of the remaining potatoes and celeriac.

4 Pour the hot stock over, then scatter the cheese and butter over the top. Cover with foil and bake for 20 minutes.

5 Remove the foil and bake for a further 20 minutes, or until the cheese has melted and the top is golden and bubbling. Serve hot.

Serving tip

This is a perfect dish for a winter day. Serve it with a tomato and green bean salad and some chunks of crusty bread.

Blue cheese

There are various types of blue cheese, from sharp and pungent varieties, including danish blue and stilton, to milder, creamy types such as cambozola and gorgonzola dolce. Use whichever you prefer in this recipe. Don't be put off if you find blue cheese too strong on its own; when cooked with other ingredients, as here, the flavour is much less assertive and will not overwhelm the dish.

Chicken and blue cheese gratin

Tarragon chicken with creamy vegetables

1 Place 4 boneless, skinless chicken breasts in a shallow non-metallic dish. Drizzle with a mixture of 1 teaspoon olive oil, 1 tablespoon lemon juice, 1 tablespoon chopped fresh tarragon and some salt and freshly ground black pepper. Turn the chicken to coat, then cover and refrigerate while you prepare the other ingredients.

2 Preheat the oven to 190°C (375°F/gas 5). Simmer 750 g (1½ lb) unpeeled small new potatoes in a saucepan of salted water for 7 minutes. Add 4 large peeled carrots and/or parsnips and simmer for 5 minutes more. Drain. Peel the potatoes, then thinly slice with the carrots or parsnips. Whisk ¾ cup (200 g/7 oz) light sour cream into 150 ml (5 fl oz) chicken stock. Stir in 1 crushed clove garlic, 4 finely chopped spring onions (scallions) and 1 tablespoon chopped fresh tarragon.

3 Layer the potatoes and carrots or parsnips alternately in a greased, shallow baking dish, spooning a little sour cream mixture over each layer. Finish with a layer of potato slices, then spread with the remaining sour cream mixture. Cover with foil and bake for 35–40 minutes. Remove from the oven and place the chicken over the potatoes. Cover and bake for a further 25–30 minutes, or until the chicken is cooked through. Serve scattered with 1 tablespoon chopped fresh tarragon.

Spicy pork and bacon pie with potato topping

Spiced lamb pie with potato topping

1 Heat 1 tablespoon extra virgin olive oil in a large frying pan. Add 2 chopped red onions, 1 red and 1 yellow capsicum (bell pepper), both seeded and chopped, 2 crushed cloves garlic and 1–2 seeded and finely chopped red chillies and sauté for 5 minutes, or until softened. Add 2 teaspoons ground cumin, 2 teaspoons ground coriander and 350 g (12 oz) lean minced (ground) lamb and cook for 3–4 minutes, or until the meat is browned. Add 1 small diced eggplant (aubergine), 250 g (8 oz) halved button mushrooms, a 410 g (14½ oz) can chopped tomatoes with their juice, 2 tablespoons tomato paste (concentrated purée) and 200 ml (7 fl oz) lamb or beef stock or red wine (or a mixture). Cover and simmer for 45 minutes.

2 Peel 1 kg (2 lb) peeled baking (floury) potatoes and cook in a saucepan of salted boiling water until tender. Mash with 1 tablespoon extra virgin olive oil and 100 ml (3½ fl oz) low-fat milk. Mix in 3 tablespoons chopped fresh coriander (cilantro) and salt and freshly ground black pepper to taste. Transfer the lamb mixture to an ovenproof dish, cover with potato mixture and bake in a preheated 200°C (400°F/ gas 6) oven for 25 minutes or until the topping is nicely browned. Serve hot.

Spicy pork and bacon pie with potato topping

2 tablespoons vegetable oil
200 g (7 oz) lean bacon, cut into
    thin strips
2 onions, finely chopped
600 g (1 lb 5 oz) pork shoulder, cut into
    bite-sized pieces
2 small eating apples, halved, seeded
    and chopped
salt and freshly ground black pepper
freshly grated nutmeg
$\frac{1}{2}$ teaspoon dried sage, plus extra for
    sprinkling
300 ml (10$\frac{1}{2}$ fl oz) unsweetened cider
400 g (14 oz) baking (floury) potatoes
3 tablespoons milk
1 tablespoon butter

serves 6
preparation 30 minutes
cooking 2 hours

per serving *1599 kJ (382 calories), 29 g protein,*
19 g total fat, 6 g saturated fat, 19 g carbohydrate

1 Heat half the oil in a large saucepan and fry the bacon until crisp. Remove from the pan, then sauté the onions in the bacon fat for about 5 minutes. Remove from the pan and heat the remaining oil. Working in batches, brown the pork all over, then return all the pork to the pan and fry for another 5 minutes.

2 Add the bacon, onions and apples, season with salt, black pepper and some nutmeg and sprinkle with the sage. Pour in the cider, bring to a boil, cover and simmer on low heat for 1$\frac{1}{2}$ hours.

3 Meanwhile, peel the potatoes, dice them, then cook in a saucepan of boiling water for 10 minutes, or until soft. Drain, then allow to steam briefly over low heat to dry off a little.

4 Heat the milk and melt the butter in it. Use a potato masher to purée the potatoes, gradually adding the milk. Season with salt, pepper and nutmeg.

5 Preheat the grill (broiler) to its highest setting. Transfer the casserole mixture to a flameproof dish and cover with the mash. Bake under the grill for 5 minutes, or until the topping is golden. Sprinkle with dried sage and serve hot.

Mix and match

Replace the potatoes, milk and butter with any of the mashed potato recipes from pages 128–29.

American-style cottage pie

500 g (1 lb) lean minced (ground) beef
1 large onion, diced
1 beef stock (bouillon) cube, crumbled
425 g (15 oz) can baked beans in
    tomato sauce
2 teaspoons worcestershire sauce
3 teaspoons maple syrup
salt and freshly ground black pepper
750 g (1½ lb) all-purpose potatoes, peeled
    and diced
3-4 tablespoons fromage frais or sour cream
fresh thyme sprigs, to garnish

serves 4
preparation 10 minutes
cooking 30 minutes

----

per serving 1800 kJ (430 calories), 37 g protein,
10 g total fat, 4 g saturated fat, 46 g carbohydrate

1 In a large frying pan, dry-fry the meat and onion over medium heat for 6-7 minutes, stirring frequently, until the meat has browned and the liquid has evaporated.

2 Add the stock cube, baked beans, worcestershire sauce and maple syrup, stirring well. Cover and simmer for 10 minutes, stirring occasionally. Moisten the mixture with a little water, if necessary, and season with black pepper.

3 Meanwhile, bring a large saucepan of water to a boil. Add the potatoes and 1 pinch salt, return to a boil and cook for 10-15 minutes, or until tender. Drain and mash with the fromage frais or sour cream, then add salt and black pepper to taste.

4 Heat the grill (broiler) to high. Spoon the meat mixture into a 6 cup (1.5 litre/52 fl oz) flameproof serving dish and spread the mashed potato over the top. Place under the grill for 5 minutes, or until the topping is golden brown. Garnish with thyme sprigs and serve.

Beef and capsicum hotpot

1 In a large frying pan, heat 2 tablespoons olive oil and sauté 1 large onion, diced, with 1 red and 1 green capsicum (bell pepper), cut into bite-sized pieces, until the onion is translucent and the capsicum is crisp-tender. Add 500 g (1 lb) lean minced (ground) beef and fry until browned and crumbling. Season with salt and freshly ground black pepper. Add 100 ml (3½ fl oz) tomato sauce (ketchup) and simmer over low heat for 10 minutes, or until all the liquid has evaporated.

2 Bring a large saucepan of water to a boil. Add 750 g (1½ lb) peeled and diced all-purpose potatoes and 1 pinch salt, return to a boil and cook for 10–15 minutes, or until tender. Drain and mash with 3–4 tablespoons fromage frais or sour cream, then add salt and black pepper to taste.

3 Heat the grill (broiler) to high. Spoon the meat mixture into a 6 cup (1.5 litre/ 52 fl oz) flameproof serving dish and spread the mashed potato mixture over the top. Place under the grill for 5 minutes, or until the topping is golden brown. Sprinkle with finely chopped fresh thyme leaves and serve hot.

American-style cottage pie

Belgian potato hotpot

1 kg (2 lb) piece of roasting beef (beef chuck)
salt and freshly ground black pepper
100 g (3½ oz) bacon
3-4 small onions, cut into wedges
leaves from 4 sprigs fresh thyme
2 dried bay leaves
1 cup (250 ml/8 fl oz) dry red wine
½ cup (125 ml/4 fl oz) beef stock
750 g (1½ lb) small boiling (waxy) or all-
    purpose potatoes, peeled and sliced
4 carrots, peeled and sliced

serves 4-6
preparation 35 minutes
cooking 2 hours 15 minutes

per serving 2456 kJ (587 calories), 63 g protein,
19 g total fat, 8 g saturated fat, 31 g carbohydrate

1 Remove the sinews and fat from the beef, then rinse the meat under cold running water. Pat dry with paper towel and rub on all sides with a little salt and black pepper.

2 Fry the bacon in a flameproof casserole dish or heavy-based saucepan over high heat without any oil. Add the beef and brown thoroughly on all sides. Add the onions and fry until well browned, stirring constantly. Sprinkle the thyme leaves over the beef and place the bay leaves on top.

3 Pour in the red wine and stir to loosen the solids from the bottom of the dish. Heat the stock in a separate pan, then pour into the dish. Cover and simmer over low heat for 90 minutes, turning the beef occasionally. Season the sauce generously with salt and black pepper.

4 Add the potatoes and carrots to the dish. Cover and simmer for a further 30 minutes, or until the vegetables are soft.

5 Discard the bay leaves. Remove the meat from the dish, carve into slices and place back in with the vegetables. Season to taste and serve hot from the dish.

Cook's tip

To retain its flavour and aroma, the meat has to be browned quickly at very high heat. The onions also need to be fried at a high temperature, but must not be burnt or they will taste bitter. Stir them frequently to stop them catching on the bottom of the pan and charring.

Five ways...

with mashed potatoes

For light, fluffy mashed potatoes every time, use baking (floury) potatoes, and always mash them with a potato masher. Using a blender or food processor will give a tough, gluey mixture.

Mashed potatoes with bacon

Mashed potatoes with bacon

serves	prep	cook
4	10 mins	20 mins

Heat 1 tablespoon vegetable oil in a frying pan. Add 100 g (3½ oz) finely diced lean bacon and 1 small red onion, cut into fine rings. Fry until the onion is golden and the bacon crisp. Stir in 1 teaspoon finely chopped fresh thyme and keep warm. Meanwhile, peel 750 g (1½ lb) baking (floury) potatoes and cut into chunks. Cook in boiling salted water for 10–15 minutes, or until soft. Drain and allow to steam briefly over low heat. Melt 2 tablespoons butter in 100 ml (3½ fl oz) hot milk, pour over the potatoes and mash coarsely, using a potato masher. Season with salt and freshly ground black pepper and stir in 2 finely chopped spring onions (scallions). Serve garnished with the bacon mixture.

per serving 1323 kJ (316 calories), 10 g protein, 19 g total fat, 8 g saturated fat, 27 g carbohydrate

Mashed potatoes with mozzarella

serves	prep	cook
4	10 mins	30 mins

Peel 750 g (1½ lb) baking (floury) potatoes and cut into chunks. Cook in boiling salted water for 10–15 minutes, or until soft. Drain, allow to steam briefly over low heat, then mash using a potato masher. Heat ½ cup (125 ml/ 4 fl oz) milk and 1 tablespoon butter and stir into the potatoes, then mix in 1 egg yolk. Season with salt, freshly ground black pepper and freshly grated nutmeg. Spread the potato mixture in a greased flameproof dish. Drain 150 g (5 oz) fresh mozzarella, cut it into thin slices and arrange over the potato. Place under a medium-hot grill (broiler) for 10 minutes, or until golden.

per serving 1274 kJ (304 calories), 16 g protein, 15 g total fat, 9 g saturated fat, 26 g carbohydrate

Cook's tip

If you prefer a softer texture, use more milk or other liquid than specified when mashing the potatoes, mixing it in gradually with a masher or whisk. Using hot (but not boiling) milk will give the best result.

Light mashed potatoes

serves 4 · prep 15 mins · cook 20 mins

Place ½ cup (125 ml/4 fl oz) milk, 1 dried bay leaf and a pinch of salt in a small saucepan. Heat gently until just boiling, then remove from the heat and set aside to infuse. Peel 1 kg (2 lb) baking (floury) potatoes and cut into chunks. Place in a saucepan and cover with boiling water. Bring to a boil, then simmer rapidly for 15-20 minutes, or until very tender. Drain the potatoes well and return them to the pan. Pour the infused milk over, discarding the bay leaf, and mash using a potato masher until completely smooth. Work in 2 tablespoons extra virgin olive oil and salt and freshly ground black pepper to taste. Serve hot.

per serving 1107 kJ (264 calories), 7 g protein, 11 g total fat, 2 g saturated fat, 35 g carbohydrate

Mashed sweet potatoes with maple and orange glaze

serves 4 · prep 15 mins · cook 45 mins

Preheat the oven to 220°C (425°F/gas 7). Peel and thickly slice 1 kg (2 lb) sweet potatoes. Place in a large saucepan with 6 quartered cloves garlic. Add ¼ teaspoon salt and enough water to just cover. Cook over medium heat for 10-15 minutes, or until soft. Drain, allow to steam briefly over low heat, then add 1 tablespoon extra virgin olive oil and season with salt and freshly ground black pepper. Mash using a potato masher to a coarse purée. Spread the mixture in a greased flameproof dish. In a small pan, bring to a boil 1 tablespoon olive oil, 3 tablespoons maple syrup and the finely grated zest of 1 orange. Drizzle over the sweet potato and bake for 25 minutes, or until golden.

per serving 1260 kJ (301 calories), 5 g protein, 10 g total fat, 1 g saturated fat, 49 g carbohydrate

Spice-glazed mashed sweet potatoes

serves 4 · prep 15 mins · cook 45 mins

Preheat the oven to 220°C (425°F/gas 7). Peel and thickly slice 1 kg (2 lb) sweet potatoes. Place in a large saucepan with 6 quartered cloves garlic. Add ¼ teaspoon salt and enough water to just cover. Cook over medium heat for 10-15 minutes, or until soft. Drain, allow to steam briefly over low heat, then add 1 tablespoon extra virgin olive oil and season with salt and freshly ground black pepper. Mash using a potato masher to a coarse purée. Spread the mixture in a greased flameproof dish. In a small saucepan, bring to a boil 1 tablespoon olive oil, 3 tablespoons honey, 1 tablespoon finely grated lemon zest, ½ teaspoon ground cinnamon and a pinch of freshly grated nutmeg. Drizzle over the sweet potato and bake for 25 minutes, or until golden.

per serving 1323 kJ (316 calories), 5 g protein, 9 g total fat, 1 g saturated fat, 53 g carbohydrate

Pan-grilled steak and potatoes

2 cloves garlic, finely chopped
1 red chilli, seeded and very finely chopped
1/2 cup (125 ml/4 fl oz) extra virgin olive oil,
  plus extra for brushing and frying
3 tablespoons red wine vinegar
1 tablespoon lemon juice
3–4 tablespoons finely chopped fresh parsley
1 tablespoon finely chopped fresh oregano
salt and freshly ground black pepper
1 large rump (sirloin) steak, about 500 g (1 lb)
  and 2.5 cm (1 inch) thick
4 unpeeled large boiling (waxy) potatoes, cut
  lengthwise into 1 cm (1/2 inch) slices

serves 4
preparation 20 minutes + 3 hours marinating
cooking 30 minutes

per serving 2286 kJ (546 calories), 31 g protein,
35 g total fat, 7 g saturated fat, 25 g carbohydrate

1 Put the garlic, chilli, olive oil, vinegar, lemon juice, parsley, oregano and some salt and black pepper in a bowl and mix well. Pour two-thirds of the marinade into a large freezer bag and set the remainder aside at room temperature.

2 Pat the steak dry with paper towel. Place into the freezer bag containing the marinade and close the bag firmly. Marinate in the refrigerator for 3 hours.

3 Cook the potatoes in a saucepan of boiling water for 10–15 minutes, or until just tender. Drain, then dry the slices well on paper towel. Brush both sides with oil and salt lightly.

4 Brush a ridged grill pan with some olive oil and heat to medium-high. Fry the steak and potatoes for 4–5 minutes per side, or until the potatoes are nicely coloured and the steak is done to your liking. Thinly slice the steak across the grain and arrange on plates with the potatoes. Drizzle with the reserved marinade and serve.

Mix and match

Wash 8 spring onions (scallions), dry with paper towel and brush with olive oil. Brown them in the grill pan together with the steak and potatoes, turning the spring onions regularly so they will not become too dark. Serve with the steak and potatoes, drizzled with the reserved marinade.

Cook's tip

The steak slices are ready when the meat yields only lightly to pressure applied with a fork.

Pan-grilled steak and potatoes

Pan-fried potatoes with veal

1 Peel and thinly slice 500 g (1 lb) small waxy or all-purpose potatoes. Quarter 250 g (8 oz) zucchini (courgettes) lengthwise then cut into chunks. Seed 1 red and 1 yellow capsicum (bell pepper) and cut into strips. Cut 3 French shallots into rings. Finely chop 1 clove garlic. Cut 250 g veal shoulder into thin strips and coat in 1 tablespoon plain (all-purpose) flour. Heat 3 tablespoons butter in a large frying pan, add the meat and fry, stirring, for about 3 minutes or until brown.

2 Add ½ cup (125 ml/4 fl oz) vegetable stock, the potatoes, zucchinis, capsicums, garlic and shallots. Cover and simmer for about 15 minutes or until the potatoes are soft. Sprinkle with 1 teaspoon each finely chopped fresh thyme, finely chopped marjoram and finely chopped rosemary and cook on low heat for another 5 minutes. Add salt and black pepper to taste, then stir in 1 tablespoon crème fraîche or sour cream.

Veal schnitzel with spinach, potatoes and herbs

1 kg (2 lb) unpeeled small new potatoes
4 veal steaks, about 140 g (5 oz) each, gently
 beaten with a meat mallet until thin
2 tablespoons plain (all-purpose) flour
salt and freshly ground black pepper
2 tablespoons extra virgin olive oil
3 tablespoons unsalted butter
400 g (14 oz) baby English spinach leaves
grated zest and juice of 1 lemon
75 ml (2½ fl oz) dry white wine
4 tablespoons chopped mixed fresh herbs,
 such as parsley, chervil, chives and tarragon
lemon wedges, to serve

serves 4
preparation 15 minutes
cooking 30 minutes

per serving 2314 kJ (553 calories), 39 g protein,
25 g total fat, 10 g saturated fat, 39 g carbohydrate

1 Cook the potatoes in a large saucepan of boiling water for 15 minutes, or until tender.

2 Meanwhile, pat the veal dry with paper towel. Season the flour with a little salt and black pepper, then toss the veal in the flour to coat the steaks lightly and evenly all over. Shake off any excess flour.

3 Heat half the oil in a large non-stick frying pan over medium heat. Add half the butter and heat until it starts to foam, then add the veal. Fry for 2-3 minutes on each side, or until the juices run clear when pierced with a skewer – you may need to cook the meat in two batches. Remove from the pan using a slotted spoon, place in a warmed serving dish and keep hot.

4 Drain the potatoes in a colander, but keep the pan handy. Add the remaining oil to the saucepan and set over a low heat. Return the potatoes to the pan and toss gently until coated with the oil. Add the spinach in batches, gently tossing and stirring to help the leaves wilt. Add the lemon juice, season with salt and black pepper and gently mix. Cover and keep warm while you make the sauce.

5 Return the frying pan to the heat and add the wine. Increase the heat so the liquid bubbles, then stir vigorously to dislodge any sediment in the pan. Boil for 1 minute, or until reduced and syrupy, then season lightly. Remove from the heat and stir in the rest of the butter until melted.

6 Scatter the herbs over the veal and drizzle with the sauce. Sprinkle the lemon zest over the potatoes and spinach. Arrange on plates and serve with lemon wedges for squeezing over.

Potatoes

Potato skins have more B vitamins, fibre, calcium, iron, phosphorus, potassium and zinc than potato flesh. The skins also provide valuable dietary fibre. The best flavour in a potato is close to the skin. When peeling potatoes, use a potato peeler rather than a knife to pare off the skin as thinly as possible, to preserve the maximum flavour and nutrition. New potatoes are usually left unpeeled.

Sausage and bean casserole with potato and parsnip topping

4 large good-quality pork sausages
410 g (14½ oz) can chopped tomatoes
410 g (14½ oz) can red kidney or borlotti (cranberry) beans, drained and rinsed
2 tablespoons tomato chutney
2 teaspoons paprika

potato and parsnip topping

750 g (1½ lb) baking (floury) potatoes, peeled and cut into cubes
1 large parsnip, about 175 g (6 oz), peeled and chopped
2 tablespoons milk
1 tablespoon extra virgin olive oil
salt and freshly ground black pepper

serves 4
preparation 15 minutes
cooking 20 minutes

-----

per serving 2202 kJ (526 calories), 22 g protein, 27 g total fat, 10 g saturated fat, 49 g carbohydrate

1 Preheat the grill (broiler) to medium. Place the sausages under the grill and cook for about 15 minutes, turning regularly, until evenly browned all over and cooked through.

2 Meanwhile, cook the potatoes and parsnip in a saucepan of boiling water for 15 minutes, or until tender.

3 Put the tomatoes in another saucepan with the beans, chutney and paprika and gently heat until bubbling.

4 Remove the sausages from the grill, but leave the grill on. Allow sausages to cool slightly, then cut each one diagonally into four thick slices. Stir them into the tomato and bean mixture and pour into a flameproof dish.

5 Drain the potatoes and parsnip, then mash with the milk and oil. Season with salt and black pepper to taste.

6 Spoon the mash evenly over the sausages and beans. Brown under the grill for 5 minutes, or until the topping is golden and crisp. Serve hot.

Sausage casserole with green beans

1 Preheat the grill (broiler) to medium. Grill 4 good-quality sausages for about 15 minutes, turning regularly, until evenly browned all over and cooked through. In a large saucepan of boiling water, cook 750 g (1 ½ lb) baking (floury) potatoes, peeled and chopped, and 1 large parsnip, peeled and chopped, for about 15 minutes or until tender. Meanwhile, trim 500 g (1 lb) green beans and cook in boiling salted water for 10 minutes. Drain, combine in a saucepan with a 410 g (14½ oz) can chopped tomatoes, 1 tablespoon finely chopped fresh marjoram and salt and freshly ground black pepper to taste, and heat until bubbling.

2 Drain the potatoes and parsnip. Mash with 2 tablespoons milk and 1 tablespoon extra virgin olive oil. Add salt and black pepper to taste. Slice the sausages into bite-sized chunks, stir into the tomato mixture, pour into a flameproof dish, spread the mashed potato over the top and grill until golden.

Sausage and bean casserole with potato and parsnip topping

Moussaka

2 eggplant (aubergines)
salt and freshly ground black pepper
1/2 cup (125 ml/4 fl oz) extra virgin olive oil,
    plus extra for brushing
2 onions, chopped
2 cloves garlic, chopped
400 g (14 oz) minced (ground) beef or lamb
1 cup (250 g/8 oz) canned chopped tomatoes
750 g (1 1/2 lb) boiling (waxy) potatoes, peeled
    and sliced 5 mm (1/4 inch) thick
2 tablespoons dry breadcrumbs
3/4 cup (200 g/7 oz) Greek-style yogurt
4 eggs
1 tablespoon finely chopped fresh oregano
1 tablespoon finely chopped fresh thyme
2/3 cup (100 g/3 1/2 oz) finely crumbled fetta
2/3 cup (100 g/3 1/2 oz) grated emmenthal
    or Swiss cheese

serves 6
preparation 30 minutes + 30 minutes soaking
cooking 2 hours 15 minutes

*per serving 2519 kJ (602 calories), 33 g protein,
40 g total fat, 14 g saturated fat, 27 g carbohydrate*

1 Cut the eggplant into slices 5 mm (1/4 inch) thick. Season generously with salt and soak in water for 30 minutes. Rinse the eggplant and pat dry with paper towel.

2 Preheat oven to 180°C (350°F/gas 4). Heat 2 tablespoons of the oil in a frying pan over medium heat. Fry the eggplant in batches for 3 minutes on each side. Remove and set aside.

3 Heat another 2 tablespoons oil in the pan and sauté the onions and garlic for 5 minutes. Add the meat and fry until browned and crumbling, stirring constantly. Mix in the tomatoes and season with salt and black pepper. Simmer over low heat until all the liquid has evaporated.

4 Heat the remaining oil in another pan and fry the potatoes in batches for about 2 minutes on each side. Set aside.

5 Brush a baking dish with oil and scatter with breadcrumbs. Cover the base with eggplant slices, then place alternating layers of potatoes and meat mixture on top, finishing with a potato layer.

6 Mix together the yogurt, eggs and herbs. Season with salt and black pepper, then spread over the potato layer. Scatter with the cheese and bake for 1 1/4 hours, or until golden. Serve hot.

Eggplant

Choose firm, plump eggplant (aubergines) that have glossy, unblemished skin. Some recipes require you to salt the sliced eggplant flesh, a process known as disgorging. This draws out any bitter juices and also improves the texture of the cooked vegetable. Rinse the eggplant slices before cooking.

Grilled steak with glazed potatoes

3 tablespoons dijon mustard
1 tablespoon honey
1 tablespoon cider vinegar
2 cloves garlic, finely chopped
¼ teaspoon freshly ground black pepper
500 g (1 lb) lean beef, such as beef fillet
750 g (1½ lb) small new potatoes,
    preferably red-skinned
1 large onion, cut into 8 wedges
1 bunch watercress, tough ends trimmed

serves 4
preparation 15 minutes + 30 minutes
    marinating
cooking 30 minutes

per serving *1769 kJ (423 calories), 39 g protein,*
13 g total fat, 5 g saturated fat, 36 g carbohydrate

1 Put the mustard, honey, vinegar, garlic and pepper in a large bowl and mix well to combine. Place the beef in a shallow bowl. Measure out 2 tablespoons of the mustard mixture and rub it all over the beef. Marinate the beef for 30 minutes at room temperature, or overnight in the refrigerator.

2 Using a vegetable peeler, remove a strip of skin from around each potato if you wish (see Cook's tip). Drop the potatoes into a large saucepan of boiling water and cook for 15 minutes, or until just tender. Drain well, then add to the bowl of mustard mixture, tossing to coat.

3 Heat the grill (broiler) to medium-high. Using a slotted spoon, transfer the potatoes to the grill pan, leaving room for the onion wedges and beef.

4 Add the onion wedges to the mustard mixture, turning to coat, then add to the grill pan with the potatoes.

5 Add the beef to the grill pan. Grill for 8 minutes, turning the beef, potatoes and onion wedges halfway through cooking. Remove the beef from the heat and allow to rest for 5 minutes before slicing. Serve with the potatoes and onion wedges on a bed of watercress.

Marinating meat

Originally used as a way of preserving meat for a few days, before refrigeration was common, marinades are now used only to heighten the flavour of food and keep it from drying out. They also have a tenderising effect. The meat can be soaked in the marinade for a few hours or overnight, or brushed on, for example while the food is grilling (broiling). Any left-over marinade can be used as a sauce if you like, but first it must be boiled for at least 3 minutes to kill any pathogens from the meat.

Cook's tip

It is not essential to peel a strip of skin from the potatoes, but it creates an attractive effect, especially if you are using red-skinned potatoes.

Irish stew

500 g (1 lb) boneless lean lamb leg steaks
1 kg (2 lb) baking (floury) potatoes, peeled
    and thickly sliced
1 large onion, sliced
500 g (1 lb) carrots, peeled and thickly sliced
2 tablespoons chopped fresh parsley, plus
    extra to garnish
1 teaspoon fresh thyme leaves, plus extra
    to garnish
1 tablespoon snipped fresh chives
freshly ground black pepper
450 ml (16 fl oz) lamb or vegetable stock
    (or half stock and half Guinness), hot
2 cos (romaine) lettuce hearts, halved,
    to serve (optional)

serves 4
preparation 20 mins
cooking 2 hours 20 mins

per serving *1682 kJ (402 calories), 36 g protein,*
8 g total fat, 4 g saturated fat, 45 g carbohydrate

1 Preheat the oven to 160°C (315°F/gas 2-3). Trim the lamb steaks of visible fat and cut each one into four pieces.

2 In a large casserole dish, make layers of the lamb, potatoes, onion and carrots, sprinkling each layer with parsley, thyme, chives and black pepper. Finish with a layer of potatoes, then pour the stock over.

3 Cover with a tight-fitting lid and bake for 2 hours, or until the meat and vegetables are tender when tested with a skewer.

4 Increase the oven temperature to 200°C (400°F/gas 6). Remove the casserole lid and cook for a further 20 minutes, or until the potatoes on top are golden brown and crisp. Meanwhile, if you like, briefly grill the lettuce halves. Serve the stew hot, sprinkled with more thyme and parsley and accompanied with the lettuce hearts.

Cook's tips

Traditional recipes for Irish stew use a tough, fatty cut of lamb. This version is updated with leaner leg steaks, although you can use lamb shoulder or lamb neck cutlets instead, if you prefer. Trim them of fat before layering them in the casserole dish.

Carrots are not traditional in Irish stew, but they are worth including for both colour and nutrition.

Some more ideas...

* Add 125 g (4½ oz) small whole button mushrooms to the casserole, layering them with the onion and carrots.

* If you want the cooking liquid to be slightly thickened, sprinkle 1 tablespoon pearl barley between the first few layers along with the herbs.

* Use turnips instead of carrots.

Irish stew

Irish stew with savoy cabbage

Replace the carrots in the recipe opposite with 1 savoy cabbage. Remove the outer
leaves and cut the cabbage into eight wedges. Remove the hard stalk and slice
the wedges into fine strips. Layer half the potatoes, half the cabbage and half the
onions in the casserole dish, seasoning each layer and sprinkling with herbs, as for
step 2 opposite. Spread the meat on top, then layer the remaining ingredients on
the meat in reverse order. Add 1 cup (250 ml/8 fl oz) each of hot meat stock and
Guinness, then cover and bake as instructed in steps 3 and 4.

Braised garlic chicken casserole

Braised garlic chicken casserole

500 g (1 lb) baking (floury) potatoes,
    peeled and cut into chunks
3 stalks celery, cut into thick slices
2 carrots, peeled and cut into chunks
40 cloves garlic
2 tablespoons extra virgin olive oil
salt and freshly ground black pepper
1 tablespoon finely chopped fresh rosemary
1 cup (250 ml/8 fl oz) chicken stock
½ cup (125 ml/4 fl oz) dry vermouth
4 boneless, skinless chicken breasts

serves 4
preparation 20 minutes
cooking 45 minutes

per serving 1898 kJ, 453 kcal, 39 g protein,
19 g fat, 25 g carbohydrates

1 Preheat the oven to 180°C (350°F/gas 4). Put the potatoes, celery, carrots and unpeeled garlic cloves in a large flameproof casserole dish. Drizzle with the olive oil, season with salt and black pepper and sprinkle with the rosemary.

2 Pour in the stock and vermouth, bring to a boil, then reduce the heat to medium and simmer for about 10 minutes. Place the chicken breasts on top of the vegetables, then cover and bake for 30 minutes.

3 Remove the garlic cloves, then squeeze them out of their skins. Purée the garlic and serve separately.

Recipe note
Don't be alarmed by the amount of garlic in this dish. When whole cloves are cooked slowly, garlic loses its sharp pungency and becomes mellow and creamy. Garlic cooked in this way (by stewing, as above, or roasting whole heads in the oven) is delicious served with roast meats and vegetables, spread on bread or toast, or as an addition to mashed potatoes.

Tomato and chicken casserole

1 Prepare the casserole as directed above, but replace the vermouth with 1 cup (250 g/8 oz) canned chopped tomatoes. Simmer the tomatoes with the vegetables for 10 minutes as in step 2, before placing the chicken on top. Cover and bake as before and serve sprinkled with 2 tablespoons finely chopped fresh parsley.

2 Serve with garlic bread: squeeze the cooked garlic cloves from their skins, mash with a fork, then mix in some finely chopped fresh flat-leaf (Italian) parsley and spread over toasted rye bread or baguette slices.

Bolognese beef casserole

350 g (12 oz) lean minced (ground) beef
1 onion, chopped
2 cloves garlic, crushed
600 g (1 lb 5 oz) boiling (waxy) potatoes,
    peeled and finely diced
2 x 410 g (14½ oz) cans chopped tomatoes
150 ml (5 fl oz) chicken stock
finely shredded zest and juice of 1 lemon
1 tablespoon soft brown sugar
salt and freshly ground black pepper
1 bulb fennel, thinly sliced (reserve the fronds
    to garnish)
1 cup (125 g/4½ oz) frozen green beans
3 tablespoons chopped fresh flat-leaf parsley
bread or rolls, to serve (optional)

serves 4
preparation 15 minutes
cooking 25 minutes

----

*per serving 1278 kJ (305 calories), 25 g protein,
7 g total fat, 3 g saturated fat, 34 g carbohydrate*

1 Place the beef, onion and garlic in a large saucepan and dry-fry over medium heat for 5 minutes, stirring frequently, until the meat is broken up and evenly browned.

2 Stir in the potatoes, tomatoes, stock, half the lemon zest and the sugar. Season with salt and black pepper. Bring to a boil, then reduce the heat, cover and simmer for 10 minutes, stirring once or twice to ensure the potatoes cook evenly.

3 Stir in the fennel, frozen beans and lemon juice. Cover and simmer for a further 5 minutes, or until the potatoes are tender and the fennel and beans are lightly cooked, but still crisp.

4 Taste and adjust the seasoning, if necessary, then spoon the mixture into serving bowls. Garnish with the remaining lemon zest and the chopped fennel fronds and parsley. Serve with bread or rolls to mop up the sauce, if you like.

Serving tip

A green salad tossed with thinly sliced red onion, a handful of fresh basil leaves, a few pitted black olives and a lemon and olive oil dressing goes well with this dish.

Some more ideas...

* Use minced (ground) turkey, chicken, pork or lamb instead of beef.

* Carrots and canned beans can be used instead of potatoes. Add a 410 g (14½ oz) can of rinsed cannellini beans or black-eyed peas, and 2 peeled and diced carrots.

* If serving this dish to young children, omit the lemon juice. Instead, serve with lemon wedges so the juice can be added to taste.

Pork korma with potatoes and spinach

Chimichurri pork skewers

1 Peel and finely chop 5 cloves garlic and place in a large non-metallic bowl with ½ cup (30 g/1 oz) chopped fresh flat-leaf parsley, 1 teaspoon dried oregano, ½ teaspoon ground cumin and ½ teaspoon paprika, 4 tablespoons red wine vinegar and 3 tablespoons extra virgin olive oil. Mix well. Add a splash of Tabasco to taste. Trim 500 g (1 lb) lean pork fillet, cut into 2 cm (¾ inch) slices, toss in the marinade and leave for at least 20 minutes, or overnight in the refrigerator.

2 Boil 2 unpeeled orange sweet potatoes for 12–15 minutes, or until just starting to soften. Remove with tongs and set aside. Add 1 cob sweetcorn to the water, boil for 5 minutes and drain. Peel the sweet potatoes and cut in half lengthwise, then widthwise into 3 cm (1¼ inches) wedges. Slice the corn cob. Thread the pork, sweet potato and corn onto metal skewers and brush with marinade. Grill or barbecue the skewers, turning frequently and basting with any remaining marinade, for 15 minutes or until the pork is cooked. Serve with lime wedges.

Note You can replace the corn with wedges of green or red capsicum (bell pepper).

Pork korma with potatoes and spinach

1 tablespoon vegetable oil
2 large onions, sliced
500 g (1 lb) lean minced (ground) pork
2 cloves garlic, crushed
8 green cardamom pods, crushed, pods
   discarded and seeds reserved
1 tablespoon cumin seeds
600 ml (21 fl oz) chicken stock, hot
750 g (1½ lb) unpeeled small new potatoes,
   halved
2 teaspoons cornflour (cornstarch)
¾ cup (80 g/2¾ oz) ground almonds
1 cup (250 g/8 oz) natural (plain) yogurt
salt and freshly ground black pepper
250 g (8 oz) baby English spinach leaves
⅓ cup (30 g/1 oz) flaked almonds, lightly
   toasted
chappatis or naan, to serve (optional)

serves 4
preparation 10 minutes
cooking 1 hour

per serving 2637 kJ (630 calories), 44 g protein,
32 g total fat, 6 g saturated fat, 41 g carbohydrate

1 Heat the oil in a large, heavy-based saucepan or flameproof casserole dish. Add the onions and sauté over medium heat for 10 minutes, then transfer to a bowl.

2 Add the pork, garlic, cardamom and cumin seeds. Cook, stirring often, for 5 minutes, or until the meat has broken up and changed colour. Return half the onions to the pan, pour in the hot stock and bring back to a boil. Reduce the heat, cover and simmer for 15 minutes.

3 Stir in the potatoes and bring back to simmering point. Cover and cook for 20 minutes, or until the potatoes are tender.

4 Blend the cornflour with the ground almonds and half the yogurt to make a paste. Pour into the curry and bring just to a boil, stirring. Reduce the heat and simmer for 1 minute until slightly thickened. Season to taste with salt and black pepper.

5 Reserve a few small spinach leaves for garnishing, and fold the rest through the korma until they are just wilted and bright green. Mix the flaked almonds with the remaining onions. Drizzle the curry with the remaining yogurt and top with the almonds, onions and reserved spinach leaves. Serve with warm chappatis or naan, if you like.

Cardamom

Cardamom is the world's most expensive spice after saffron and vanilla. Each small green seed capsule contains up to 20 sticky black seeds and must be harvested by hand. The ground spice quickly loses its flavour and aroma, so it is best to buy whole seed pods and to grind the seeds yourself with a mortar and pestle or in a coffee grinder. When buying cardamom, look for green seed pods rather than white ones (which have been bleached).

Argentine beef stew

½ cup (125 ml/4 fl oz) vegetable oil
1 tablespoon butter
1 kg (2 lb) topside or round steak, cut into
    bite-sized pieces
2 onions, finely chopped
2 cloves garlic, finely chopped
1 dried bay leaf
½ teaspoon marinated green peppercorns
salt and freshly ground black pepper
cayenne pepper
dried basil
dried marjoram
1 cup (250 ml/8 fl oz) dry white wine
2 cups (500 ml/16 fl oz) beef stock
500 g (1 lb) boiling (waxy) potatoes, peeled
    and cut into small dice
2 cups (300 g/10½ oz) peeled and finely
    diced pumpkin
2 green capsicums (bell peppers), finely diced
410 g (14½ oz) can corn kernels, drained
2 peaches
200 g (7 oz) dark grapes, preferably seedless
1 cup (250 g/8 oz) canned chopped tomatoes

serves 6
preparation 20 minutes
cooking 1 hour 20 minutes

----

per serving *2484 kJ (593 calories), 43 g protein,*
30 g total fat, 7 g saturated fat, 32 g carbohydrate

1 Heat the oil and butter in a large saucepan. Brown the beef in batches on all sides over medium-high heat. Add the onions and garlic and fry with the meat for 3 minutes. Add the bay leaf and green peppercorns, then season with salt, black pepper, cayenne pepper, dried basil and dried marjoram to taste. Pour in the wine and stock, then cover and simmer for 30 minutes.

2 Add the potatoes, pumpkin, capsicums and corn, then cover and simmer for another 20 minutes.

3 Meanwhile, blanch the peaches in hot water. Peel off the skins, cut in half and remove the stones. Cut the peaches into thick wedges. Cut the grapes in half and remove any seeds using a small sharp kitchen knife.

4 Carefully mix the peaches, grapes and tomatoes into the stew and cook for a further 5 minutes to heat through. Season to taste and serve.

Recipe note
This traditional Argentinian recipe is known in its homeland as carbonada criolla, or creole stew. 'Criollo' is the name given to a person born in Argentina but of Spanish descent. Argentinian food evolved separately from other Latin American cuisines because of the strong influence of Spanish, French, Italian and other European cuisines.

Beef hotpot with small potato dumplings

Beef hotpot with small potato dumplings

2 tablespoons vegetable oil
2 large onions, finely chopped
800 g (1 lb 12 oz) topside or round steak, or
    stewing steak, cut into bite-sized pieces
salt and freshly ground black pepper
1 tablespoon plain (all-purpose) flour
2 carrots, peeled and cut into 5 cm (2 inch)
    chunks
200 g (7 oz) baby or small turnips, trimmed
    and quartered if necessary (optional)
1 cup (250 ml/8 fl oz) beef stock

dumplings

300 g (10½ oz) baking (floury) potatoes,
    peeled and finely grated
1 egg, beaten
1¼ cups (125 g/4½ oz) dry breadcrumbs
1 tablespoon flour, plus extra for dusting
1 tablespoon finely chopped fresh parsley
plain (all-purpose) flour, for dusting
salt and freshly ground black pepper

serves 4
preparation 20 minutes
cooking 2 hours 15 minutes

----

*per serving 2370 kJ (566 calories), 53 g protein,
20 g total fat, 5 g saturated fat, 42 g carbohydrate*

1 Heat the oil in a large saucepan and sauté the onions over medium heat for 5 minutes, or until translucent. Add the beef and brown on all sides. Season with salt and black pepper and dust the flour over the meat, stirring well. Add the carrots and turnips, if using, pour in the stock and bring to a boil. Reduce the heat, cover and simmer for 1½ hours.

2 Meanwhile, make the dumplings. In a bowl, mix together the potatoes, egg, breadcrumbs, flour and parsley until well combined. Season with salt and black pepper. With flour-dusted hands, shape the mixture into small dumplings and sprinkle them with flour.

3 Return the stew to a boil. Spread the dumplings over the meat, then reduce the heat, cover and simmer for a final 30 minutes without lifting the lid. Serve hot.

Some more ideas...

✳ Replace the dumplings with either of the dumpling recipes on page 154.

✳ Omit the dumplings and serve the stew with any of the mashed potato recipes from pages 128–29.

Beef and mushroom hotpot

Substitute 250 g (8 oz) mushrooms for the carrots in the recipe above and also add 100 g (3½ oz) lean diced bacon. Before browning the beef, fry the bacon in the saucepan until crisp, then remove with a slotted spoon. Cut the mushrooms in half and sauté in the bacon fat with the onions for 5 minutes, then remove. Heat the oil in the pan and brown the meat as outlined in step 1 above. Season and dust with the flour. Add the bacon, onions and mushrooms, pour in the stock and cook as for step 1. Prepare and cook the dumplings as directed in steps 2 and 3.

Liver and bacon casserole with potato crust

750 g (1½ lb) boiling (waxy) potatoes,
    peeled and thinly sliced
2 tablespoons vegetable oil
400 g (14 oz) lamb or beef liver, sliced
2 slices (strips) bacon, rind removed,
    finely chopped
2 onions, finely chopped
1 swede (rutabaga), diced
2 carrots, peeled and diced
2 tablespoons plain (all-purpose) flour
450 ml (16 fl oz) beef, lamb or chicken stock,
    preferably homemade
1 tablespoon chopped fresh sage or
    ½ teaspoon dried sage
3 teaspoons wholegrain mustard
salt and freshly ground black pepper
1 tablespoon butter

serves 4
preparation 30 minutes
cooking 1 hour

per serving *2149 kJ (513 calories), 35 g protein,*
23 g total fat, 7 g saturated fat, 41 g carbohydrate

1   Preheat the oven to 190°C (375°F/gas 5). Place the potatoes in a large saucepan and pour in enough boiling water to cover them. Bring back to a boil, then cook for 4–5 minutes, or until they are just tender. Drain well but gently to ensure the slices do not break.

2   While the potatoes are cooking, heat the oil in a non-stick frying pan and brown the liver slices on both sides for about 1 minute, turning once. Transfer to a casserole dish.

3   Sauté the bacon, onions, swede and carrots in the frying pan over medium heat for 10 minutes, or until the bacon and onions are golden. Sprinkle the flour over the mixture and stir it in, then stir in the stock. Add the sage, 2 teaspoons mustard and salt and black pepper to taste. Bring to a boil, stirring.

4   Pour the bacon and vegetable mixture over the liver. Arrange the potato slices on top, overlapping them neatly and covering the casserole completely. Gently melt the butter in a small saucepan and stir in the remaining mustard. Brush the mustard butter over the potatoes and season lightly.

5   Bake for 45 minutes, or until the potatoes are browned and tender. Serve straight from the dish.

Cook's tips

To prepare liver, soak it (if using strongly flavoured pig's or ox liver) to soften the taste. Drain, pat dry with paper towel and carefully snip and peel away the fine membrane. With a sharp knife, cut the liver diagonally into even, thin slices. Snip out any tough internal tubes with sharp scissors, then proceed as directed.

Liver can be tough if overcooked. To prevent this, either cook it very briefly over high heat, or braise it very slowly in a casserole.

Liver and bacon casserole with potato crust

Liver and mushroom casserole

Prepare the potatoes and liver as in the recipe opposite, but replace the carrots
with 250 g (8 oz) mushrooms. Slice them and fry with the bacon and onions as in
step 3, then dust with flour and add the stock. Replace the sage and mustard seeds
with 2 tablespoons finely chopped fresh parsley and 1 tablespoon finely chopped
fresh thyme. Season with salt and black pepper and add to the liver. Cover the
casserole with the potato slices as in step 4, brush with melted butter and sprinkle
with 1 teaspoon crushed coriander seeds. Season again and bake as directed.

Five ways...

with croquettes and dumplings

Croquettes – sausage-shaped portions of fried potato – and potato dumplings, which are usually steamed or boiled, make comforting and filling accompaniments to meat and vegetable main courses.

Basic potato dumplings

serves **4**

prep **15** *mins*

cook **45** *mins*

Peel, wash and cook 350 g (12 oz) baking (floury) potatoes, then drain and cool. Peel another 1 kg (2 lb) baking (floury) potatoes and grate them into a bowl of cold water; drain, place in a tea towel (dish towel) and squeeze out all the water. Place in a bowl and grate the cooked potatoes into the bowl. Pour in ½ cup (125 ml/4 fl oz) hot milk, add salt and 1 beaten egg and mix well. If the mixture is too moist, stir in a few tablespoons dry breadcrumbs. Shape into 8 large or 12 small dumplings using wet hands. Add to a large saucepan of salted boiling water and shake so the dumplings float freely. Quickly bring back to a boil, then cook on medium heat for 25-30 minutes, or until a skewer inserted in a dumpling comes out clean. Remove with a slotted spoon, drain and serve hot.

per serving *1157 kJ (276 calories), 11 g protein, 3 g total fat, 1 g saturated fat, 49 g carbohydrate*

Potato and semolina dumplings

serves **4**   *prep* **45** *mins*   *cook* **45** *mins*

Peel 1 kg (2 lb) roasting (floury) potatoes and grate them into a bowl full of cold water. Drain, place in a tea towel (dish towel) and squeeze out all the water. Place in a bowl. In a saucepan bring ½ cup (125 ml/4 fl oz) milk to a boil. Stir in 3 tablespoons semolina and slowly cook into a thick mass on medium heat, stirring constantly. Season with salt and freshly grated nutmeg, add to the potatoes and mix well. Shape into 8 dumplings using wet hands. Add to a large saucepan of salted boiling water and shake so the dumplings float freely. Quickly bring back to a boil, then cook on medium heat for 30 minutes, or until a skewer inserted in a dumpling comes out clean. Remove with a slotted spoon and drain. Serve hot, sprinkled with chopped fresh parsley if desired.

per serving *900 kJ (215 calories), 8 g protein, 2 g total fat, 1 g saturated fat, 41 g carbohydrate*

Japanese potato and meat croquettes

Japanese potato and meat croquettes

serves **4** prep **15** mins cook **40** mins

Peel, cook and mash 600 g (1 lb 5 oz) baking (floury) potatoes; set aside. Sauté 1 grated onion in 1 tablespoon vegetable oil over medium heat until light golden. Add 300 g (10 ½ oz) minced (ground) beef and stir until well coloured. Stir in 2 tablespoons soy sauce, 3 teaspoons grated fresh ginger, 2 crushed cloves garlic and 1 tablespoon mirin (rice wine) or sherry and cook until all the liquid has evaporated. Mix through the mashed potato and form into logs, using about 2 tablespoons for each. Beat 2 eggs in a bowl. Dip the logs into the eggs, then into a dish of plain (all-purpose) flour, then into the egg again, then a dish of coarse dry breadcrumbs – preferably panko (Japanese breadcrumbs). Place a frying pan over medium heat and add enough vegetable oil to come halfway up the side of the croquettes. When the oil is hot, cook the croquettes in batches until golden on each side. Serve with tonkatsu sauce, Japanese mustard or hot English mustard.

per serving *1383 kJ (330 calories), 24 g protein, 13 g total fat, 4 g saturated fat, 27 g carbohydrate*

Potato puffs

serves **4** prep **30** mins cook **30** mins

Preheat the oven to 200°C (400°F/gas 4). Boil 750 g (1 ½ lb) peeled baking (floury) potatoes for 20 minutes, or until soft. Drain well, return to the saucepan and let the moisture evaporate for 2 minutes on low heat. Squeeze twice through a potato press into a bowl (never use a blender or food processor, or the potatoes will be gluey). Stir in 3 tablespoons butter, 3 beaten egg yolks and some salt. Mix well, then pack into a piping (icing) bag and pipe rosettes or other decorative shapes onto an ovenproof platter or a baking tray lined with baking (parchment) paper. Brush with 2 whisked egg yolks, lightly dust with paprika and bake for 8 minutes, or until golden. Serve hot.

per serving *1229 kJ (294 calories), 8 g protein, 18 g total fat, 10 g saturated fat, 25 g carbohydrate*

Potato croquettes

serves **4** prep **45** mins cook **45** mins

Boil 750 g (1 lb 10 oz) peeled baking (floury) potatoes for 20 minutes, or until soft. Drain well, return to the pot and let the moisture evaporate for 2 minutes on low heat. Squeeze twice through a potato press into a bowl (never use a blender or food processor, or the potatoes will be gluey). Add 3 beaten egg yolks, 3 tablespoons dry breadcrumbs, salt and freshly grated nutmeg and mix well. Using lightly floured hands, shape into long rolls 2 cm (³⁄₄ inch) thick, then cut into 5 cm (2 inch) lengths. In a shallow bowl, lightly whisk 2 egg whites. Spread 4 tablespoons flour on a flat plate, and 4 tablespoons dry breadcrumbs on another. Turn the croquettes first in flour, then in the egg whites and finally in breadcrumbs. Heat oil in a deep-fryer or large saucepan to 190°C (375°F). Fry batches of croquettes until golden, turning occasionally so they don't stick together. Drain on paper towel and keep warm while cooking the rest.

per serving *1131 kJ (270 calories), 12 g protein, 5 g total fat, 1 g saturated fat, 44 g carbohydrate*

Venison and mushroom pie with sweet potato topping

2 tablespoons olive oil

200 g (7 oz) baby onions, peeled and left whole

500 g (1 lb) boneless haunch or shoulder of venison, diced (see Cook's tips)

150 g (5 oz) small button mushrooms

3 stalks celery, thickly sliced

1 tablespoon fresh thyme leaves

300 ml (10$\frac{1}{2}$ fl oz) full-bodied red wine

150 ml (5 fl oz) strong beef stock

1$\frac{1}{2}$ tablespoon cornflour (cornstarch)

mashed sweet potato

1 kg (2 lb) sweet potatoes, peeled and diced

1 tablespoon wholegrain mustard

grated zest and juice of 1 orange

salt and freshly ground black pepper

serves 4

cooking 1 hour 15 minutes

preparation 20 minutes

---

per serving 2061 kJ (492 calories), 37 g protein,
12 g total fat, 2 g saturated fat, 46 g carbohydrate

Cook's tips

If you prefer, use beef instead of venison; choose a cut suitable for use in a casserole. Ask the butcher to bone and dice the meat for you.

The pie can be made ahead and chilled, then reheated in a preheated 190°C (375°F/gas 5) oven for 45 minutes or until piping hot.

1 Heat the oil in a large saucepan and add the onions. Cover and cook over low heat for 8–10 minutes, shaking the pan occasionally, until the onions are lightly browned all over.

2 Remove the onions using a slotted spoon. Add the venison to the pan and brown over medium-high heat for 2–3 minutes, or until nicely browned all over, stirring frequently.

3 Return the onions to the pan with the mushrooms, celery and thyme. Pour in the wine and stock. Bring to a boil, then reduce the heat, cover and simmer for 45 minutes, or until the venison is tender.

4 Meanwhile, steam the sweet potatoes for 25 minutes or until tender. Alternatively, cook them in boiling water for 15 minutes, then drain.

5 Preheat the oven to 190°C (375°F/gas 5). Tip the sweet potatoes into a bowl and mash with the mustard, orange zest and juice, and salt and black pepper to taste. Set aside.

6 Blend the cornflour with 2 tablespoons cold water. Stir into the venison mixture and cook, stirring, until slightly thickened. Season to taste. Spoon the filling into a 5 cup (1.25 litre/44 fl oz) pie dish.

7 Spread the mashed sweet potatoes over the venison filling to cover it completely. Bake for 20 minutes and serve hot.

Mix and match

Cover the venison filling with mashed potato and butternut pumpkin (squash). Steam 500 g (1 lb) each peeled baking (floury) potatoes and butternut pumpkin for 25 minutes, or cook in boiling water for 15 minutes, or until tender. Mash with 1 tablespoon butter and 2 tablespoons snipped fresh chives, spread over the filling and bake as directed in the main recipe.

Tex-mex shepherd's pie

2 teaspoons olive oil
4 spring onions (scallions), thinly sliced
6 cloves garlic, crushed
1 large green capsicum (bell pepper),
    seeded and chopped
300 g (10½ oz) lean minced (ground) lamb
1 teaspoon chilli powder
1½ teaspoons ground coriander
1½ teaspoons ground cumin
410 g (14½ oz) can chopped tomatoes
100 ml (3½ fl oz) beef stock, hot
410 g (14½ oz) can red kidney beans, drained
    and rinsed
750 g (1½ lb) baking (floury) potatoes,
    peeled and sliced
2 tablespoons chopped fresh coriander
    (cilantro) leaves

serves 4
preparation 15 minutes
cooking 40 minutes

per serving 1450 kJ (346 cal), 27 g protein, 9 g fat,
40 g carbohydrate

1 Preheat the oven to 220°C (425°F/gas 7). Heat the oil in a large frying pan over low heat. Add the spring onions and half the garlic and cook for 2 minutes, stirring frequently. Add the capsicum, increase the heat to medium and cook for 5 minutes, stirring until the capsicum is just tender.

2 Add the lamb and spices and cook for 2-3 minutes, stirring to break up the meat, until it is no longer pink. Stir in the tomatoes, stock and kidney beans and bring to a boil. Reduce the heat to a simmer, cover and cook for 5 minutes, or until the mixture is thick.

3 Meanwhile, cook the potatoes with the remaining garlic in a saucepan of lightly salted boiling water for 10 minutes, or until tender. Drain the potatoes, reserving 3 tablespoons of the cooking liquid. Return the potatoes and garlic to the pan with the reserved liquid and mash them roughly using a potato masher or large fork. Stir in the chopped coriander.

4 Spoon the lamb mixture into a deep pie dish, about 6 cups (1.5 litres/52 fl oz) capacity. Spoon the mashed potatoes over the top. Bake for 15 minutes, or until golden. Serve hot.

Cook's tips

This dish can be assembled ahead of time up to the end of step 3, then baked for 15 minutes, or until heated through, before serving.

If you like, replace the lamb with lean minced (ground) beef.

Bangers and mash

1 tablespoon vegetable oil

8 large good-quality sausages, about
     500 g (1 lb) in total

175 g (6 oz) baby onions, halved

1 large clove garlic, crushed

175 g (6 oz) button mushrooms, halved

1 red capsicum (bell pepper), seeded and
     thinly sliced

200 ml (7 fl oz) beef stock

150 ml (5 fl oz) full-bodied red wine

1 tablespoon redcurrant or blackberry jelly

3 sprigs fresh thyme

salt and freshly ground black pepper

2 teaspoons cornflour (cornstarch)

750 g (1½ lb) baking (floury) potatoes,
     peeled and cut into chunks

½ cup (125 ml/4 fl oz) milk

2 teaspoons extra virgin olive oil

1 tablespoon chopped fresh parsley

steamed broccoli, to serve

serves 4
preparation 25 minutes
cooking 35 minutes

---

per serving 2273 kJ (543 calories), 41 g protein,
18 g total fat, 6 g saturated fat, 36 g carbohydrate

1 Heat the oil in a deep non-stick frying pan. Add the sausages and fry over medium heat, turning occasionally, for 10 minutes, or until lightly browned all over.

2 Add the onions and cook for 5 minutes, or until they are golden and the sausages are nicely browned all over. Transfer the sausages to a plate and set aside. Drain off the excess oil from the pan.

3 Gently sauté the garlic, mushrooms and capsicum in the pan for a few minutes, until softened. Pour in the stock and wine and add the redcurrant or blackberry jelly and 2 thyme sprigs. Season to taste with salt and black pepper. Mix the cornflour with 1 tablespoon cold water and stir into the liquid in the pan. Bring to a boil, stirring until slightly thickened, then reduce the heat and return the sausages to the pan. Simmer gently for 10 minutes, then remove the thyme sprigs.

4 Meanwhile, cook the potatoes in a saucepan of boiling water for 15–20 minutes, or until very tender.

5 Drain the potatoes well, then return to the saucepan. Heat the milk in a small saucepan until hot, pour over the potatoes and mash until smooth. Beat in the olive oil, parsley and salt and black pepper to taste.

6 Divide the mashed potatoes among warmed plates and top with the sausages, vegetables and sauce. Sprinkle with the leaves from the remaining thyme sprig and serve with broccoli.

'Bangers'

This British term for sausages came about after World War II, when, due to meat rationing, sausages had a high water content. When fried, they would often explode in the pan, earning them the nickname 'bangers'.

Pepper steak with mashed potatoes and leeks

2 tablespoons mixed or black peppercorns, coarsely crushed
4 fillet steaks, each about 2.5 cm (1 inch) thick and 150 g (5 oz), trimmed
olive oil, for brushing
chopped fresh parsley or snipped fresh chives, to garnish
steamed green beans, to serve

leek and mustard mashed potatoes

1 kg (2 lb) baking (floury) potatoes, peeled and cut into chunks
2 teaspoons olive oil
200 g (7 oz) young leeks, white part only, finely shredded
½ cup (125 ml/4 fl oz) low-fat milk
1 tablespoon wholegrain mustard
1 tablespoon butter
salt and freshly ground black pepper

serves 4
preparation 25 minutes
cooking 35 minutes

per serving 2123 kJ (507 calories), 42 g protein, 19 g total fat, 7 g saturated fat, 41 g carbohydrate

1 Cook the potatoes in a saucepan of boiling water for 15-20 minutes, or until very tender.

2 Meanwhile, spread the crushed peppercorns on a plate and press the steaks into them until coated on all sides. Set aside.

3 Heat the olive oil for the mashed potato mixture in a non-stick frying pan. Add the leeks and cook, stirring constantly, for 3-5 minutes or until tender. Transfer to a plate lined with a double thickness of paper towel to drain. Heat the milk in a small saucepan until hot.

4 When the potatoes are tender, drain well and return to the pan. Pour the hot milk over the potatoes, then mash until completely smooth. Add the leeks, mustard and butter, and season with salt and black pepper to taste. Beat well to mix, then cover and keep warm.

5 Heat a ridged cast-iron grill pan over high heat until hot, then reduce the heat to medium-high. Brush the steaks with oil, place in the pan and cook for 3 minutes on each side for rare; 3 ½ minutes each side for medium-rare; 4 minutes each side for medium; or 5 minutes each side for well done.

6 Spoon a mound of mashed potatoes on each of four warmed plates and place a steak next to it. Drizzle any pan juices over the steaks and sprinkle with parsley or chives. Serve at once, with green beans.

Cook's tip

When using a ridged cast-iron grill pan, always heat the pan slowly until very hot, then reduce the temperature if specified in the recipe. Lightly oil the food, not the pan. Move the food after a few seconds, so it does not stick, then leave to brown. Turn over and repeat.

Leeks

Leeks are a member of the onion family. To prepare them, remove most of the green tops (save these for the stockpot, if you like) and make slits in the outer layers to enable you to flush out any grit under cold running water. If more cleaning seems necessary once you have sliced the leeks, rinse them further or stand them in a bowl of cold water for 15-20 minutes.

Sausage with lentils and potato and pumpkin mash

¾ cup (175 g/6 oz) French-style green
    (puy) lentils
3 cups (750 ml/26 fl oz) chicken stock
1 large onion, roughly chopped
600 g (1 lb 5 oz) baking (floury) potatoes,
    peeled and quartered
300 g (10½ oz) butternut pumpkin (squash),
    peeled and chopped
4 pork sausages, about 300 g (10½ oz)
    in total
410 g (14½ oz) can chopped tomatoes
3 tablespoons milk
salt and freshly ground black pepper
1 tablespoon balsamic vinegar
3 tablespoons chopped fresh flat-leaf parsley

serves 4
preparation 20 minutes
cooking 35 minutes

per serving *1828 kJ (461 calories), 30 g protein,*
14 g total fat, 5 g saturated fat, 56 g carbohydrate

1 Preheat the grill (broiler) to medium. Rinse the lentils and place in a saucepan with 600 ml (21 fl oz) of the stock and the onion. Bring to a boil, then reduce the heat, cover and simmer for 25 minutes.

2 While the lentils are simmering, cook the potatoes in a large saucepan of boiling water for 10 minutes. Add the pumpkin and cook for a further 10 minutes, or until both vegetables are tender.

3 Meanwhile, brown the sausages under the grill for 15 minutes, turning them several times so they brown evenly.

4 Slice the sausages thickly and add them to the lentils, together with the tomatoes and their juice. If the lentils have absorbed all the liquid, add the remaining stock. Cover and cook for a further 10 minutes.

5 Drain the potatoes and pumpkin and mash them with the milk. Season with salt and black pepper to taste. Spoon the mashed potato mixture onto plates and top with the lentil mixture. Drizzle with vinegar, sprinkle with parsley and serve.

Cook's tip

This dish traditionally uses Toulouse
sausage, a French type made with
pork, smoked bacon, wine and garlic.
Any well-flavoured thick sausage can
be substituted.

Puy lentils

Puy lentils, or *lentilles vertes de Puy*, come from a defined area in France and have their own *appelation controlée*. They are small and green and are regarded as the best-tasting lentils. Other countries produce similar types. Like all lentils, puy lentils do not need to be soaked before cooking.

African lamb ragoût with okra

1 tablespoon olive oil

500 g (1 lb) well-trimmed lean leg of lamb,
    cut into large chunks

1 onion, finely chopped

4 cloves garlic, finely chopped

1 cup (250 g/8 oz) canned chopped tomatoes

500 g (1 lb) orange sweet potatoes, peeled
    and cut into bite-sized chunks

2 tablespoons smooth peanut butter

½ teaspoon salt

½ teaspoon cayenne pepper

250 g (8 oz) okra, stalks trimmed, cut
    crosswise if large

serves 4

preparation 15 minutes

cooking 1 hour

per serving *1736 kJ (415 calories), 36 g protein,*
19 g total fat, 5 g saturated fat, 27 g carbohydrate

1 Preheat the oven to 180°C (350°F/gas 4). In a large flameproof casserole dish, heat half the oil over medium-high heat. Add the lamb and sauté for 5 minutes, or until browned all over. Transfer to a plate using a slotted spoon.

2 Reduce the heat to medium and add the remaining oil. Sauté the onion and garlic for 2 minutes. Stir in ⅓ cup (80 ml/2 ½ fl oz) water and cook until the onion is golden brown and tender.

3 Stir in the tomatoes, sweet potatoes, peanut butter, salt, cayenne pepper and 1½ cups (375 ml/13 fl oz) water and bring to a boil. Return the lamb to the dish, then cover with a tight-fitting lid. Transfer to the oven and bake for 25 minutes.

4 Remove the dish from the oven and stir in the okra. Bake for a further 15-20 minutes, or until the lamb and okra are tender, then serve immediately.

Cook's tip

When buying okra, make sure
the pods are light green and firm.
They should yield to gentle pressure
from your finger.

Lamb stew with green beans

1 Replace the sweet potatoes in the recipe above with 500 g (1 lb) boiling (waxy) potatoes and the okra with 300 g (10½ oz) fine green beans. Peel and dice the sweet potatoes and set aside. Sauté the onion and garlic in the hot olive oil for about 5 minutes, then add the lamb and brown as instructed in step 1.

2 Add the sweet potatoes and briefly fry them with the meat, then continue as directed in step 2. Instead of cayenne pepper, use salt and freshly ground black pepper to season the stew, then sprinkle with 1 tablespoon finely chopped fresh thyme. Add the trimmed green beans to the stew after 25 minutes of cooking, then simmer on the stovetop for 25 minutes more.

African lamb ragoût with okra

Indian beef and potato curry

Meatballs with spinach

1 Put 500 g (1 lb) minced (ground) beef in a bowl. Chop 1 onion, 3 cloves garlic and a 2.5 cm (1 inch) piece peeled ginger. Add 1 teaspoon ground turmeric, 1 teaspoon each cumin seeds and coriander seeds, roughly crushed, and ½ teaspoon dried red chilli flakes. Divide the onion, garlic and spices into two batches. Add one batch to the beef with some salt and 1 beaten egg. Mix well and shape into small balls. Brown on all sides (in batches if necessary) for about 10 minutes in 2 tablespoons olive oil, then remove.

2 Fry the remaining onion, garlic and spices for 2 minutes. Add 500 g (1 lb) boiling (waxy) potatoes, peeled and diced, and fry briefly. Add 300 ml (10½ fl oz) beef stock, a 410 g (14½ oz) can chopped tomatoes and salt and black pepper to taste. Add the meatballs and briefly bring to a boil, then reduce the heat, cover and simmer for about 25 minutes. Add 3 cups (150 g/5 oz) baby spinach leaves and briefly heat. Serve hot.

Indian beef and potato curry

500 g (1 lb) lean minced (ground) beef
1 onion, finely chopped
500 g (1 lb) boiling (waxy) potatoes,
    peeled and diced
3 cloves garlic, chopped
2.5 cm (1 inch) piece fresh ginger, peeled
    and finely chopped
1 cinnamon stick, halved
1 teaspoon ground turmeric
1 teaspoon cumin seeds, roughly crushed
1 teaspoon coriander seeds, roughly crushed
$\frac{1}{2}$ teaspoon dried red chilli flakes
410 g (14$\frac{1}{2}$ oz) can chopped tomatoes
300 ml (10$\frac{1}{2}$ fl oz) beef or lamb stock
salt and freshly ground black pepper
3 cups (150 g/5 oz) baby English
    spinach leaves
fresh mint leaves, to garnish

raita

$\frac{2}{3}$ cup (150 g/5 oz) low-fat natural
    (plain) yogurt
$\frac{1}{3}$ small cucumber, finely diced
1 tablespoon chopped fresh mint

serves 4
preparation 10–15 minutes
cooking 35 minutes

per serving *1424 kJ (340 calories), 35 g protein,*
10 g total fat, 4 g saturated fat, 28 g carbohydrate

1 Fry the beef and onion in a large saucepan over medium heat for 5 minutes, or until evenly browned, stirring to break up the meat. Add the potatoes, garlic, ginger and spices and fry for 2 minutes, stirring.

2 Add the tomatoes and stock and season to taste with salt and black pepper. Bring to a boil, then cover and simmer for 20 minutes, stirring occasionally.

3 Meanwhile, make the raita. Mix the yogurt, cucumber and mint together with a little seasoning. Spoon into a small bowl and chill until required.

4 Stir the spinach leaves into the curry and heat through for 1 minute, then taste and add more salt and black pepper, if needed. Spoon the curry onto warmed plates and scatter with mint leaves. Serve immediately, with the chilled raita.

Some more ideas…

✳ If you don't have the individual dried spices, use 2 tablespoons mild curry paste instead.

✳ The curry can be cooked in the oven if you prefer. Brown the beef and onion in a flameproof casserole dish, then add the other ingredients and bring to a boil. Cover and bake in a preheated 180°C (350°F/gas 4) oven for 1 hour. Mix in the spinach, then cover and bake for a final 10 minutes.

Chicken and apple pie

1 tablespoon vegetable oil

1 large onion, sliced

500 g (1 lb) boneless, skinless chicken breasts, cut into chunks

3 carrots, thickly sliced

1 cup (250 ml/8 fl oz) chicken stock

1 cup (250 ml/8 fl oz) dry apple cider

1 teaspoon wholegrain mustard

1 tablespoon chopped fresh tarragon or 1 teaspoon dried tarragon

2 sweet eating apples, cored and thickly sliced

1 tablespoon cornflour (cornstarch)

salt and freshly ground black pepper

topping

750 g (1½ lb) baking (floury) potatoes, peeled and cut into large chunks

2⅔ cups (200 g/7 oz) shredded savoy cabbage

4 tablespoons milk

1 tablespoon butter

4 spring onions (scallions), finely chopped

serves 4
preparation 30 minutes
cooking 30 minutes

per serving *2102 kJ (502 calories), 36 g protein, 17 g total fat, 6 g saturated fat, 53 g carbohydrate*

Cook's tips

Adding a green vegetable such as cabbage to a mashed potato topping is a tasty and clever way to increase the vegetable content of a meal. It may also appeal to children who do not always like vegetables.

In Ireland, the combination of mashed potatoes and cabbage is known as colcannon.

1 Heat the oil in a large, deep, non-stick frying pan. Add the onion and sauté over low heat for 5 minutes, or until softened.

2 Add the chicken and cook over medium heat, stirring occasionally, for 5 minutes, or until it is no longer pink. Stir in the carrots.

3 Mix together the stock, cider, mustard and tarragon, then pour into the pan. Bring to a boil, reduce the heat, cover and simmer for 10 minutes. Stir in the apples and cook, covered, for an additional 10 minutes, or until the chicken and carrots are tender, and the apples have softened but still hold their shape.

4 Meanwhile, make the topping. Cook the potatoes in a saucepan of boiling water for 15 minutes, or until just tender. Cook the cabbage in a separate pan of boiling water for 4-5 minutes, or until just tender but not soft; drain well.

5 Drain the potatoes and return them to the pan. Add the milk and butter and mash until smooth. Stir in the cabbage and spring onions, and season to taste with salt and black pepper. Cover to keep warm.

6 Preheat the grill (broiler) to high. Using a slotted spoon, transfer chicken, apples and vegetables to a 7 cup (1.75 litre/61 fl oz) baking dish. Set aside.

7 Mix the cornflour with 1 tablespoon cold water, stir into the cooking liquid left in the frying pan and bring to a boil, stirring until thickened. Season with salt and black pepper, then pour over the chicken mixture.

8 Pile the topping over the chicken mixture, spreading it evenly to cover. Place under the grill and cook for 4-5 minutes, or until golden brown. Serve immediately.

Mix and match

Instead of cabbage and spring onions, use leeks in the potato topping. Cook 2 sliced leeks (white part only) in the butter until tender. Mash the potatoes with the milk, then mix in the buttery leeks.

Pan-fried potatoes and beef

500 g (1 lb) small unpeeled new potatoes,
    finely diced
2 carrots, thinly sliced
2 tablespoons olive oil
1 onion, finely chopped
2 cloves garlic, finely chopped
250 g (8 oz) cooked beef, cut into
    bite-sized pieces
310 g (11 oz) can sweetcorn kernels, drained
salt and freshly ground black pepper

serves 4
preparation 15 minutes
cooking 35 minutes

per serving *1424 kJ (340 calories), 23 g protein,*
15 g total fat, 3 g saturated fat, 29 g carbohydrate

1 Cook the potatoes in a saucepan of boiling water for about 8 minutes, then add the carrots and cook for a further 2 minutes. Drain well.

2 Heat the oil in a large frying pan. Sauté the onion over medium heat for about 3 minutes, then add the garlic and sauté for another 2 minutes. Add the drained potatoes and carrots and season with salt and black pepper. Fry for about 10 minutes, stirring constantly.

3 Add the beef and sweetcorn and heat through for another 5 minutes, using a spatula to press the mixture against the bottom of the pan to create a crust. Season to taste with salt and black pepper and serve hot.

Cook's tips

This is a good recipe for using up any left-over roast beef.

If you prefer, replace the canned corn with the kernels cut from a cob of fresh sweetcorn.

Some more ideas...

✳ Replace the cooked beef with 1 roast chicken that has been skinned, boned and cut into bite-sized pieces. Add to the pan with the corn in step 3 and cook as before.

✳ To accompany this dish, try a salad of crisp mixed leaves with a dressing made from ½ cup (125 ml/4 fl oz) extra virgin olive oil, 2–3 tablespoons red wine vinegar, ¼ teaspoon mustard, 1 finely chopped French shallot, salt, freshly ground black pepper and 1 tablespoon finely chopped fresh herbs.

Malaysian chicken curry

5 cloves garlic, crushed

5 cm (2 inch) piece fresh ginger, finely grated

2 red onions, finely chopped

2 tablespoons Malaysian curry powder
   (or use a medium curry powder)

1.5 kg (3 lb) chicken pieces

3 tablespoons vegetable oil

2 cups (500 ml/16 fl oz) coconut milk

500 g (1 lb) boiling (waxy) potatoes, peeled
   and cut into large chunks

4 spring onions (scallions), finely sliced

2 red chillies, finely sliced (optional)

rice, to serve

serves 4

preparation 15 minutes + 30 minutes resting

cooking 50 minutes

per serving *4837 kJ (1155 calories), 76 g protein,*
83 g total fat, 38 g saturated fat, 28 g carbohydrate

1 Process the garlic, ginger, onions and 2-3 tablespoons water in a food processor to form a paste. Mix in the curry powder. Rub this paste over the chicken pieces, cover and allow to marinate in the refrigerator for 30 minutes.

2 Heat the oil in a large frying pan or wok over medium heat. Add the chicken pieces with all of the marinade and brown on each side, taking care not to burn the paste. Add the coconut milk, scraping up all the spices from the bottom of the pan, and simmer for 15 minutes.

3 Add the potatoes and simmer for another 20 minutes, or until the potatoes are cooked and the sauce has thickened. Stir in the spring onions and garnish with the chilli (if using). Serve immediately, with rice.

Chicken and potato curry

1 Remove the skin from 8 chicken pieces (about 1.5 kg (3 lb) in total). Slash the flesh of each joint in 3–4 places, right to the bone. Combine ½ teaspoon ground turmeric, 2 tablespoons grated fresh ginger, the juice of ½ lemon and 1 pinch salt, then rub all over the chicken joints. Cover and set aside for 30 minutes in a cool place.

2 Heat 2 tablespoons vegetable oil over medium heat in a large, heavy-based frying pan. Add 1 dried red chilli, halved, 1 teaspoon brown or black mustard seeds and ½ teaspoon each fennel seeds and cumin seeds, and let them splutter and pop for a few minutes; do not allow to burn. Stir in ½ teaspoon ground cinnamon and 1 tablespoon plain (all-purpose) flour. Add 3 crushed cloves garlic, ½ green capsicum (bell pepper), thinly sliced, and 1 sliced large onion and cook for a few minutes, stirring. Stir in the chicken and a 410 g (14½ oz) can chopped tomatoes. Cover and cook for 15 minutes.

3 Meanwhile, cook 2 peeled all-purpose potatoes in a saucepan of boiling water for 5 minutes, then drain and cut into bite-sized pieces. Blanch 2 cups (150 g/5 oz) thinly sliced green cabbage in a separate pan of boiling water for 1 minute, then drain. Add the potatoes and cabbage to the chicken. Cover the pan again and simmer over low–medium heat for 20–25 minutes, or until the chicken is cooked through and tender. Add 1 cup (150 g/5 oz) frozen peas and warm through for a few minutes before serving.

Malaysian chicken curry

Greek-style braised lamb and potatoes

Roast lamb with zucchini

Substitute 2 small zucchini (courgettes) and 1 red capsicum (bell pepper) for
the cherry tomatoes in the recipe opposite. Cut the zucchini into thick slices and
the capsicum into bite-sized pieces. Spread them in the baking dish together with
the meat, potatoes and onions. Proceed as directed in step 2 and bake as before.

Greek-style braised lamb and potatoes

500 g (1 lb) well-trimmed lean lamb leg steak
2 onions, cut into quarters
500 g (1 lb) unpeeled new potatoes,
    cut in half if large
1 large lemon, cut into 8 wedges
1 tablespoon olive oil
12 cloves garlic, peeled
6 sprigs fresh rosemary
6 sprigs fresh thyme
salt and freshly ground black pepper
200 g (7 oz) cherry or baby roma (plum)
    tomatoes, cut in half
3 teaspoons mint sauce or 1½ tablespoons
    mint jelly, melted

serves 4
preparation 20 minutes
cooking 1 hour

*per serving 1437 kJ (343 calories), 32 g protein,
13 g total fat, 4 g saturated fat, 24 g carbohydrate*

1 Preheat the oven to 200°C (400°F/gas 6). Cut the lamb into 2.5 cm (1 inch) chunks and arrange in a large baking dish with the onions and potatoes.

2 Squeeze the juice from four of the lemon wedges, whisk with the oil and drizzle over the meat and vegetables. Add all eight lemon wedges, the garlic and half the herb sprigs to the dish. Season with salt and black pepper, cover tightly with foil and bake for 45 minutes.

3 Remove dish from the oven and increase the temperature to 220°C (425°F/gas 7). Discard the foil and herb sprigs from the dish and add the tomatoes and remaining herb sprigs. Baste the lamb and vegetables with the mint sauce or melted mint jelly. Roast for a further 15-20 minutes, or until the lamb and vegetables are browned and tender.

4 Divide the lamb and vegetables among serving plates, drizzle with any roasting juices and serve.

Cook's tip

If the meat and vegetables did not produce enough juice during cooking, pour 1 glass of dry white wine into the dish and simmer it briefly in the hot oven. Season to taste with salt and black pepper.

Mix and match

Instead of onions, you could use 300 g (10½ oz) French shallots, peeled but left whole.

Five ways...
with roast potatoes

Crisp and golden outside, light and fluffy inside, roast potatoes are the classic accompaniment to roast meat or poultry, and they also go well with fish and other seafood.

Spiced garlic and ginger potatoes

serves **4** | prep **5** mins | cook **35** mins

Preheat the oven to 200°C (400°F/gas 6). Cut a 3 cm (1¼ inch) unpeeled piece of fresh ginger into 3 slices. Cut 750 g (1½ lb) unpeeled small new potatoes into chunks. Heat 1 tablespoon olive oil in a large non-stick frying pan and sauté the ginger with 8 unpeeled garlic cloves, 1½ teaspoons fennel seeds, 1½ teaspoons cumin seeds and 1½ teaspoons ground turmeric for 1 minute. Add the potatoes and cook, stirring, for 5 minutes, or until golden brown. Transfer the mixture to a roasting pan, pour in 100 ml (3½ fl oz) water, then bake for 25–30 minutes, or until the potatoes are well browned and the liquid has evaporated, turning the potatoes occasionally. Discard the ginger. Squeeze the garlic out of the cloves onto the potatoes, and season with salt and 1 tablespoon lemon juice.

NOTE Instead of garlic cloves, you can also use garlic chives. Snip the stalks into short lengths and sprinkle over the potatoes just before serving.

per serving 787 kJ (188 calories), 6 g protein, 6 g total fat, 1 g saturated fat, 28 g carbohydrate

Roast new potatoes with thyme

serves **4** | prep **5** mins | cook **35** mins

Preheat the oven to 230°C (450°F/gas 8). Pour 2 tablespoons olive oil into a large, shallow baking dish and place in the oven to heat. Cook 500 g (1 lb) unpeeled small new potatoes in a large saucepan of boiling water for 5 minutes. Drain well. Remove the baking dish from the oven and add the potatoes to the hot oil; they should sizzle. Stir well to coat in the hot oil, then sprinkle with coarse sea salt and 1–2 tablespoons fresh thyme leaves. Roast on the top shelf of the oven for 20 minutes, until golden.

NOTE These potatoes are delicious with baked fish parcels. Place 4 firm white fish fillets (such as ocean perch) on separate sheets of foil. Season with salt and freshly ground black pepper. Place 2 lemon slices and a few fresh dill sprigs on each and dot with small pieces of butter. Fold into parcels and bake on the middle shelf of the oven for 20 minutes.

per serving 1618 kJ (387 calories), 34 g protein, 20 g total fat, 8 g saturated fat, 17 g carbohydrate

Spiced garlic and ginger potatoes

New potatoes with lemon and rosemary

serves **4** | prep **5** mins | cook **25** mins

Preheat the oven to 230°C (450°F/gas 8). Pour 2 tablespoons olive oil into a large, shallow baking dish and place in the oven to heat. Cook 500 g (1 lb) unpeeled small new potatoes in a large saucepan of boiling water for 5 minutes. Drain well. Remove the baking dish from the oven and add the potatoes to the hot oil; they should sizzle. Stir well to coat in the hot oil, then sprinkle with the finely grated zest of 1 lemon, the leaves from 2–3 large fresh rosemary sprigs and some salt and freshly ground black pepper. Roast on the top shelf of the oven for 20 minutes, until golden.

per serving *687 kJ (164 calories), 3 g protein, 9 g total fat, 1 g saturated fat, 17 g carbohydrate*

Potato wedges with herbs

serves **4** | prep **15** mins | cook **45** mins

Preheat the oven to 200°C (400°F/gas 6). Line a baking tray with baking (parchment) paper. In a large saucepan, melt 2–3 tablespoons butter, then leave to cool briefly. Stir in 100 ml (3½ fl oz) vegetable oil, 1 teaspoon dried thyme, 1 teaspoon dried marjoram, 1 teaspoon onion flakes and some salt and freshly ground black pepper. Cut 1 kg (2 lb) unpeeled boiling (waxy) potatoes into quarters and toss them in batches through the herb oil mixture, then place face-down on the baking tray. Drizzle with the remaining herb oil and bake for 45 minutes, or until golden brown. Sprinkle with 2 tablespoons finely chopped fresh parsley and serve hot, with sour cream.

per serving *2039 kJ (487 calories), 6 g protein, 36 g total fat, 11 g saturated fat, 34 g carbohydrate*

Roast root vegetables

serves **4** | prep **15** mins | cook **55** mins

Preheat the oven to 200°C (400°F/gas 6). Pour 2 tablespoons vegetable oil into a large, non-stick roasting pan and 1 tablespoon vegetable oil into another large, non-stick roasting pan. Place in the oven to heat. Cut 250 g (½ lb) baby parsnips and 250 g (½ lb) baby carrots in half lengthwise. Place in a large saucepan of boiling water and cook for 3 minutes, then drain. Meanwhile, peel 500 g (1 lb) baking (floury) potatoes and chop into evenly sized pieces. Cook in a large saucepan of boiling water for 5 minutes. Drain well and return to the pan, then cover and shake vigorously to roughen the surface of the potatoes (this helps to make them crisp). Add the potatoes to the roasting pan containing the 2 tablespoons of oil and the parsnips and carrots to the other roasting pan, turning to coat them in the oil. Roast for 30 minutes, then turn all the vegetables and roast for 20 minutes more, or until tender.

per serving *1048 kJ (250 calories), 5 g protein, 14 g total fat, 1 g saturated fat, 26 g carbohydrate*

Pot-au-feu

3 chicken legs, about 175 g (6 oz) each
4 leeks, white part only, sliced into 5 cm
    (2 inch) lengths
1 bulb garlic, broken into cloves
1 bouquet garni (see Cook's tip)
2 teaspoons salt
2 teaspoons freshly ground black pepper
10 cups (2.5 litres/87 fl oz) chicken stock
1 white cabbage, about 500 g (1 lb)
500 g (1 lb) beef tenderloin roast
500 g (1 lb) carrots, peeled and cut into
    5 cm (2 inch) lengths
500 g (1 lb) small unpeeled boiling (waxy)
    potatoes, halved
4 tablespoons finely chopped fresh parsley

serves 8
preparation 20 minutes
cooking 1 hour 10 minutes

per serving 1400 kJ (335 calories), 39 g protein,
11 g total fat, 4 g saturated fat, 20 g carbohydrate

1 Rinse the chicken legs and pat dry with paper towel. Place in a large pot with the leeks, garlic, bouquet garni, salt and black pepper. Add the stock, ensuring all the ingredients are covered (top up with water if necessary). Bring to a boil, then reduce the heat to medium and simmer for 30 minutes.

2 Meanwhile, wash the cabbage and cut it into eight pieces, removing the core. Tie kitchen string around the meat to help keep its shape while cooking.

3 Add the cabbage and meat to the broth with the carrots and potatoes and simmer for an additional 30-35 minutes, or until the meat is still slightly pink on the inside. Remove the meat, wrap in foil and leave to rest for 5 minutes. Untie the string and carve the meat into thin slices.

4 Remove the chicken legs from the pot, pick off the meat and discard the skin and bones. Discard the bouquet garni and skim the fat off the broth. Season the broth with salt and black pepper to taste, if needed.

5 Transfer the beef, chicken meat and vegetables to eight shallow soup bowls. Pour the hot broth into the bowls and serve sprinkled with the parsley.

Cook's tip

*To make a bouquet garni, tie up
6 fresh sprigs flat-leaf parsley,
6 fresh thyme sprigs and a bay leaf
to make a little bunch. Alternatively,
buy dried bouquet garni sachets.*

Recipe note

Pot-au-feu (French for 'pot on the fire') is a type of boiled dinner. In the past, it was usually a continuous dish; a pot would always be on the fire, and various ingredients – meat, vegetables and herbs – would be added to it. Now it is cooked for a specific meal and is often served with strong dijon mustard.

Chicken and potato hash

500 g (1 lb) small boiling (waxy) potatoes

1½ tablespoons vegetable oil

1 onion, chopped

1 green capsicum (bell pepper), seeded and chopped

1 red capsicum (bell pepper), seeded and chopped

1 cup (150 g/5 oz) diced cooked skinless chicken

1 large clove garlic, crushed

1 teaspoon paprika

½ teaspoon dried thyme

salt and freshly ground black pepper

fresh herbs of your choice, to garnish (optional)

apple wedges, to serve

Tabasco or sweet chilli sauce, to serve

serves 4

preparation 15 minutes

cooking 50 minutes

---

per serving 1048 kJ (250 calories), 13 g protein, 12 g total fat, 2 g saturated fat, 23 g carbohydrate

1 Cook the unpeeled potatoes in a saucepan of boiling water for 20-25 minutes, or until tender. Drain, allow to cool, then cut into small dice.

2 Heat the oil in a large frying pan over medium heat. Add the onion and sauté for 4 minutes, or until slightly softened. Add the capsicums and cook gently for 4-5 minutes.

3 Stir in the diced potato and cook for 5 minutes, or until it is beginning to brown. Add the chicken and garlic, then sprinkle with the paprika, thyme and some salt and black pepper.

4 Press the mixture into an even layer over the bottom of the pan, using a spatula or the back of a wooden spoon to squash it down. Cook, without stirring, for 5 minutes, until the bottom is nicely browned and crisp.

5 Break up the mixture, then leave to cook for 5 minutes until a crust forms on the bottom. Garnish with herbs, if you like, and serve with apple wedges and Tabasco or sweet chilli sauce.

Cook's tips

Use a boiling (waxy) variety of potato with a firm flesh, such as bintje or pink-eye, which will hold its shape while cooking. If you like, you can peel off the skins after boiling the potatoes.

Left-over chicken from a roast is perfect for this crisp golden hash. This easy dish is ideal for a one-pot dinner or brunch.

Mix and match

Roast beef and potato hash is also delicious — instead of chicken, use left-over roast beef and some cooked greens, such as broccoli florets, instead of capsicums.

Chicken and sweet potato hash

Potato hash with mushrooms

Replace the sweetcorn and sun-dried tomatoes in the recipe opposite with 2 finely
diced slices bacon (bacon strips) and 250 g (8 oz) thickly sliced button mushrooms.
Heat the oil in a large non-stick frying pan and sauté the bacon for 5 minutes. Add
the mushrooms and fry for another 5 minutes. Add the potatoes, sweet potatoes and
leeks and fry for 5 minutes more. Stir in the chicken, season with salt and freshly
ground black pepper, but omit the paprika. Heat through for 5 minutes and serve.

Chicken and sweet potato hash

300 g (10½ oz) boiling (waxy) potatoes, peeled and cut into small bite-sized chunks
500 g (1 lb) orange sweet potatoes, peeled and cut into small bite-sized chunks
2 leeks, white part only, sliced
2 tablespoons vegetable oil
1½ cups (250 g/8 oz) cooked skinless chicken meat, diced
1¼ cups (170 g/6 oz) frozen sweetcorn, thawed with boiling water and drained
8 sun-dried tomatoes packed in oil, drained and chopped
1 teaspoon paprika
salt

yogurt garlic sauce
⅔ cup (150 g/5 oz) natural (plain) yogurt
1 small clove garlic, crushed
½ teaspoon paprika

serves 4
preparation 15 minutes
cooking 15 minutes

per serving 1805 kJ (431 calories), 26 g protein, 17 g total fat, 3 g saturated fat, 43 g carbohydrate

1 Cook the potatoes and sweet potatoes in a large saucepan of boiling water for 2 minutes. Add the leeks and cook for a further 1 minute. Drain well.

2 Heat the oil in a large non-stick frying pan and add the leeks and potatoes. Cook over medium heat, stirring frequently, for 3-4 minutes, or until beginning to brown.

3 Add the chicken, corn, sun-dried tomatoes, paprika and salt to taste. Mix thoroughly and continue cooking for 3-5 minutes, pressing down well to make a cake in the pan, and turning it over in chunks, until brown and crisp on both sides.

4 Put all the yogurt garlic sauce ingredients in a bowl and mix together well. Serve portions of hash topped with the yogurt sauce.

Cook's tip

This is a great dish to make with left-over roast chicken, or with turkey. Sweet potatoes are a colourful addition to the potatoes traditionally used in a hash, and corn adds a delightful texture. Serve with a crisp mixed salad and crusty bread.

Mix and match

To make a fruity, spicy chicken or turkey hash, sauté 1 chopped onion, 1 chopped red capsium (bell pepper) and 1 chopped red-skinned eating apple in 2 tablespoons vegetable oil for 2 minutes. Stir in 1 tablespoon curry powder or paste and 2 tablespoons raisins or sultanas (golden raisins). Add 500 g (1 lb) cooked all-purpose potatoes and/or cooked sweet potatoes, cut into chunks, and cook over medium heat until beginning to brown. Mix in 1½ cups (250 g/8 oz) cooked skinless chicken or turkey and 1 tablespoon mango chutney, and cook for 3–5 minutes, pressing into a cake and turning in chunks. Serve topped with yogurt garlic sauce (left) or tzatziki.

Baked chicken pieces
with spicy potatoes

4 tablespoons vegetable oil
1 teaspoon dried thyme
2½ teaspoons sweet paprika
salt and freshly ground black pepper
4 unpeeled boiling (waxy) potatoes, cut into
   bite-sized pieces
1.5 kg (3 lb) skinless chicken pieces
1½ cups (150 g/5 oz) dry breadcrumbs
½ cup (60 g/2¼ oz) plain (all-purpose) flour
1 teaspoon dried sage
1 teaspoon dried oregano
⅔ cup (150 g/5 oz) sour cream

serves 4
preparation 20 minutes
cooking 1 hour

*per serving 4658 kJ (1113 calories), 84 g protein,
61 g total fat, 19 g saturated fat, 58 g carbohydrate*

1 Preheat the oven to 180°C (350°F/gas 4). In a small
bowl, mix together 1 tablespoon oil, the thyme and ½ teaspoon
paprika. Season with salt and black pepper to taste and brush
all over the potatoes.

2 Wash the chicken pieces and pat dry with paper towel.
Put the remaining oil in a bowl. In another bowl, mix together
the breadcrumbs, flour, sage, oregano, remaining paprika,
2 teaspoons salt and ½ teaspoon black pepper. Turn the
chicken pieces first in the oil, then in the breadcrumb mixture.

3 Spread the potatoes and chicken pieces in a large baking
dish, or on a baking tray spread with baking (parchment) paper,
and bake for 1 hour, or until golden and cooked. Serve hot, with
sour cream.

Cook's tip

*To turn stale bread into dry breadcrumbs, remove
the crusts and place the slices in one layer on a
baking tray. Bake at 130°C (250°F/gas 1) for
15 minutes or until the bread is dry; do not allow
it to colour. Alternatively, leave the slices in a
warm place for a day or two, covered with paper
towels, until dry. Crush with a rolling pin or in a
food processor and store in an airtight container.*

Chicken with potatoes and vegetables

Preheat the oven to 180°C (350°F/gas 4). Line a baking tray with baking
(parchment) paper. Prepare the chicken pieces as directed in step 2 above.
Cut 500 g (1 lb) new potatoes in half lengthwise and place face-down on the
baking tray. Brush with 2 tablespoons olive oil and season with salt. Add the
chicken pieces to the tray as directed above and bake for 30 minutes. Meanwhile,
cut 2 zucchini (courgettes) and 1 red and 1 green capsicum (bell pepper) into
bite-sized pieces. Brush with oil, add to the baking tray and season with salt
and black pepper. Bake for a final 30 minutes.

Baked chicken pieces with spicy potatoes

Potato pizza with chicken and rocket

Chicken with potatoes and bacon

1 Cook 500 g (1 lb) small boiling (waxy) potatoes in a large saucepan of lightly salted boiling water for 20 minutes, or until tender. Drain and quarter. Meanwhile, half-fill a large frying pan with water. Add 3 skinless chicken breast fillets, about 175 g (6 oz) each, and poach over medium heat for 10–15 minutes until cooked through. Remove the chicken from the pan, cover, allow to cool slightly, then slice on the diagonal. Cook 4 chopped slices rindless bacon (bacon strips) in a dry frying pan over medium heat until crisp. Drain on paper towels.

2 Put the potatoes, chicken, half the bacon, ⅔ cup (100 g/3½ oz) semi-dried tomatoes and 5 cups (150 g/5 oz) mixed salad leaves into a large bowl and gently toss with ½ cup (125 g/4 fl oz) creamy salad dressing, the remaining bacon and 3 quartered hard-boiled eggs, then serve warm or cold.

Potato pizza with chicken and rocket

500 g (1 lb) unpeeled small new potatoes
2 tablespoons olive oil, plus extra for brushing
2 red onions, halved and very thinly sliced
75 g (2½ oz) pancetta, diced
2 cups (175 g/6 oz) sliced button mushrooms
leaves from 2 sprigs rosemary
freshly ground black pepper
2 ready-made pizza bases, each about 22 cm
    (8½ inches) across
90 ml (3 fl oz) milk
1½ cups (250 g/9 oz) shredded cooked
    skinless chicken breast
100 g (3½ oz) rocket (arugula)
2 tablespoons shaved parmesan

serves 4
preparation 30 minutes
cooking 25 minutes

per serving 2163 kJ (517 calories), 30 g protein
27 g total fat, 6 g saturated fat, 39 g carbohydrate

1 Preheat the oven to 220°C (425°F/gas 7). Put two baking trays or pizza trays (or use pizza tiles, if you have them) in the oven to heat.

2 Using a mandolin, a fine slicing disk in a food processor or a very sharp knife, cut the potatoes into wafer-thin slices. Cook in a large saucepan of boiling water for 1-2 minutes, or until just tender, then drain.

3 Heat the oil in a large saucepan and lightly fry the onions with the pancetta for 2-3 minutes, or until softened. Add the mushrooms and cook for an additional 2 minutes. Add the potatoes and rosemary, season with black pepper and gently toss, taking care not to break up the potatoes.

4 Lightly oil one side of each pizza base and place, oiled side down, on the preheated trays. Spread the potato mixture evenly over the bases. Trickle the milk over the topping on both pizzas. Bake for 15 minutes, or until the potatoes are tender and golden.

5 Remove the pizzas from the oven, cut them into quarters and place two quarters on each plate. Divide the chicken among the pizza pieces, scatter the rocket and parmesan shavings over the top and serve.

Cook's tip

Traditionally, pizzas are cooked in wood-fired ovens, which are extremely hot and produce a lovely crisp base. The best way to replicate this at home is to put the dough straight onto a preheated tray or pizza stone (many kitchen stores sell them). You can also buy a special two-piece pizza pan that has a perforated disc on which the pizza cooks, so that air circulates underneath, ensuring a crisp crust.

Shepherd's pie

1 tablespoon olive oil
500 g (1 lb) lean minced (ground) lamb
1 large onion, finely chopped
3 carrots, finely chopped
3 stalks celery, thinly sliced
2 leeks, white part only, thinly sliced
1 tablespoon tomato passata (puréed tomatoes)
1 tablespoon worcestershire sauce
350 ml (12 fl oz) lamb or beef stock
$\frac{1}{3}$ cup (100 g/3$\frac{1}{2}$ oz) split red lentils
3 tablespoons chopped fresh parsley,
    plus parsley sprigs to garnish
peas, to serve

potato and parsnip topping

500 g (1 lb) baking (floury) potatoes, peeled
    and cut into chunks
500 g (1 lb) parsnips, peeled and cut
    into chunks
75 ml (2$\frac{1}{2}$ fl oz) milk
1 tablespoon butter
salt and freshly ground black pepper

serves 4
preparation 30 minutes
cooking 1 hour

per serving *2239 kJ (534 calories), 42 g protein,*
19 g total fat, 8 g saturated fat, 49 g carbohydrate

1   Preheat the oven to 200°C (400°F/gas 6). Heat the oil in a large heavy-based saucepan. Add the lamb and cook over high heat for 5 minutes, or until lightly browned, stirring well with a wooden spoon to break up the meat. Push the meat to one side of the pan and add the onion. Reduce the heat to low and cook for 10 minutes, stirring occasionally, until the onion is softened and lightly browned.

2   Add the carrots, celery and leeks and stir well, then add the tomato passata, worcestershire sauce, stock and lentils. Increase the heat and bring to a boil, stirring frequently. Partially cover with a lid, then reduce the heat to low and simmer for about 20 minutes, stirring occasionally.

3   While the lamb mixture is cooking, prepare the topping. Place the potatoes and parsnips in a saucepan and pour in boiling water to cover by 5 cm (2 inches). Bring back to a boil, then reduce the heat and simmer for 15-20 minutes, or until very tender. Heat the milk in a small saucepan until hot.

4   Drain the potatoes and parsnips well, then return them to the pan. Pour the hot milk over and mash with a potato masher until completely smooth. Beat in the butter and season to taste with salt and black pepper.

5   Remove the lamb mixture from the heat, then stir in the chopped parsley and salt and black pepper to taste. Spoon into a large baking dish (about 10 cups/2.5 litres/87 fl oz in capacity). Top with the mashed vegetables, spreading them in an even layer. Bake for 20 minutes, or until bubbling and lightly browned. Garnish with parsley sprigs and serve hot, with peas.

Recipe note
In this version of an old family favourite, the lamb filling contains lots of vegetables and red lentils, giving a rich flavour and texture. A generous serving of peas will make the meal even more nutritious.

Shepherd's pie

Mix and match

Replace the lamb with lean minced (ground) beef or pork. Omit the leeks and stir
1⅔ cups (250 g/9 oz) fresh or frozen peas into the meat mixture after it has simmered
for 15 minutes. In the topping, replace the parsnips with celeriac (celery root).

Stir-fried potatoes with lamb and ginger

2 teaspoons sesame oil

1 tablespoon lemon juice

2 tablespoons finely chopped fresh ginger

3 tablespoons chopped fresh mint

350 g (12 oz) lean lamb leg or neck fillet,
cut into thin slices

750 g (1½ lb) small boiling (waxy) potatoes

3 tablespoons vegetable oil

2 zucchini (courgettes), sliced on the diagonal

6 spring onions (scallions), sliced on the
diagonal

1 cup (150 g/5 oz) shelled fresh or frozen peas,
thawed if necessary

1 tablespoon salt-reduced soy sauce

4 tablespoons beef or vegetable stock

2 teaspoons honey

salt and freshly ground black pepper

serves 4
preparation 15 minutes
cooking 25 minutes

*per serving 1859 kJ (444 calories), 28 g protein,
22 g total fat, 5 g saturated fat, 33 g carbohydrate*

1 In a shallow dish, whisk together the sesame oil, lemon juice, half the ginger and 1 tablespoon mint. Add the lamb and stir well, then cover and leave to marinate while you prepare the remaining ingredients.

2 Put the potatoes in a large saucepan and pour over enough boiling water to cover them. Bring back to a boil, half-cover the pan with a lid and simmer for 12 minutes, or until almost tender when pierced with a sharp knife. Drain and leave until cool enough to handle. Cut the potatoes into slices slightly thicker than 5 mm (¼ inch), then cut the slices into sticks. Put them in a bowl, drizzle with 1 tablespoon of the vegetable oil and gently toss to coat. (This will stop the potatoes sticking together during frying.)

3 Heat 1 tablespoon of the remaining oil in a wok or large frying pan. When the oil is hot, add the lamb and stir-fry over high heat for 1 minute or until just browned, but still fairly rare. Quickly remove and set aside.

4 Add the remaining oil to the wok. When hot, add the zucchini and stir-fry for 1 minute, then add the potato sticks. Cook for 3–4 minutes, stirring constantly, until lightly browned, taking care not to break up the potatoes. Add the spring onions and stir-fry for 1 minute more.

5 Reduce the heat to medium and add the peas, soy sauce, stock, honey and remaining ginger. Return the lamb with any juices to the pan. Stir-fry for 2–3 minutes, or until the liquid is bubbling and all the ingredients are tender and hot. Season to taste with salt and black pepper, scatter the remaining mint over the top and serve.

Cook's tip
*If time permits, marinate the lamb
for 2–3 hours to intensify the flavour.*

Fish and seafood

Potatoes pair well with the tender flesh of fish and seafood. This chapter presents recipes for both everyday meals and special occasions and also gives hints on selecting and cooking seafood.

Thai fish cakes with lime and honey dip

350 g (12 oz) baking (floury) potatoes,
    peeled and cut into chunks
350 g (12 oz) firm white fish fillets
juice of 1 lime
1 lemongrass stalk, white part only, thinly
    sliced and lightly crushed
2 teaspoons Thai red curry paste
3 spring onions (scallions), thinly sliced
3 cloves garlic, chopped
3 tablespoons chopped fresh coriander
    (cilantro)
1 teaspoon peeled and chopped fresh ginger
4 tablespoons plain (all-purpose) flour
1 cup (100 g/3½ oz) fresh wholemeal
    (whole grain) breadcrumbs
2 eggs
2 tablespoons olive oil

lime and honey dipping sauce

juice of 3 limes
2 tablespoons honey
1 teaspoon peeled and chopped fresh ginger
2 teaspoons salt-reduced soy sauce
¾ teaspoon Thai red curry paste
1 large mild red chilli, seeded and thinly sliced

cucumber and mint salad

1 iceberg lettuce, finely shredded
½ cucumber, diced
¾ cup (35 g/1¼ oz) finely shredded fresh
    mint leaves

serves 8
preparation 40 minutes + 1 hour chilling
cooking 25 minutes

per serving *1004 kJ (240 calories), 15 g protein,
8 g total fat, 1 g saturated fat, 28 g carbohydrate*

1 Cook the potatoes in a saucepan of boiling water for 15-20 minutes, or until tender. Drain well, then mash.

2 Meanwhile, place the fish in a shallow saucepan with enough cold water to cover and add half the lime juice. Bring to a boil, reduce the heat to low and simmer for 1 minute. Remove from the heat, cover and leave to cool for 4 minutes. Drain the fish and flake the flesh with a fork, discarding the skin and bones, and place in a bowl. Add the potatoes and mix together with a fork. Mix in the lemongrass, curry paste, spring onions, garlic, coriander, ginger and the remaining lime juice.

3 Tip the flour onto a plate and the breadcrumbs onto a second plate. Lightly beat the eggs in a shallow bowl. Take about 1 tablespoon of the fish mixture and shape into a patty. Turn it first in the flour, dip into the egg, then coat with the breadcrumbs. Shape and coat the remaining fish cakes in the same way, making 24 in total. Chill for 1 hour.

4 Heat half the oil in a non-stick frying pan. Add half the fish cakes and cook over medium heat for about 3 minutes on each side, or until golden. Remove and keep warm while you cook the rest of the fish cakes, using the remaining oil.

5 Meanwhile, put all the dipping sauce ingredients in a small pan and heat gently for 1 minute without boiling. Mix together the salad ingredients in a bowl. Arrange the fish cakes on individual plates, with the salad. Serve each plate with a tiny dish of the dipping sauce.

Lemongrass

To prepare lemongrass, peel it down to the first purple ring, then chop only the tender inner part. The fibrous outer leaves can be used to flavour stocks and soups; discard before serving. When a stalk is being used whole, for example in a soup, it is often first bruised with a rolling pin or the flat side of a knife to release its delicate lemon flavour.

Indian-style fish

Indian-style fish

1 kg (2 lb) small unpeeled new potatoes
4 plaice, sole or trout fillets, or thin white fish
  fillets, about 150 g (5 oz) each
salt and freshly ground black pepper
2 cm (¾ inch) piece fresh ginger, peeled and
  finely chopped
½ red onion, finely chopped
1 mild red chilli, seeded and finely chopped
4 tablespoons coconut milk
4 tablespoons chopped fresh mint
2 zucchini (courgettes), cut into large dice
1 tablespoon sesame seeds
2 teaspoons yellow mustard seeds
2 teaspoons soy sauce

serves 4
preparation 20 minutes
cooking 20 minutes

*per serving 1574 kJ (376 calories), 37 g protein,
9 g total fat, 4 g saturated fat, 37 g carbohydrate*

1 Preheat the oven to 180°C (350°F/gas 4). Cook the potatoes in a saucepan of boiling water for 15 minutes, or until tender.

2 Meanwhile, cut out four large pieces of baking (parchment) paper or foil, each large enough to enclose a fish fillet. Lay a fillet on each sheet and season with salt and black pepper.

3 In a bowl, mix together the ginger, onion, chilli, coconut milk and half the mint, then spread over the fish. Fold over the paper or foil and pleat or twist the ends to seal securely. Put the parcels on a large baking tray and bake for 10-12 minutes, or until the fish flakes easily with a fork.

4 When the potatoes and fish are almost ready, steam the zucchini for 4 minutes in a steamer above the potatoes.

5 Heat a frying pan. Add the sesame and mustard seeds, cover and fry over medium heat for 2-3 minutes, or until lightly toasted, shaking the pan frequently.

6 Take the pan off the heat, stir in the soy sauce, then cover and set aside until the seeds stop 'popping'. Stir the zucchini into the seed mixture.

7 Drain the potatoes and toss with the remaining mint. Arrange the fish parcels on serving plates and serve with the zucchini and potatoes.

Indian-style salmon fillets

Prepare the potatoes and zucchini (courgettes) as directed in the recipe above. Replace the fish with 4 salmon fillets, about 150 g (5 oz) each. Rinse, pat dry and place on four large pieces of baking (parchment) paper or foil, then season with salt and freshly ground black pepper. Replace the coconut milk with the juice from 2 limes, and mix in a bowl with the ginger, onion, chilli and 2 tablespoons mint. Spread the mixture over the salmon, wrap to make parcels and bake for about 15 minutes. Complete the dish as directed in steps 4–7.

Foil-cooked trout with roast potatoes and cucumber sauce

750 g (1½ lb) unpeeled new potatoes,
    quartered lengthwise
1 tablespoon olive oil
4 sprigs fresh tarragon
4 small whole trout, about 300 g (10½ oz)
    each, scaled and cleaned
freshly ground black pepper
1 orange, cut into 8 slices
1 lemon, cut into 8 slices
4 tablespoons orange juice
baby rocket (arugula) leaves, to garnish

cucumber sauce

1 cup (200 g/7 oz) grated cucumber
²/₃ cup (150 g/5 oz) low-fat natural (plain)
    yogurt
2 tablespoons chopped fresh mint

serves 4
preparation 20 minutes
cooking 35 minutes

----

per serving 1964 kJ (469 calories), 63 g protein,
9 g total fat, 2 g saturated fat, 31 g carbohydrate

1 Preheat the oven to 200°C (400°F/gas 6) and place two baking trays in the oven to heat.

2 Cook the potatoes in a large saucepan of boiling water for 5 minutes. Drain and return to the pan. Drizzle with the oil and toss quickly to coat.

3 Spread the potatoes in a single layer on one of the hot baking trays and roast for 10 minutes. Turn the potatoes over and roast for another 10 minutes, then turn them again and roast for a further 5 minutes, or until crisp and tender.

4 Meanwhile, tuck a tarragon sprig inside each trout with some black pepper. Cut out four squares of foil, each large enough to wrap a fish. Cut the orange and lemon slices in half. Divide half the orange and lemon slices among the foil squares, lay the fish on top and cover with the remaining citrus slices. Sprinkle 1 tablespoon orange juice over each fish. Wrap the foil to enclose the fish completely, twisting the ends to seal securely. Place the parcels on the second hot baking tray and bake for 20 minutes with the potatoes.

5 While the fish and potatoes are cooking, make the cucumber sauce. Place the grated cucumber in a sieve and press to squeeze out any liquid. Tip into a small bowl, mix in the yogurt and mint and season with black pepper.

6 Arrange the fish, citrus slices and roast potatoes on individual warm plates. Garnish with rocket leaves and serve with the cucumber sauce.

Selecting fish

When choosing whole fish, look for shiny skin or scales and firm, resilient flesh. The eyes should be clear and protruding, and the gills a bright pink or red colour. The fish should smell fresh, not overly 'fishy'; saltwater fish should smell of the sea. Fillets and steaks should be firm and moist, with fresh-looking, translucent flesh.

Foil-cooked trout with roast potatoes and cucumber sauce

Ocean perch with oven potatoes

Prepare the potatoes as directed in the recipe opposite. Rinse 4 fillets of ocean perch or other firm white fish, pat dry and place on four large pieces of foil. Drizzle with lemon juice and add salt and black pepper to taste. Top each with a few dots of butter and 3 sprigs fresh dill. Wrap to make parcels, place on a hot baking tray and bake with the potatoes for about 15 minutes. For the cucumber sauce, use 2 tablespoons finely chopped fresh dill instead of the mint, and add 1 crushed clove garlic. Serve the fish with the potatoes and cucumber sauce.

Potato pizza with tuna, chorizo and black olives

Potato pizza with sardines

Prepare the potato dough as directed in the recipe opposite. Replace the shallots with 1 red onion, peeled and shaved into fine rings. Replace the chorizo and tuna with 2 x 115 g (4 oz) cans sardines in oil, drained and flesh flaked apart with a fork. Spread the rolled-out, blind-baked dough with the tomato passata, then scatter with the raw onion, uncooked capsicum, sardines and olives. Cover with foil and bake for about 45 minutes, removing the foil after 25 minutes. Serve hot.

Potato pizza with tuna, chorizo and black olives

300 g (10½ oz) all-purpose potatoes, peeled and diced
2 tablespoons milk
1 scant cup (115 g/4 oz) plain (all-purpose) flour
pinch of salt
55 g (2 oz) cold butter, chopped
1 tablespoon chopped fresh basil

tuna and chorizo topping

8 French shallots
100 g (3½ oz) chorizo sausage, thinly sliced
1 red capsicum (bell pepper), seeded and thinly sliced
1 yellow capsicum (bell pepper), seeded and thinly sliced
½ cup (125 ml/4½ oz) tomato passata (puréed tomatoes)
180 g (6 oz) can tuna in springwater, drained and flaked
12 pitted black olives, halved

serves 4
preparation 25 minutes + 30 minutes chilling
cooking 50 minutes

----

per serving 1739 kJ (415 calories), 19 g protein, 20 g total fat, 10 g saturated fat, 38 g carbohydrate

1 Cook the potatoes in a saucepan of boiling water for 8-10 minutes, or until just tender. Drain well, then mash with the milk. Set aside to cool.

2 Sift the flour and salt into a large bowl. Add the butter and rub in with your fingertips until the mixture resembles fine breadcrumbs. Add the mashed potato and basil and mix to form a soft dough. Wrap in plastic wrap and chill for at least 30 minutes before rolling out.

3 Meanwhile, preheat the oven to 190°C (375°F/gas 5) and put a large non-stick baking tray in the oven to heat. To make the topping, put the shallots in a heatproof bowl and pour in enough boiling water to cover. Leave for 5 minutes, then drain. When cool enough to handle, peel and quarter the shallots.

4 Roll out the potato dough to a 28 cm (11 inch) round. Lightly oil one side of the dough and place, oiled side down, on the hot baking tray. Bake for 20-25 minutes, or until light golden.

5 Meanwhile, gently cook the chorizo in a non-stick frying pan. When the oil starts to run from the sausage, add the shallots and cook for 2-3 minutes, or until the shallots are glazed. Add the capsicums and cook for 1-2 minutes to soften.

6 Spread the tomato passata evenly over the pastry round, leaving a bit of a border. Top with the chorizo mixture and scatter the tuna and olives over.

7 Bake for 15 minutes, or until the exposed pastry edge is golden brown. Serve hot, cut into wedges.

Serving tip

This pizza is delicious served with a salad of watercress and cherry or grape tomatoes.

Fish casserole with pesto potatoes

750 g (1½ lb) baking (floury) potatoes,
    peeled and diced
600 ml (21 fl oz) milk
2 tablespoons butter
2 tablespoons ready-made pesto
600 g (1 lb 5 oz) skinless firm white fish fillet
1 bay leaf
2 young leeks, white part only, thinly sliced
3 tablespoons plain (all-purpose) flour
½ cup (125 ml/4 fl oz) fish stock
125 g (4½ oz) cooked and peeled prawns
    (shrimp)
2 tablespoons crème fraîche or sour cream
salt and freshly ground black pepper
2 tablespoons dry breadcrumbs
2 tablespoons grated parmesan

serves 4
preparation 20 minutes
cooking 40 minutes

per serving 2639 kJ (630 calories), 52 g protein,
27 g total fat, 15 g saturated fat, 44 g carbohydrate

1 Cook the potatoes in a saucepan of boiling water for 15 minutes, or until tender. Drain, allow to steam briefly, then place in a bowl. Heat 100 ml (3½ fl oz) of the milk and melt half the butter in it. Mash the potatoes with a potato masher, adding the milk mixture. Finally, stir the pesto into the potatoes.

2 Meanwhile, wash the fish and place in a non-stick saucepan, putting the bay leaf on top. Pour the remaining milk over the fish and briefly bring to a boil. Reduce the heat and simmer for 6-8 minutes, then remove the fish and cut into bite-sized pieces. Strain the milk and set aside, discarding the bay leaf.

3 Preheat the grill (broiler) to medium.

4 Heat the remaining butter in a large saucepan and sauté the leeks for about 8 minutes. Stir in the flour and cook for 1 minute, then add the stock and boil until the liquid is reduced by half. Gradually stir in the strained milk. Cook, stirring, on low heat for an additional 3 minutes.

5 Stir in the fish, prawns and crème fraîche, season to taste with salt and black pepper and heat for another 2 minutes, taking care the fish does not fall apart.

6 Spread the mixture into a flameproof dish and cover with the pesto mashed potato. Smooth the surface and sprinkle with the breadcrumbs and parmesan. Place under the hot grill for about 5 minutes to heat through. Serve hot.

White fish and oily fish

White fish are saltwater fish that have the oil concentrated mainly in the liver. They include cod, haddock, whiting, bass, ray, skate, bream and snapper, as well as flat fish such as plaice, dory and sole. The oil in oily fish is distributed throughout their flesh. This makes them more nutritious than white fish, but higher in kilojoules (calories). Saltwater oily fish include tuna, anchovies, herring and sardines. Salmon and trout are freshwater oily fish.

Fish casserole with pesto potatoes

Fish pie with cabbage and mashed potatoes

Prepare the potatoes and fish as directed in the recipe opposite. Substitute 400 g (14 oz) finely shredded savoy cabbage for the leeks. Blanch in a saucepan of boiling water for 5 minutes, drain, rinse with cold water and drain again. Stir 2 cups (150 g/ 5 oz) of the cabbage into the mashed potato instead of the pesto. Heat 1 tablespoon butter in a large frying pan and sauté the remaining cabbage for about 6 minutes. Proceed as outlined in steps 4 and 5. Spread the potato mixture over the pie, but omit the breadcrumbs and parmesan. Heat under the grill (broiler) for 5 minutes.

Herb-crumbed fish with oven-baked wedges

750 g (1½ lb) baking (floury) potatoes, peeled
1 teaspoon olive oil
1 egg white
4 firm white fish fillets, about 150 g
    (5 oz) each
1 tablespoon mayonnaise or aïoli (see page 213)
¾ cup (60 g/2¼ oz) fresh white breadcrumbs
3 teaspoons butter, melted
3 teaspoons grated parmesan
1 tablespoon chopped fresh chives
1 tablespoon chopped fresh flat-leaf parsley,
    plus extra sprigs to garnish
salt and freshly ground black pepper
lemon wedges, to serve

serves 4
preparation 20 minutes
cooking 40 minutes

*per serving 1670 kJ (399 calories), 39 g protein,
10 g total fat, 4 g saturated fat, 36 g carbohydrate*

1 Preheat the oven to 200°C (400°F/gas 6). Gently cook the potatoes in a saucepan of boiling water for 5 minutes. Drain, then dry thoroughly with paper towel. Cut each potato lengthwise into slices about 2 cm (³/₄ inch) thick, then cut each slice into two or three thick wedges.

2 Brush a non-stick baking tray with some of the oil. Beat the egg white until frothy. Toss the chips in the egg white, gently shake off any excess, then spread out on the baking tray. Bake for 35 minutes, turning halfway through cooking.

3 Meanwhile, prepare the fish. Use the remaining oil to oil another non-stick baking tray. Place the fish fillets, skin side down, on the baking tray and spread 1 teaspoon mayonnaise or aïoli over each fillet.

4 Mix together the breadcrumbs, butter, parmesan, chives and parsley and season with salt and black pepper. Spread the crumb mixture evenly over the fish, pressing on gently.

5 Bake the fish on the top shelf of the oven for the final 10-15 minutes of the chips' cooking time. Divide the fish and chips among serving plates, garnish with parsley sprigs and serve with lemon wedges.

Health tip
You can enjoy this delicious variation on traditional fish and chips without worrying about the fat content – the secret to the golden wedges is to coat them with egg white, not fat.

Fish and parsley sauce with mashed potatoes, leek and zucchini

4 firm white fish fillets, about 150 g
    (5 oz) each
½ small bunch (20 g/¾ oz) fresh parsley,
    plus chopped fresh parsley, to garnish
1 small onion, thinly sliced
1 carrot, thinly sliced
6 black peppercorns
300 ml (10½ fl oz) milk
750 g (10½ lb) baking (floury) or all-purpose
    potatoes, peeled and cut into chunks
1 large whole leek, thinly sliced (including the
    green top)
2 zucchini (courgettes), cut into thin sticks
1 tablespoon butter
2½ tablespoons plain (all-purpose) flour
finely grated zest and juice of ½ lemon
salt and freshly ground black pepper
lemon wedges, to serve

serves 4
preparation 25 minutes
cooking 25 minutes

per serving 1703 kJ (407 calories), 40 g protein,
11 g total fat, 6 g saturated fat, 37 g carbohydrate

1 Put the fish fillets in a large frying pan. Remove the leaves from the parsley stalks and add the stalks to the pan with the onion, carrot, peppercorns and milk. Bring just to a boil, then cover and simmer very gently for 5 minutes. Remove from the heat and leave for 5 minutes to complete the cooking.

2 Meanwhile, put the potatoes in a saucepan of boiling water and simmer for 10 minutes. Add the white part of the leek to the pan, then set a colander containing the zucchini and the green part of the leek on top of the pan, over the potatoes. Cook for 5 minutes, or until the vegetables are tender.

3 Transfer the fish to a heatproof plate and remove the skin. Keep warm. Strain the cooking liquid and reserve.

4 Melt the butter in a saucepan, stir in the flour and cook for 1 minute. Gradually stir in the strained cooking liquid and bring to a boil, stirring until the sauce is thickened and smooth. Finely chop the parsley leaves and stir into the sauce with the lemon zest. Season to taste with salt and black pepper. Keep hot.

5 Drain the potatoes and white leeks and mash with the lemon juice and some seasoning. Stir in the green leek tops and zucchini. Transfer the fish fillets to serving plates and spoon the sauce over. Garnish with chopped parsley and serve with the mashed potato mixture and lemon wedges.

Cook's tip

Fish cooks very quickly, so it needs to be watched carefully; if overcooked, it loses flavour and becomes dry. Properly cooked fish is moist, tender to the bite and full of flavour. Test the fish when it begins to look opaque. Gently prod it with the prongs of a fork; when the flesh flakes easily, the fish is done.

Fish with gremolata crust and saffron mashed potatoes

2 lemons

²/₃ cup (55 g/2 oz) fresh white breadcrumbs

3 tablespoons chopped fresh parsley

2 cloves garlic, crushed

salt and freshly ground black pepper

4 skinless thick firm white fish fillets, about
     150 g (5 oz) each

olive oil, for brushing

2 teaspoons wholegrain mustard

3 roma (plum) tomatoes, quartered

1 large zucchini (courgette), thinly sliced
     diagonally

1 tablespoon olive oil

1 kg (2 lb) baking (floury) potatoes, peeled
     and cut into chunks

1 teaspoon saffron threads

3 tablespoons milk

serves 4

preparation 20 minutes

cooking 25 minutes

per serving *2227 kJ (532 calories), 41 g protein,*
19 g total fat, 3 g saturated fat, 47 g carbohydrate

1 Preheat the oven to 200°C (400°F/gas 6). Finely grate the zest and squeeze the juice from one of the lemons. To make the gremolata, mix the zest in a small bowl with the breadcrumbs, parsley and garlic. Season to taste with salt and black pepper.

2 Place the fish fillets in a large, lightly oiled baking dish. Spread the mustard evenly over the fish, then sprinkle with the lemon juice. Arrange the tomatoes and zucchini around the fish. Cut the remaining lemon into four wedges and add them to the dish.

3 Spoon the gremolata mixture over the fish and press down lightly. Drizzle with the olive oil and bake for 25 minutes, or until the fish flakes easily and the topping is crisp.

4 Meanwhile, place the potatoes in a saucepan, cover with boiling water and add the saffron. Cook for 15-20 minutes, or until tender. Drain the potatoes and mash with the milk. Season to taste with salt and black pepper. Serve the fish with the saffron mashed potatoes, tomatoes and zucchini.

Some more ideas...

✱ For a special occasion, bake the fish in individual ovenproof dishes. Slice the tomatoes, and replace the zucchini with 1 chopped red or yellow capsicum (bell pepper). Put a fish fillet in each dish and arrange the sliced tomatoes on top. Scatter with freshly ground black pepper and then the gremolata mixture. Bake for 20 minutes and garnish with lemon wedges.

✱ Skinless salmon fillets can be used instead of white fish. Replace the lemon zest with orange zest and add some snipped fresh chives to the gremolata topping.

Seafood hotpot with saffron and vegetables

1 tablespoon olive oil

2 carrots, thickly sliced

2 stalks celery, chopped

1 large onion, sliced

1 clove garlic, crushed

350 g (12 oz) unpeeled new potatoes, halved if large

1¼ cups (310 ml/10¾ fl oz) vegetable or fish stock

10–12 saffron threads

500 g (1 lb) skinless firm white fish or salmon fillets

150 g (5 oz) green beans, halved

½ cup (125 ml/4 fl oz) dry white wine

125 g (4 oz) raw or cooked prawns (shrimp), peeled (and thawed if frozen)

1 tablespoon cornflour (cornstarch)

1 tablespoon milk

salt and freshly ground black pepper

2 tablespoons chopped fresh herbs, such as chives, parsley, tarragon or thyme

rice or crusty bread, to serve (optional)

serves 4
preparation 15 minutes
cooking 35 minutes

per serving *1340 kJ (320 calories), 36 g protein, 8 g total fat, 2 g saturated fat, 20 g carbohydrate*

1 Heat the oil in a large flameproof casserole dish. Add the carrots, celery and onion, then cover and cook over low heat for 5 minutes.

2 Add the garlic and potatoes and cook, uncovered, for a further 5 minutes, stirring occasionally.

3 Pour in the stock and stir in the saffron. Cover and simmer for 10 minutes, or until the vegetables just start to soften.

4 Meanwhile, remove any bones from the fish and cut into 4 cm (1½ inch) chunks. Add to the dish with the beans and wine. If using raw prawns, add them now. Cover and simmer for a further 7 minutes.

5 Mix the cornflour into the milk until smooth, then gently stir the mixture into the dish. If using cooked prawns, add them now. Allow the sauce to bubble gently and thicken slightly, taking care the fish does not break up and that the prawns are cooked right through if fresh, and thoroughly heated if pre-cooked. Season to taste with salt and black pepper, stir in the herbs and serve with rice or bread, if you like.

Saffron

Saffron is the dried stamens of a type of crocus. The stamens – known as 'threads' – must be harvested by hand; this is what makes saffron the most expensive spice. Luckily, only a small amount – as little as a pinch – is needed to flavour a dish. The threads are a vibrant red-orange; the deeper the colour, the better the quality. Saffron threads are preferable to the ground form, which can be adulterated with cheaper spices such as turmeric.

Seafood hotpot with saffron and vegetables

Aïoli (garlic mayonnaise)

Before making aïoli, ensure all your ingredients are at room temperature. Crush 4 halved cloves garlic and some salt in a mortar. Stir in 2 egg yolks, then gradually add about 300 ml (10½ fl oz) extra virgin olive oil, stirring constantly until the mixture emulsifies into a mayonnaise. Season to taste with some lemon juice and salt. If the aïoli is too thick, gradually stir in 1–2 tablespoons warm water.

Grilled sole with new potatoes

4 small sole, about 225 g (8 oz) each, skinned
    and cleaned
750 g (1½ lb) unpeeled small new potatoes
1 large sprig fresh mint, plus extra sprigs,
    to garnish
2 tablespoons butter
finely grated zest and juice of 1 large lemon
salt and freshly ground black pepper
500 g (1 lb) baby spinach leaves
freshly grated nutmeg (optional)
lemon wedges, to serve

serves 4
preparation 15 minutes
cooking 15 minutes

*per serving 1717 kJ (410 calories), 49 g protein,
11 g total fat, 6 g saturated fat, 27 g carbohydrate*

Cook's tip

*If sole is unavailable, use other flat
fish (such as flounder or dory), or
thin white fish fillets.*

1 Preheat the grill (broiler) to high. Cut a piece of foil to fit the grill tray and lay the fish on top (if your grill is small, you may need to cook the fish in two batches).

2 Cook the potatoes in a saucepan of boiling water with the mint sprig for 15 minutes, or until the potatoes are just tender.

3 Meanwhile, melt the butter in a small saucepan and mix in the lemon zest and juice. Season with salt and black pepper. Brush some of the lemon butter over the fish and grill for 5-6 minutes, or until the flesh close to the bone flakes easily when pierced with a knife. Carefully turn the fish over, brush again with the lemon butter and grill for 5-6 minutes more.

4 While the fish cooks, steam the spinach for 2-3 minutes, or until just wilted. Season to taste with salt, black pepper and nutmeg, if you like.

5 Drain the potatoes and place in a warmed serving dish. Add plenty of black pepper, toss gently and garnish with mint sprigs. Transfer the sole to warmed serving plates and spoon over any cooking juices from the grill tray. Garnish with lemon wedges and serve with the potatoes and spinach.

Some more ideas...

* Instead of spinach, serve the fish with broccoli florets steamed for 2-3 minutes, until just tender.

* Smooth, creamy mashed potatoes flavoured with herbs are another good accompaniment for grilled white fish. Boil 1 kg (2 lb) peeled baking (floury) potatoes for 15-20 minutes, or until tender. Drain thoroughly, then mash until smooth. Mix in 100 ml (3½ fl oz) hot milk and 1 tablespoon butter. Season with salt and black pepper, then mix in 3 tablespoons chopped fresh herbs – a combination of parsley, chives and lovage is particularly good.

Five ways...

with fish cakes

Fish cakes and croquettes are delicious for a snack or light meal. They're also an excellent way to use up left-over mashed potatoes, as long as they have not been mashed with a lot of milk or butter.

Potato and fish patties with pesto

serves **4**   prep **20** mins   cook **35** mins

Peel, cook and mash 400 g (14 oz) baking (floury) potatoes. Gently poach 375 g (13 oz) skinless firm white fish fillets in a frying pan with 100 ml (3½ fl oz) hot milk, salt and freshly ground black pepper for 5 minutes, or until the fish flakes when tested. Reserve the milk, remove the fish and flake the flesh, discarding any bones. Mix into the potatoes with 3 finely chopped spring onions (scallions), finely grated zest of 1 lemon, 2 tablespoons pesto and 1½ tablespoons poaching milk. Season and leave to cool. Shape into 8 thick flat patties and dust with plain (all-purpose) flour. Spread 1 cup (100 g/3½ oz) fresh breadcrumbs and 3 tablespoons grated parmesan on a plate. Beat 1 large egg in a shallow bowl. Coat the patties in egg, then crumbs. Chill until ready to cook. Bake for 20 minutes in a preheated 190°C (375°F/gas 5) oven on a non-stick baking tray with 8 small halved tomatoes.

per serving 1703 kJ (407 calories), 34 g protein, 12 g total fat, 4 g saturated fat, 40 g carbohydrate

Salmon cakes with creamy tomato and garlic sauce

serves **4**   prep **15** mins   cook **20** mins

Cook ¼ cup (30 g/1 oz) sun-dried tomatoes (not packed in oil) and 2 peeled cloves garlic in a small saucepan of boiling water for 3 minutes. Drain, reserving 4 tablespoons liquid. Put the tomatoes and garlic in a food processor with the reserved cooking liquid, 100 g (3½ oz) low-fat natural (plain) yogurt and ½ teaspoon hot chilli sauce; purée until smooth. Boil 1 large peeled and thinly sliced baking (floury) potato with 2 peeled cloves garlic for 7 minutes, until tender. Drain, place in a large bowl and mash together. Stir in a drained 410 g (14½ oz) can pink salmon, 2 tablespoons dry breadcrumbs, ½ cup (30 g/1 oz) finely chopped fresh dill and 1 tablespoon chopped capers. Shape into 8 flat round patties. Heat 1 tablespoon olive oil in a large non-stick frying pan over medium heat. Coat the salmon cakes in ½ cup (50 g/1¾ oz) dry breadcrumbs and fry in batches for 3 minutes per side, until golden. Serve with the sauce.

per serving 1093 kJ (261 calories), 20 g protein, 10 g total fat, 2 g saturated fat, 22 g carbohydrate

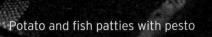
Potato and fish patties with pesto

Fish and potato croquettes

serves **4**   prep **20** mins   cook **25** mins

Peel, cook and finely mash 400 g (14 oz) baking (floury) potatoes. In a bowl, mix a drained 410 g (14 ½ oz) can pink salmon with 2 tablespoons dry breadcrumbs, ½ cup (30 g /1 oz) finely chopped fresh dill and 1 tablespoon chopped capers. Knead in the mashed potatoes and 2 egg yolks. Season with salt and freshly ground black pepper, fold in 2 stiffly beaten egg whites, then shape into small oval croquettes. Cook in hot oil in a deep-fryer or large saucepan until golden.

per serving 2270 kJ (542 calories), 21 g protein, 44 g total fat, 7 g saturated fat, 17 g carbohydrate

Baked salmon fish cakes with parsley sauce

Preheat the oven to 190°C (375°F/gas 5). Peel, cook and mash 750 g (1 ½ lb) baking (floury) potatoes. Poach 350 g (12 oz) salmon fillets in a frying pan in 1 ¼ cups (310 ml/10 ¾ fl oz) hot milk for 8 minutes, or until opaque. Reserve the milk. Remove the fish; skin, bone and flake flesh into a bowl. Mix in the mashed potatoes, 2 tablespoons tomato sauce (ketchup) and 1 tablespoon chopped fresh chives. Season and shape into 8 cakes. Chill for 1 hour if possible. Beat 1 egg in a shallow bowl with 2 tablespoons cold water. Spread 1 ½ cups (150 g/5 oz) dry breadcrumbs on a plate. Dip the fish cakes in the egg, then lightly coat with crumbs. Place on a non-stick baking tray and bake for 20–30 minutes. Meanwhile, strain the reserved milk into a small saucepan and add 3 tablespoons plain (all-purpose) flour and 1 ½ tablespoons butter. Stir until smooth and thickened; simmer for 20 minutes. Add salt, freshly ground black pepper and 2 tablespoons chopped fresh parsley. Briefly brown the fish cakes under a hot grill (broiler) until golden. Serve on a bed of the parsley sauce.

serves **4**

prep **25** mins

cook **45** mins

per serving 2266 kJ (541 calories), 32 g protein, 18 g total fat, 8 g saturated fat, 62 g carbohydrate

Salt cod fritters

serves **4**   soak **2** days   prep **20** mins   cook **50** mins

Soak 150 g (5 oz) salt cod for 2 days in cold water, changing the water after the first day. Peel, cook and mash 500 g (1 lb) baking (floury) potatoes. In a saucepan, bring 2 cups (500 ml/16 fl oz) milk to a simmer with 1 sliced onion, 1 bay leaf and grated zest of 1 lemon. Add the cod, cut into chunks; cook for 20 minutes. Add 100 g (3 ½ oz) firm white fish fillet and simmer for 10 minutes, or until the cod is soft. Drain the fish, discarding the milk. Cool the fish slightly and remove the skin and bones. Mash roughly and add the mashed potatoes, 2 crushed cloves garlic, 1 tablespoon chopped fresh parsley, 2 teaspoons chopped fresh chives and 1 tablespoon mild mustard. Season well and roll into small balls, about 1 tablespoon at a time. Roll in plain (all-purpose) flour, then 2 beaten eggs, then in dry breadcrumbs. Deep-fry in hot oil in a deep saucepan or wok until golden. Serve with lemon wedges and a good mayonnaise.

per serving 1275 kJ (305 calories), 24 g protein, 9 g total fat, 4 g saturated fat, 32 g carbohydrate

Seafood pie with potato pastry

1¼ cups (150 g/5 oz) plain (all-purpose) flour
½ teaspoon ground turmeric
½ cup (100 g/3½ oz) cold mashed potatoes
100 g (3½ oz) cold butter, diced
1 tablespoon milk, to glaze
1 tablespoon dry breadcrumbs

filling

400 g (14 oz) skinless firm white fish fillets
200 g (7 oz) peeled raw prawns (uncooked shrimp) or mixed seafood (including mussels and squid)
2 leeks, white part only, thinly sliced
1 cup (150 g/5 oz) frozen peas, thawed
2 tablespoons chopped fresh flat-leaf parsley
leaves from 2 sprigs fresh thyme
grated zest of 1 lemon
¼ cup (30 g/1 oz) cornflour (cornstarch)
2 cups (500 ml/16 fl oz) milk
salt and freshly ground black pepper

serves 4
preparation 20 minutes + 45 minutes cooling
cooking 35 minutes

----

per serving 2696 kJ (644 calories), 43 g protein, 30 g total fat, 18 g saturated fat, 49 g carbohydrate

1 Sift the flour and turmeric into a bowl. Using a fork, mix in the mashed potatoes until blended. Rub in the butter, then draw together into a dough, adding trickles of cold water if necessary to bind it together. Wrap in plastic wrap and rest in the refrigerator for 20 minutes.

2 Meanwhile, prepare the filling. Cut the fish into small chunks and place in a 5 cup (1.25 litre/44 fl oz) pie dish. Mix in the prawns or mixed seafood, leeks, peas, parsley, thyme and lemon zest.

3 In a bowl, blend the cornflour with a little milk. Heat the remaining milk until almost boiling, then stir it into the cornflour paste. Return the mixture to the pan and cook, stirring, until the sauce thickens. Season to taste with salt and black pepper and pour over the fish filling. Set aside to cool for 15 minutes. Meanwhile, preheat the oven to 200°C (400°F/gas 6).

4 Roll out the pastry between two sheets of plastic wrap so it is large enough to fit the top of the pie dish. Remove the top sheet of plastic and use the second sheet to help you lay the pastry over the filling. Remove the plastic wrap.

5 Press and trim the pastry edges to neaten, then make a small slash in the centre of the lid to allow steam to escape. Brush the pastry with the glazing milk, then sprinkle with the breadcrumbs. Place on a baking tray and bake for 10 minutes, then reduce the oven temperature to 180°C (350°F/gas 4) and bake for an additional 15 minutes, or until golden on top.

Cook's tip

When buying seafood, compare prices and select the best-value produce for the day. If you are trying a new variety, be sure to ask whether it is suitable for the recipe you are planning to cook.

Seafood pie with potato pastry

Potato and tuna casserole

1 Preheat the oven to 180°C (350°F/gas 4). Peel 2 carrots and 500 g (1 lb) boiling (waxy) potatoes, then slice 5 mm (¼ inch) thick. Place in a saucepan with 1 cup (250 ml/8 fl oz) hot vegetable stock and cook for 10 minutes. Drain well.

2 Combine the juice of 1 lemon, 2 tablespoons tarragon mustard and salt and freshly ground black pepper. Spread the mixture over 500 g (1 lb) diced tuna fillet and leave for 10 minutes. In a saucepan, cook 2 finely chopped French shallots, 2–3 chopped spring onions (scallions) and the finely sliced white part of 1 leek in 2 tablespoons butter for 5 minutes. Add the tuna and cook for 5 minutes, then mix in the potatoes and carrots. Place in a large greased baking dish. Combine ¾ cup (200 g/7 oz) natural (plain) yogurt, 2 tablespoons tarragon mustard, 150 g (5 oz) crème fraîche or sour cream, 3 tablespoons dry white wine and 2 eggs; spread over the casserole. Sprinkle with ⅔ cup (100 g/3½ oz) grated emmenthal cheese and bake for 20–25 minutes, or until golden. Garnish with snipped fresh chives.

Fisherman's stew

3 tablespoons olive oil
2 onions, finely chopped
3 garlic cloves, crushed
2 stalks celery, finely sliced
½ teaspoon dried red chilli flakes
2 teaspoons smoked paprika
1½ cups (375 ml/12 fl oz) dry white wine
2 x 410 g (14½ oz) cans chopped tomatoes
2 bay leaves
500 g (1 lb) boiling (waxy) potatoes,
    peeled and diced
600 g (1 lb 5 oz) mixed seafood such as
    skinless fish fillets (boned and diced),
    peeled raw prawns (uncooked shrimp),
    squid, scallops, mussels, clams (vongole)
1 teaspoon sugar
1 tablespoon lemon juice
½ cup (15 g/½ oz) chopped fresh flat-leaf
    parsley
salt and freshly ground black pepper
2 lemons, cut into wedges

serves 4
preparation 20 minutes
cooking 40 minutes

per serving *2099 kJ (501 calories), 34 g protein,*
17 g total fat, 3 g saturated fat, 36 g carbohydrate

1 Heat the oil in a saucepan over medium heat. Sauté the onions, garlic and celery until soft but not coloured. Stir in the chilli flakes and paprika, then add the wine and cook until the liquid has reduced by half. Add the tomatoes, bay leaves and potatoes and bring to a boil. Reduce the heat and simmer for 15 minutes, or until the potatoes are soft.

2 Add the seafood, pushing it gently into the liquid. Cover and simmer for 5 minutes, or until the seafood is just cooked. Gently stir in the sugar, lemon juice, parsley and some salt and black pepper. Serve with lemon wedges.

Storing fish

All fish are highly perishable, especially once they have been cut. Fish is generally best eaten within 24 hours of purchase. Oily fish spoil more quickly than white fish because their oils oxidise, causing the flesh to go rancid. To store fish, remove its wrappings, gut it if necessary, rinse under cold running water and pat dry. Then rewrap loosely in a plastic bag and store in the coldest part of the refrigerator.

Portuguese-style fish stew

1½ tablespoons olive oil

2 onions, sliced into rings

750 g (1½ lb) boiling (waxy) potatoes, peeled and sliced into rounds

500 g (1 lb) tomatoes, sliced into rounds

600 g (1 lb 5 oz) skinless firm white fish fillets, cut into large chunks

salt and freshly ground black pepper

1 sprig fresh thyme, plus extra sprigs to garnish (optional)

1 bay leaf

200 ml (7 fl oz) fish stock

serves 4

preparation 15 minutes

cooking 1 hour

per serving *1551 kJ (371 calories), 37 g protein, 11 g total fat, 2 g saturated fat, 31 g carbohydrate*

1 Heat 1 tablespoon of the oil in a large flameproof casserole dish and cook the onions gently for about 15 minutes, or until transparent. Lift out the onions and set aside. Remove the casserole dish from the heat.

2 Add layers of potato slices, tomatoes, fish and onions to the dish until all the ingredients are used up, seasoning each layer with salt and black pepper as you go. Place the thyme and bay leaf on top.

3 Pour the fish stock and the rest of the oil over the top. Return the dish to the heat and bring just to the boil. Reduce the heat, cover and simmer for 40 minutes, or until the fish and potatoes are tender. Remove the bay leaf and thyme, then serve the dish garnished with fresh thyme, if you like.

Mix and match

Cook 1 seeded and sliced red capsicum (bell pepper) and 2 crushed cloves garlic with the onions in step 1, and in step 2 sprinkle the layers with a pinch of chilli powder for a spicy flavour.

Potato charlottes with smoked trout

1 Cook 400 g (14 oz) unpeeled boiling (waxy) potatoes in a saucepan of boiling
salted water for 20 minutes, or until just tender. Drain, leave to cool, then peel
the potatoes and crush with a fork. Blend 2 tablespoons olive oil and 1 tablespoon
white wine vinegar with some salt and black pepper. Add 2 teaspoons chopped
fresh dill, stir well, then pour the mixture over the potatoes.

2 Place half this potato mixture in four lightly greased 150 ml (5 fl oz) ramekins,
pressing it down well. Flake 125 g (4½ oz) smoked trout and lay it on top of the
potatoes. Drizzle 1 tablespoon lemon juice over the charlottes. Cover with the
rest of the potatoes and press down. Refrigerate overnight and until just before
serving. When ready to serve, run a knife around the edge of each ramekin and
carefully ease the charlottes onto serving plates. Garnish with lemon wedges.

Portuguese-style fish stew

Potato and celeriac purée with seared scallops and chorizo

400 g (14 oz) baking (floury) potatoes,
    peeled and cut into 1.5 cm (½ inch) dice
1 large celeriac (celery root), peeled and
    cut into 1 cm (½ inch) dice
2 cloves garlic, peeled
3 tablespoons pure (light/single) cream
½ cup (125 ml/4 fl oz) milk
salt and freshly ground black pepper
24 scallops, without roe
grated zest and juice of 1 lemon
2 tablespoons olive oil
2 chorizo sausages, sliced
2 tablespoons chopped roasted hazelnuts
extra virgin olive oil, for drizzling

serves 4
preparation 20 minutes
cooking 30 minutes

----

*per serving 1629 kJ (389 calories), 15 g protein,
27 g total fat, 8 g saturated fat, 20 g carbohydrate*

1 Put the potatoes, celeriac and garlic in a saucepan over medium heat with enough water to just cover them. Bring to a boil, then reduce the heat and simmer for 20 minutes, or until the celeriac is very tender. Drain.

2 Process the celeriac and potatoes in a food processor with the cream and most of the milk, gradually adding the remaining milk if necessary to obtain a smooth purée. Season well with salt and black pepper.

3 Mix the scallops in a bowl with the lemon juice and zest, half the olive oil and some salt and black pepper.

4 Heat the remaining olive oil in a frying pan over medium heat and fry the chorizo slices on each side until golden. Remove the chorizo and wipe the pan clean. Place the pan back on the stovetop and quickly sear the scallops on each side over high heat.

5 Divide the purée among four plates and top with the chorizo and scallops. Sprinkle with the hazelnuts and drizzle with extra virgin olive oil.

Cook's tips

It is best to buy scallops on the shells; unscrupulous sellers sometimes soak shelled scallops in water overnight to plump them. This makes them double in size, but they shrink back as soon as they hit the pan.

Raw scallops should be kept for no more than 24 hours; cooked, they can be kept for up to 2 days.

Smoked fish and potato pie

3 cups (750 ml/26 fl oz) milk, plus
    3 tablespoons extra
500 g (1 lb) smoked fish fillets
1 bay leaf
1 large leek, white part only, halved lengthwise
    and sliced
500 g (1 lb) boiling (waxy) potatoes, peeled
    and cut into slices 5 mm (¼ inch) thick
¼ cup (30 g/1 oz) cornflour (cornstarch)
3 cups (85 g/3 oz) watercress leaves
salt and freshly ground black pepper
½ cup (50 g/1¾ oz) coarsely grated mature
    cheddar
chopped fresh parsley, to garnish

serves 6
preparation 20 minutes
cooking 55 minutes

----

per serving 1175 kJ (281 calories), 26 g protein,
10 g total fat, 6 g saturated fat, 22 g carbohydrate

1 Pour the 3 cups (750 ml/26 fl oz) milk into a wide frying pan. Add the fish and bay leaf. Bring to a gentle simmer, then cover and cook for 5 minutes, or until the fish is just cooked.

2 Lift out the fish with a slotted spoon and leave to cool slightly. Peel away the skin, remove any bones, break the flesh into large flakes and set aside. Strain the milk and reserve 600 ml (21 fl oz), as well as the bay leaf.

3 Put the leek in the frying pan and add the reserved milk and bay leaf. Cover and simmer for 10 minutes, or until the leek is tender.

4 Preheat the oven to 190°C (375°F/gas 5). Meanwhile, cook the potato slices in a saucepan of boiling water for 8 minutes, or until they are just tender but not breaking up. Drain.

5 Remove the bay leaf from the leeks and discard. Mix the cornflour with the extra 3 tablespoons milk to make a smooth paste. Add to the leek mixture and cook gently, stirring until slightly thickened. Remove from the heat and stir in the watercress, which will wilt. Season to taste with salt and black pepper and gently fold in the fish.

6 Transfer the mixture to an 8 cup (2 litre/70 fl oz) pie dish. Arrange the potato slices on top, overlapping them slightly. Sprinkle with the cheese and season with salt and black pepper. Bake for 25-30 minutes, or until the filling is bubbling and the potatoes are turning golden.

7 Sprinkle the top of the pie with parsley and allow to stand for about 5 minutes before serving.

Smoked fish

Smoking was originally a way of preserving fish. There are two kinds of smoked fish. Hot-smoked fish (such as kippers and smoked mackerel) are bought cooked and ready to eat, though they are often warmed through for serving. Some cold-smoked fish, such as smoked salmon, are eaten raw; others need to be cooked further. Smoking, whether hot or cold, does not destroy the nutrients in the fish.

Some more ideas...

* Reduce the amount of smoked fish in the recipe opposite to 400 g (14 oz), and add 2 chopped hard-boiled eggs to the fish filling at the end of step 5.

* Use 2 sliced leeks. Omit the watercress and instead add 2¾ cups (125 g/4 oz) baby spinach leaves to the potato slices for the last 1–2 minutes of their cooking. Drain well. Make a layer of potatoes and spinach in the pie dish. Spoon the hot fish and leek sauce over, sprinkle with the cheese and heat under a medium-hot grill (broiler) for 5–10 minutes, or until bubbling and golden.

* Chop 1 red capsicum (bell pepper), 1 small onion and 2 cloves garlic. Sauté in 1 tablespoon olive oil for 5 minutes. Add 250 g (8 oz) thinly sliced fennel bulb and sauté for 5 minutes more. Stir in a 410 g (14½ oz) can chopped tomatoes, season with salt and black pepper, then cover and simmer for 25 minutes. Cut the potatoes into chunks instead of slices, cook for 10 minutes and drain. Pour the fennel mixture into the pie dish. Lay the skinned fish on top (cut to fit if necessary) and top with the potatoes. Sprinkle with ½ teaspoon dried red chilli flakes and 3 tablespoons grated parmesan. Bake for 20 minutes, or until golden and bubbling.

Coconut prawn and vegetable curry

Fish boulangère

1 Preheat the oven to 190°C (375°F/gas 5). Peel and thinly slice 1 onion or 1 bulb fennel and 750 g (1½ lb) boiling (waxy) potatoes. Combine 1 teaspoon fresh thyme leaves and 2 tablespoons snipped fresh chives. Layer the potatoes and onion in a large, greased baking dish, sprinkling some thyme and chives and a little salt and freshly ground black pepper between each layer. Heat 400 ml (14 fl oz) fish stock and stir in the grated zest and juice of 1 lemon. Pour over the vegetables, cover with foil and bake for 45 minutes, or until the potatoes are almost tender.

2 Remove the skin and bones from 500 g (1 lb) thick firm white fish cutlets or fillets, then cut into chunks. Arrange over the potatoes in a single layer, replace the foil and bake for a further 15 minutes. Scatter 2 cups (300 g/10½ oz) shelled fresh or thawed frozen peas (or fresh or thawed frozen broad (fava) beans) over the fish. Halve 200 g (7 oz) cherry or baby roma (plum) tomatoes and arrange over the casserole, cut side up. Sprinkle with coarsely ground black pepper, replace the foil and bake for a final 10 minutes. Scatter with snipped fresh chives and serve.

Coconut prawn and vegetable curry

200 g (7 oz) small, even-sized boiling (waxy) potatoes, scrubbed

salt and freshly ground black pepper

1½ tablespoons vegetable oil

1 onion, sliced

3 cloves garlic, finely chopped

2 tablespoons mild curry paste

150 ml (5 fl oz) can coconut cream

1 cup (250 ml/8 fl oz) canned chopped tomatoes

200 g (7 oz) carrots, peeled and sliced

200 g (7 oz) bite-sized cauliflower florets

200 ml (7 fl oz) vegetable stock

200 g (7 oz) green beans, cut into short lengths

200 g (7 oz) peeled raw prawns (uncooked shrimp), thawed and drained if frozen

2 tablespoons chopped fresh coriander (cilantro) leaves

serves 4
preparation 20 minutes
cooking 40 minutes

---

per serving 1327 kJ (317 calories), 16 g protein, 19 g total fat, 8 g saturated fat, 19 g carbohydrate

1 Cook the potatoes in a saucepan of lightly salted boiling water for 10 minutes. Drain and set aside.

2 Meanwhile, heat the oil in a large heavy-based saucepan, add the onion and fry gently for 5 minutes, stirring from time to time. Add the garlic and curry paste and cook for a further 2 minutes, stirring constantly.

3 Stir in the coconut cream, then add the tomatoes. Simmer uncovered for 2-3 minutes, or until the mixture resembles a fairly thick paste.

4 Add the carrots, cauliflower florets and stock, bring to the boil, then cover and simmer for 15 minutes. Add the beans and potatoes and cook for a further 8 minutes.

5 Stir in the prawns and simmer for 2-3 minutes, or until they turn pink. Season to taste with salt and black pepper, stir in the chopped coriander and serve immediately.

Cook's tips

If your potatoes are a bit big, cut them in half before adding them in step 4.

This curry is mild enough for anyone to enjoy, which makes it a great choice when introducing children to spicy foods.

Mix and match

Spinach is also delicious in this curry. Reduce the stock to 150 ml (5 fl oz) and add 250 g (8 oz) spinach leaves, washed, drained and roughly chopped, with the beans.

Smoked fish hash with savoy cabbage

1 kg (2 lb) baking (floury) potatoes, peeled
    and cut into 5 mm (¼ inch) dice
2 teaspoons curry paste, or to taste
2 tablespoons vegetable oil
300 ml (10½ fl oz) fish or vegetable stock
300 g (10½ oz) smoked fish fillet
175 g (6 oz) spring onions (scallions), chopped
1½ cups (115 g/4 oz) finely shredded savoy
    cabbage
3 tablespoons chopped fresh flat-leaf parsley,
    plus extra sprigs to garnish
4 tablespoons Greek-style yogurt
salt and freshly ground black pepper

serves 4
preparation 25 minutes
cooking 20 minutes

per serving 1538 kJ (368 calories), 24 g protein,
13 g total fat, 3 g saturated fat, 37 g carbohydrate

1 Put the potatoes in a bowl. Add the curry paste and toss to coat the potatoes evenly all over.

2 Heat the oil in a large non-stick frying pan, add the potatoes and fry over medium heat for 20 minutes, turning occasionally.

3 Meanwhile, pour the stock into a saucepan and bring to a boil. Reduce the heat, then add the fish. Cover and simmer very gently for 8-10 minutes, or until the fish flakes easily with a fork. Remove the fish, allow to cool slightly, then flake the flesh, discarding any skin and bones. Discard the cooking liquid.

4 Add the spring onions and cabbage to the potatoes and sauté for a further 3-5 minutes, or until the potatoes are cooked and crisp and the cabbage has wilted.

5 Stir in the fish, parsley and yogurt, and season to taste with salt and black pepper. Continue cooking gently until very hot, stirring occasionally. Serve hot, garnished with parsley sprigs.

Curry paste and powder

Both curry paste and curry powder are a blend of many spices, but they are used differently. Dry curry powder cannot be fried in oil because it burns and turns acrid, so it must be added to foods that are already simmering in a liquid. For fried dishes it is best to use a curry paste. Various types and strengths are available. If you don't have curry paste on hand, make your own by adding a few teaspoons of water to curry powder and stirring vigorously until it has absorbed the water and the mixture is moist.

Some more ideas...

✳ Use sweet potatoes instead of the potatoes.

✳ Instead of the parsley, use 1–2 tablespoons chopped fresh coriander (cilantro) or tarragon.

✳ For a salmon hash with broccoli and peas, use salmon fillet in place of the smoked fish and gently poach as instructed in step 3. Cook the potatoes as directed, but omit the curry paste. In step 5, add 3 cups (175 g/6 oz) steamed broccoli florets and 1 cup (155 g/5 oz) cooked frozen peas to the potatoes with the flaked salmon, yogurt, 2 tablespoons chopped fresh flat-leaf parsley and 2 tablespoons snipped fresh chives.

Smoked fish hash with savoy cabbage

Fish and mushroom pie with mashed potato crust

Fish, pea and cheesy potato bake

1 Preheat the oven to 190°C (375°F/gas 5). Cook 500 g (1 lb) small new potatoes in a saucepan of boiling water for 10 minutes, or until just tender. Drain and set aside. Cut 500 g (1 lb) skinless smoked cod fillets into large chunks and arrange in a greased large shallow baking dish. Season with freshly ground black pepper and sprinkle with 1 tablespoon snipped fresh chives. Pour in 150 ml (5 fl oz) hot fish stock, then scatter with 1½ cups (200 g/7 oz) shelled fresh (or thawed frozen) peas and 4 finely sliced small leeks, white part only.

2 Thinly slice the potatoes and arrange them in an even layer over the fish and vegetables. Season with more black pepper, then cover and bake for 30 minutes. Remove the dish from the oven and increase the temperature to 230°C (450°F/gas 8). Sprinkle ½ cup (60 g/2¼ oz) grated sharp-tasting cheddar over the potatoes, then bake for 5–10 minutes more, or until the potatoes are crisp and golden.

Fish and mushroom pie with mashed potato crust

500 g (1 lb) baking (floury) potatoes, peeled and cut into chunks
4 tablespoons Greek-style yogurt
1 tablespoon butter
1 small onion, sliced
400 g (14 oz) firm white fish fillets
2 cups (500 ml/16 fl oz) milk
2 bay leaves
4 sprigs fresh parsley, chopped
1/4 cup (30 g/1 oz) cornflour (cornstarch)
1/2 teaspoon mustard powder
freshly grated nutmeg
125 g (4 1/2 oz) cooked peeled prawns (shrimp)
1 cup (90 g/3 1/4 1/2 oz) finely sliced button mushrooms
1 cup (85 g/3 oz) small pasta shells, cooked and drained
3 tablespoons chopped fresh parsley
freshly ground black pepper

serves 4
preparation 20 minutes
cooking 50 minutes

------

per serving 1790 kJ (428 calories), 38 g protein, 14 g total fat, 8 g saturated fat, 38 g carbohydrate

1 Preheat the oven to 180°C (350°F/gas 4). Cook the potatoes in a saucepan of boiling water for 15-20 minutes, or until tender. Drain well, then mash with the yogurt. Set aside and keep warm.

2 Meanwhile, melt the butter in a flameproof casserole dish. Add the onion and gently sauté for 5 minutes, or until soft. Place the fish fillets on top, pour 1 1/4 cups (435 ml/15 1/4 fl oz) of the milk over and add the bay leaves and parsley. Cover, transfer to the oven and bake for 15 minutes, or until the fish flakes easily with a fork. Remove the dish from the oven, then lift out the fish with a slotted spoon and set aside. Reserve the poaching liquid.

3 Put the cornflour and mustard powder in a saucepan. Stir in the remaining milk and mix to a smooth paste. Strain the poaching milk from the casserole dish into the saucepan, reserving the onion. Add nutmeg to taste and bring to a boil, stirring well all the while. Reduce the heat and simmer for 5 minutes, or until the sauce is smooth and thick. Remove the bay leaves.

4 Flake the fish, discarding the skin and any bones. Stir into the sauce with the reserved onion, prawns, mushrooms, pasta, parsley, and black pepper to taste. Pile the mixture back into the casserole dish and spoon the mashed potatoes over the top, evenly spreading the mixture right to the edge. Rough up the surface with a fork and bake for a final 20 minutes, or until the sauce is bubbling and the surface is browned. Serve hot.

Serving tip

This dish is good served with steamed carrots, baby corn and sugarsnap peas.

Vegetarian

Potatoes go well with all other vegetables,
as well as with vegetarian sources of protein.
This chapter offers delicious ideas for both
committed vegetarians and those simply
seeking to add more vegetables to their diet.

Frittata with corn and capsicum

675 g (1 lb 8 oz) boiling (waxy) potatoes, peeled, quartered lengthwise and thinly sliced across
1 red, yellow or orange capsicum (bell pepper), seeded and chopped
2 tablespoons olive oil
1 onion, halved and thinly sliced
1²⁄₃ cups (250 g/8 oz) drained canned or thawed frozen sweetcorn
6 eggs
4 tablespoons finely chopped fresh parsley
salt and freshly ground black pepper

serves 4
preparation 10 minutes
cooking 25 minutes

-----

per serving 1593 kJ (381 calories), 17 g protein, 18 g total fat, 4 g saturated fat, 36 g carbohydrate

Cook's tip

Known in Italy as frittata, or in Spain as tortilla, flat omelettes can be served hot or cold with salad for brunch, lunch or supper. They also make ideal picnic fare. This delicious version can be kept for a day in the refrigerator, but remove it 30 minutes before serving as it tastes best at room temperature.

1 Put the potatoes in a saucepan, cover with boiling water and return to a boil. Reduce the heat, then add the capsicum and simmer for 3 minutes, or until the potatoes are just starting to cook. Drain well, cover and keep hot.

2 Meanwhile, heat a 25 cm (10 inch) non-stick frying pan over high heat. Add the oil and swirl it around. When the oil is hot, reduce the heat to medium and sauté the onion for 3 minutes, or until softened.

3 Add the potatoes, capsicum and corn and sauté for 8 minutes, or until the potatoes are just tender. Remove from the heat.

4 In a large bowl, beat the eggs with the parsley, then season with salt and black pepper. Using a slotted spoon, add the vegetables to the eggs, stirring them in thoroughly.

5 Place the pan back over medium heat. When the pan is hot, pour in the egg mixture, spreading out the vegetables evenly. Cook the frittata, shaking the pan frequently, for 3-4 minutes, or until the edges are set and the top is beginning to look set.

6 Meanwhile, preheat the grill (broiler) to its hottest setting. Place the frittata under the grill for 2 minutes, or until the eggs are just set. Pierce the top of the mixture with a knife to check that the frittata is cooked through.

7 Remove the pan from the heat and leave the frittata to set for 2 minutes, then slide it onto a serving plate. Serve hot or at room temperature, cut into wedges.

Some more ideas...

✳ Take a tip from Spanish tapas bars and serve frittata at room temperature, cut into bite-sized pieces, as a snack with drinks.

✳ For a simple potato and capsicum frittata, omit the sweetcorn and use 3 capsicums (bell peppers) of any colour and 2 onions.

Potato, fennel and zucchini frittata

Prepare the potatoes as directed in step 1 of the recipe opposite. Replace the capsicum, onion and corn with 1 finely sliced bulb fennel, 1 finely sliced zucchini (courgette) and 100 g (3½ oz) finely sliced button mushrooms. Sauté them together for about 3 minutes in 2 tablespoons olive oil, then add the potatoes and sauté for 8 minutes more. Complete the frittata as directed.

Frittata with corn and capsicum

Vegetable patties
with coriander sauce

300 g (10½ oz) boiling (waxy) potatoes
½ celeriac (celery root), about 200 g (7 oz)
2 carrots
4 tablespoons plain (all-purpose) flour
2 egg yolks
2 tablespoons sour cream
salt and freshly ground black pepper
freshly grated nutmeg
1 tablespoon finely chopped fresh dill
1 tablespoon finely chopped fresh parsley
2 tablespoons olive oil

coriander sauce

½ cup (125 ml/4 fl oz) milk
1 small onion, quartered
1 bay leaf
5 black peppercorns
1 tablespoon butter
1-2 tablespoons plain (all-purpose) flour
2 tablespoons sour cream
⅓ cup (80 ml/2½ fl oz) pure (light/single)
    cream
1 teaspoon ground coriander
1 teaspoon finely chopped fresh coriander
    (cilantro)
2 tablespoons finely chopped fresh parsley

serves 4
preparation 25 minutes
cooking 35 minutes

----
per serving 1680 kJ (401 calories), 9 g protein,
27 g total fat, 12 g saturated fat, 33 g carbohydrate

1 To make the sauce, briefly bring the milk, onion, bay leaf and peppercorns to a boil in a small saucepan, then remove from the heat, cover and leave to infuse for about 10 minutes. Strain and set aside.

2 Heat the butter in a saucepan, then add the flour and cook for 30 seconds, stirring constantly. Gradually stir in the infused milk. Add the sour cream and cream, then briefly bring to a boil and allow to thicken. Remove from the heat and stir in the ground coriander. Season to taste with salt and black pepper. Keep warm, adding the fresh coriander and parsley only just before serving.

3 Peel and coarsely the grate the potatoes, celeriac and carrots; pat dry and place in a bowl. Stir the flour, egg yolks and sour cream through. Season generously with salt, black pepper and nutmeg, then stir in the dill and parsley.

4 Heat 1 tablespoon oil in a frying pan. Add a tablespoon of the vegetable mixture to the pan and flatten into a patty. Make another three patties in the same way and fry for 4 minutes on each side, or until golden. Drain well on paper towel and keep warm while cooking four more patties in the remaining oil. Serve hot, with the coriander sauce.

Coriander

All parts of this plant are edible. The pungent leaves should be added to dishes just before serving, as long cooking destroys their flavour. The pounded roots and tender stems are often included in Southeast Asian curry pastes. The seeds may be used whole or ground and are often roasted to enhance their flavour. The fresh herb is also known as cilantro, but the seeds are always referred to as coriander seeds.

Ravioli with potato filling

4 cups (500 g/1 lb) strong (bread) flour,
  plus extra for kneading
4 eggs, beaten
1 tablespoon extra virgin olive oil

filling

500 g (1 lb) all-purpose potatoes, peeled,
  boiled and mashed
3 tablespoons cottage cheese, sieved
5 spring onions (scallions), thinly sliced
2 tablespoons chopped fresh parsley
4 teaspoons chopped fresh thyme
4 tablespoons grated parmesan
4 cloves garlic, chopped
salt and freshly ground black pepper
1 egg, beaten
500 g (1 lb) ripe tomatoes, diced, or a 410 g
  (14$\frac{1}{2}$ oz) can chopped tomatoes, drained
1 tablespoon extra virgin olive oil

serves 6
preparation 1$\frac{1}{2}$ hours + 1 hour resting
cooking 10 minutes

----

per serving 2113 kJ (505 calories), 21 g protein,
14 g total fat, 4 g saturated fat, 74 g carbohydrate

Cook's tip

*The ravioli can be cooked in advance,
then cooled and chilled until needed.
Add the tomatoes, oil and remaining
garlic, thyme and parmesan shortly
before serving, and reheat in a
preheated 200°C (400°F/gas 6)
oven for about 5 minutes, or until
the topping is lightly browned.*

1 Put the flour and 1 pinch salt in a bowl and make a well in the centre. Add the eggs and oil. Gradually work in the flour, first using a fork, then your hands, and adding 1-2 tablespoons water, if necessary, to make a firm dough. Knead firmly for 5-10 minutes, or until smooth. Cover with plastic wrap and leave at room temperature to rest for 1 hour.

2 To make the filling, mix the mashed potatoes in a bowl with the cottage cheese, spring onions, parsley, and half the thyme, parmesan and garlic. Season with salt and black pepper, then mix in the egg and set aside.

3 Cut the pasta dough into quarters. Keep three portions covered while you roll out one piece very thinly into a rectangle measuring about 20 x 50 cm (8 x 20 inches). Keep this piece covered while you roll out a second portion to the same size.

4 Dot teaspoonfuls of the filling in mounds over one sheet of pasta, placing them about 5 cm (2 inches) apart. You should have 21 mounds, in seven rows of three. Brush between the mounds of filling with water, then top with the second sheet of pasta. Press the dough together between the mounds, then cut along the sealed area using a fluted pastry wheel or sharp knife. Separate the ravioli and place on a lightly floured plate. Repeat with the remaining pasta and filling.

5 If the ravioli are to be left for any length of time, dust them with flour, cover loosely with plastic wrap and refrigerate. Cook within 24 hours, or freeze.

6 When you're ready to cook the ravioli, gently warm the tomatoes, with salt and black pepper to taste, in a saucepan over low heat. Cook the ravioli in a large saucepan of boiling water for about 3 minutes, or until just tender. Drain well.

7 Arrange the ravioli in warmed serving dishes and top with the tomatoes, and the remaining garlic, thyme and parmesan. Drizzle with the olive oil and serve.

Ravioli with potato filling

Folded potato ravioli

To make folded 'ravioli', cook 250 g (8 oz) fresh lasagne sheets, a few at a time, in rapidly boiling water for 3 minutes, or following the packet instructions. Refresh in cold water and drain well. Place some filling from the recipe opposite on one half of a sheet, fold it over and lay it in a greased baking dish. Repeat with the remaining lasagne and filling. Heat the tomatoes with the remaining garlic and thyme and the olive oil. Pour over the pasta and sprinkle with the remaining parmesan. Bake at 200°C (400°F/gas 6) for 10 minutes, or until piping hot.

Roasted vegetable crumble

Potato pie with tomatoes and olives

1 Preheat the oven to 200°C (400°F/gas 6). Cook 750 g (1½ lb) unpeeled baking (floury) potatoes in a saucepan of boiling water for 20–30 minutes, or until soft. Drain and peel. Squeeze the still-warm potatoes through a potato press (potato ricer) into a bowl and allow to cool slightly.

2 Knead in 1¼ cups (125 g/4 oz) grated pecorino cheese, ¾ cup (100 g/3½ oz) plain (all-purpose) flour and 2 beaten eggs. Season with salt and grated nutmeg to taste, spoon into a greased 25 cm (10 inch) quiche dish and shape the edge into a rim. Scatter with fresh basil leaves, 500 g (1 lb) sliced tomatoes, 2 chopped French shallots, 2 slivered cloves garlic and 12 pitted and halved black olives. Sprinkle with salt and freshly ground black pepper and top with 200 g (7 oz) sliced mozzarella. Bake for 30 minutes, or until the cheese has melted.

Roasted vegetable crumble

6 small red onions, quartered

400 g (14 oz) orange sweet potatoes, peeled and cut into 3 cm (1¼ inch) chunks

2 tablespoons olive oil

1 clove garlic, crushed

1 teaspoon fresh thyme

2 large zucchini (courgettes), cut into 3 cm (1¼ inch) slices

100 g (3½ oz) baby button mushrooms

350 g (12 oz) roma (plum) tomatoes, quartered lengthwise

crumble topping

½ cup (75 g/2½ oz) wholemeal (whole grain) flour

25 g (1 oz) chilled butter, diced

1 tablespoon chilled water

⅔ cup (75 g/2½ oz) fresh wholemeal (whole grain) breadcrumbs

½ cup (50 g/1¾ oz) grated parmesan

¼ cup (30 g/1 oz) mixed chopped nuts

2 tablespoons sunflower seeds

2 tablespoons pepitas (pumpkin seeds)

1 teaspoon fresh thyme

serves 4
preparation 20 minutes
cooking 1 hour 15 minutes

per serving 2125 kJ (508 calories), 19 g protein, 28 g total fat, 9 g saturated fat, 46 g carbohydrate

1 Preheat the oven to 190°C (375°F/gas 5). Put a baking dish or roasting tin measuring about 30 x 20 x 4 cm (12 x 8 x 1½ inches) in the oven and allow it to heat for 10 minutes. Put the onions and sweet potatoes in a bowl, drizzle with 1 tablespoon oil and gently toss to coat. Tip into the heated dish and roast for 30 minutes, turning the vegetables after 15 minutes.

2 In the same bowl, mix the remaining oil with the garlic and thyme. Add the zucchini, mushrooms and tomatoes and gently toss to coat. Tip into the dish and roast for 20 minutes more.

3 Meanwhile, make the crumble topping. Put the flour in a bowl and rub in the butter using your fingertips. Add the water and mix together with a fork to make large crumbs. Stir in the breadcrumbs, cheese, nuts, seeds, pepitas and thyme.

4 Sprinkle the crumble mixture over the vegetables. Bake for 15-20 minutes, or until the topping is golden brown and all the vegetables are tender. Remove from the oven and leave to stand for 3-4 minutes before serving.

Mix and match

Other root vegetables, such as parsnips, carrots and beetroot (beets), are also good cooked in this dish. Cut them into 3 cm (1¼ inch) chunks before roasting.

Potato and leek quiche with chilli crust

1⅓ cups (175 g/6 oz) plain (all-purpose) flour
2 red chillies, seeded and finely chopped
2 teaspoons chopped fresh thyme
1 egg
80 ml (⅓ cup/2½ fl oz) vegetable oil
1 tablespoon lukewarm water

filling

350 g (12 oz) unpeeled small new potatoes
2 small leeks, white part only, cut into 1 cm
    (½ inch) slices
½ cup (65 g/2¼ oz) grated gruyère
2 tablespoons snipped fresh chives
salt and freshly ground black pepper
1¼ cups (55 g/2 oz) roughly chopped rocket
    (arugula)
2 eggs
150 ml (5 fl oz) milk

serves 4
preparation 30 minutes + 30 minutes resting
cooking 1 hour

----
per serving *2235 kJ (534 calories), 19 g protein,*
30 g total fat, 8 g saturated fat, 47 g carbohydrate

1 Sift the flour and a pinch of salt into a large bowl. Add the chillies and thyme and make a well in the centre. Whisk together the egg, oil and water, then add to the dry ingredients and mix quickly with a fork to make a dough.

2 Turn the dough out onto a lightly floured surface and knead briefly until just smooth. Place in a bowl, cover with a damp cloth and leave to rest for 30 minutes.

3 Meanwhile, make the filling. Cook the potatoes in a saucepan of boiling water for 5 minutes, then place the leeks over the potatoes and steam for a further 6-7 minutes, or until the potatoes are almost tender. Drain thoroughly and leave until cool enough to handle.

4 Preheat the oven to 200°C (400°F/gas 6). Place a baking tray in the oven to heat.

5 On a lightly floured work surface, roll out the pastry thinly and use it to line a 20 cm (8 inch) round, fluted loose-based flan tin (tart pan). Scatter half the cheese over the pastry case.

6 Thickly slice the potatoes and toss in a bowl with the leeks, remaining cheese and the chives. Season with salt and black pepper. Arrange half the potato and leek mixture in the pastry case. Scatter the rocket over, then top with the remaining potato and leek mixture.

7 Lightly beat the eggs in a small bowl. Heat the milk to just below boiling point, then gradually and gently whisk it into the eggs.

8 Place the flan tin on the hot baking tray. Pour the warm egg custard into the pastry case and bake for 10 minutes. Reduce the oven temperature to 180°C (350°F/gas 4) and bake for a further 30-35 minutes, or until the filling is lightly set. Leave the quiche in the tin for 5 minutes before serving.

Potato and leek quiche with chilli crust

Potato and emmenthal quiche

1 Prepare the dough as outlined in step 1 opposite and allow to rest in the refrigerator for 30 minutes. Meanwhile, preheat the oven to 200°C (400°F/gas 6). In a bowl, mix together 600 g (1 lb 5 oz) peeled and finely grated boiling (waxy) potatoes, 1 tablespoon finely chopped fresh parsley and 1 small red onion, shaved into fine rings. Season with salt and freshly ground black pepper.

2 Grease a 20 cm (8 inch) pie dish and line it with the dough, then spread the potato mixture over the top. Mix together 200 ml (7 fl oz) milk, 150 g (5 oz) crème fraîche or sour cream, 1 pinch freshly grated nutmeg and some black pepper, then spread over the potato mixture. Sprinkle with 1 cup (125 g/4 oz) grated emmenthal or Swiss cheese, dot with butter and bake as directed.

Vegetables with melted brie dressing

100 g (3½ oz) thin green beans, halved
1 kg (2 lb) baking (floury) potatoes,
    scrubbed and cut into big wedges
1½ tablespoons olive oil
1 teaspoon paprika
1 teaspoon sea salt
coarsely crushed black peppercorns
2 tablespoons sesame seeds
1 small iceberg lettuce, torn into
    bite-sized pieces
1 red onion, thinly sliced
½ cucumber, chopped
250 g (8 oz) baby roma (plum)
    or cherry tomatoes, halved
juice of 1 lemon
salt and freshly ground black pepper

brie dressing

250 g (8 oz) brie
4 tablespoons milk
1 tablespoon finely chopped fresh tarragon
ground white pepper

serves 4
preparation 15 minutes
cooking 1 hour

per serving *2152 kJ (514 calories), 23 g protein,*
30 g total fat, 14 g saturated fat, 39 g carbohydrate

1 Preheat the oven to 200°C (400°F/gas 6). Heat a roasting tin in the oven. Drop the beans into a large saucepan of boiling water and blanch for 2 minutes. Using a slotted spoon, scoop the beans into a colander and refresh under cold running water. Add the potatoes to the saucepan and cook for 3 minutes, then drain.

2 Put the potatoes in a bowl. Add the oil, paprika, salt and some crushed black peppercorns and gently toss to coat. Tip the potatoes into the hot roasting tin and roast for 15 minutes. Sprinkle with the sesame seeds and roast for an additional 30 minutes, turning once or twice, until crisp and browned.

3 When the potatoes are ready, remove from the oven and keep hot. Put the green beans, lettuce, onion, cucumber and tomatoes in a mixing bowl. Add the lemon juice and salt and black pepper to taste and toss well.

4 To make the dressing, slice off and discard the rind from the brie. Dice the cheese, put in a saucepan with the milk and heat gently, stirring until melted and well blended. Stir in the tarragon and a little white pepper and cook for a few seconds.

5 Spoon the salad into bowls. Top with the roasted potatoes and drizzle with the warm brie dressing.

Some more ideas...

✳ Instead of a dressing, simply top the hot roasted potatoes with the diced brie, which will melt with the heat from the potatoes.

✳ Try other cheeses in the dressing, such as camembert, blue brie or Danish blue.

✳ For a fondue-style dressing, place 1⅓ cups (175 g/6 oz) grated gruyère in a saucepan with 1 crushed clove garlic and 90 ml (3 fl oz) dry white wine. Mix 1 teaspoon cornflour (cornstarch) with 2 teaspoons water and stir it into the cheese mixture. Bring to a boil, stirring constantly until melted and smooth. Drizzle over the salad and roasted potatoes.

Potato tart with asparagus

butter, for greasing
1 tablespoon dry breadcrumbs
300 g (10½ oz) all-purpose potatoes, peeled
1 tablespoon vegetable oil
salt
500 g (1 lb) thin asparagus, trimmed
3 spring onions (scallions), finely chopped
1 cup (250 ml/8 fl oz) pure (light/single) cream
3 eggs
freshly ground black pepper
4 tablespoons grated gruyère

serves 4
preparation 20 minutes
cooking 40 minutes

----

*per serving 1619 kJ (387 calories), 15 g protein,
29 g total fat, 15 g saturated fat, 17 g carbohydrate*

1 Preheat the oven to 200°C (400°F/gas 6). Grease a 24 cm (9½ inch) flan tin (tart pan) and line it with the breadcrumbs.

2 Cut or shave the potatoes into thin slices. Layer the potatoes in the tin, overlapping the slices and pressing them down lightly. Drizzle with the oil and bake for 10 minutes, then sprinkle with some salt.

3 Set aside 12 asparagus spears and cut the remainder into 2.5 cm (1 inch) lengths. Scatter the chopped asparagus and spring onions over the potatoes and arrange the spears on top.

4 In a small bowl, mix together the cream, eggs and some salt and black pepper. Stir in the gruyère and pour over the asparagus mixture. Bake for a further 30 minutes, or until the egg mixture is golden and lightly set. Leave to stand in the tin for 5 minutes before removing. Serve warm.

Cook's tip

To prepare asparagus, gently bend the spears; they will break at a natural divide between the tough and more tender parts. Discard the lower end of the spear.

Asparagus

Asparagus spears should be firm and round, with tightly closed tips of deep green, purple or white. Purple spears are larger and less fibrous than green ones. When asparagus is grown shielded from sunlight, white spears develop. These have a very delicate flavour, milder than either green or purple. Choose spears of uniform size to ensure even cooking.

Five ways...
with sauces for gnocchi

Rich, filling potato gnocchi make a good alternative to pasta and can be stored in the fridge or freezer and used straight from frozen. Pair them with one of these sauces for delicious comfort food.

Tomato and basil sauce

serves 4

prep 10 mins

cook 20 mins

Heat 1 tablespoon olive oil in a large saucepan and sauté 1 finely chopped onion for 4 minutes. Add 1 finely chopped clove garlic and sauté for 1 minute more. Dice 750 g (1½ lb) roma (plum) tomatoes and add to the pan with 50 ml (1½ fl oz) full-bodied red wine, 1 bay leaf and 1 sprig fresh thyme. Season with salt and freshly ground black pepper, then cover and simmer for 15 minutes. Remove the bay leaf and thyme and strain the sauce. Just before serving, stir in 2 tablespoons fresh basil leaves and season to taste. Spoon over hot cooked gnocchi, sprinkle with grated parmesan and serve.

per serving *409 kJ (98 calories), 4 g protein, 6 g total fat, 1 g saturated fat, 6 g carbohydrate*

Cook's tip
The essential oils in fresh basil evaporate quickly, so use your fingertips to pluck the leaves into smaller pieces rather than chopping them with a knife. Do not bring the sauce to a boil again after adding the basil.

Thyme and cheese sauce

serves 4 **steep 1 hour** **prep 15 mins** **cook 10 mins**

Spread 1 cup (100 g/3½ oz) grated pecorino cheese, 1 cup (125 g/4 oz) grated gruyère and ½ cup (50 g/1¾ oz) grated parmesan in a small flameproof bowl. Add the leaves from 2–3 sprigs fresh thyme, pour 150 ml (5 fl oz) milk over and steep for 1 hour. Warm 100 ml (3½ fl oz) milk in a small saucepan, then remove from the heat and mix in 2 egg yolks and 3 tablespoons butter. Bring a wide saucepan of water to a boil and place the bowl with the cheeses into the water. Melt the cheese, stirring constantly. Gradually stir in the warm milk mixture, then season to taste with salt, freshly ground black pepper and nutmeg. Mix through hot cooked gnocchi and garnish with fresh sage leaves. If making your own gnocchi, add some thyme and sage to the dough before shaping, to complement the sauce.

per serving *1876 kJ (448 calories), 25 g protein, 38 g total fat, 23 g saturated fat, 4 g carbohydrate*

Gnocchi with tomato and basil sauce

Blue cheese and walnut sauce

serves **4** · prep **5** mins · cook **15** mins

Spread ⅔ cup (85 g/3 oz) walnut pieces on a baking tray and toast in a 180°C (350°F/gas 4) oven for 5 minutes, or until lightly browned. Remove from the oven and leave to cool, then chop coarsely. Meanwhile, put ¾ cup (100 g/3½ oz) crumbled blue cheese in a saucepan. Add 2 tablespoons pure (light/single) cream, mix well and heat gently for 2-3 minutes, stirring constantly, without boiling. Cook gnocchi, then drain, reserving 1½ tablespoons of the cooking water. Tip the gnocchi into a warm serving dish. Add the reserved cooking water to the blue cheese mixture, mix well, then pour over the gnocchi and gently mix through. Add the walnuts and some freshly ground black pepper and serve.

per serving 977 kJ (234 calories), 8 g protein, 22 g total fat, 7 g saturated fat, 1 g carbohydrate

Grilled vegetable sauce

serves **4** · prep **10** mins · cook **15** mins

Preheat the grill (broiler) to high. Halve 1 large red capsicum (bell pepper) and remove the seeds. Place under the grill, skin side up, and cook for 5-10 minutes, or until blistered and blackened, then place in a plastic bag until cool enough to handle. Cut 125 g (4 oz) tomatoes into wedges, slice 1 eggplant (aubergine) lengthwise and grill both for 5 minutes, or until slightly charred, turning so they cook evenly. Put the tomatoes in a large serving bowl. Allow the eggplant slices to cool slightly, then cut into 2.5 cm (1 inch) strips and add to the tomatoes. Peel the capsicum halves, cut into 2.5 cm (1 inch) strips and add to the bowl. Add 2 tablespoons extra virgin olive oil, 2 tablespoons shredded fresh basil, 1 tablespoon chopped capers and 1 large crushed clove garlic and mix well. Season to taste with salt and freshly ground black pepper. Mix through hot cooked gnocchi, sprinkle with 4 tablespoons grated parmesan and serve.

per serving 558 kJ (133 calories), 4 g protein, 12 g total fat, 3 g saturated fat, 3 g carbohydrate

Fresh sage, rocket and fetta sauce

serves **4** · prep **10** mins · cook **20** mins

Place a large frying pan over medium-high heat. Finely chop 50 g (1¾ oz) pancetta, 2 cloves garlic and 2 French shallots and add to the pan with 8 shredded fresh sage leaves. Sauté for 6-8 minutes, or until the pancetta is golden brown and the shallots are soft. Drain a 410 g (14½ oz) can of chickpeas and add to the pan with a 410 g (14½ oz) can chopped tomatoes and 1 pinch sugar. Bring to a boil, reduce the heat and simmer for 10 minutes, or until the sauce has thickened slightly. Season with freshly ground black pepper. Mix through hot cooked gnocchi with 2 cups (50 g/1¾ oz) shredded rocket (arugula). Sprinkle with ⅔ cup (100 g/3½ oz) crumbled fetta and serve.

per serving 762 kJ (182 calories), 12 g protein, 9 g total fat, 5 g saturated fat, 13 g carbohydrate

Pasta with potato, beans and pesto

Pasta with potato and goat's cheese

Prepare the potatoes, broccoli, broad (fava) beans, green beans and zucchini (courgettes) as in the recipe opposite and cook as directed. Cook 300 g (10½ oz) small pasta shells until al dente. Meanwhile, prepare the pesto, but omit the parmesan and tomatoes. Drain the vegetables and pasta well, then gently mix together. Top with pesto, crumble 150 g (5 oz) goat's cheese over the top and serve.

Pasta with potato, beans and pesto

600 g (1 lb 5 oz) unpeeled small new potatoes,
   halved or quartered
4 cups (250 g/8 oz) broccoli florets
250 g (8 oz) fresh or thawed frozen broad
   (fava) beans (see Cook's tip)
175 g (6 oz) thin green beans, trimmed
2 zucchini (courgettes), cut into bite-sized
   chunks
300 g (10½ oz) tubular or hollow pasta shapes
fresh basil sprigs, to garnish

tomato pesto sauce

4-5 cloves garlic, chopped
2 tablespoons pine nuts
2 cups (100 g/3½ oz) fresh basil leaves
½ cup (50 g/1¾ oz) grated parmesan
4 tablespoons extra virgin olive oil
2 ripe tomatoes, diced

serves 4
preparation 15 minutes
cooking 20 minutes

----

per serving 2909 kJ (695 calories), 28 g protein,
29 g total fat, 6 g saturated fat, 77 g carbohydrate

1 Cook the potatoes in a saucepan of boiling water for 15 minutes, or until tender but not soft. Add the broccoli, broad beans, green beans and zucchini and simmer together for a further 5 minutes.

2 Meanwhile, cook the pasta in a saucepan of boiling water for 10-12 minutes, or according to the packet instructions, until al dente.

3 While the vegetables and pasta are cooking, make the pesto sauce. Pound the garlic with the pine nuts and 1 pinch salt in a mortar using a pestle. Add the basil and continue pounding until the ingredients form a green paste, then work in the parmesan and olive oil. Finally, work in the tomatoes. Alternatively, put all the ingredients, except the oil, in a food processor or blender and process to a paste, then gradually add the oil with the motor running.

4 Drain the pasta and vegetables and toss together. Top with the pesto, garnish with basil sprigs and serve.

Cook's tip

Broad beans are at their most tender when double peeled. To do this, boil or steam the shelled beans, then, when they are cool enough to handle, slip off the leathery grey-green skins to reveal the bright green bean inside.

Some more ideas...

❋ For a Sicilian-style pesto, use blanched almonds instead of the pine nuts. Cut them into fine slivers and add to the pounded mixture.

❋ To boost the flavour when fresh basil is not at its best, add a few sprigs of fresh mint, flat-leaf parsley and/or rocket (arugula) to the pesto.

Potato tortilla with fetta

500 g (1 lb) boiling (waxy) potatoes
3 tablespoons vegetable oil
1⅓ cups (200 g/7 oz) frozen peas, thawed
2 young leeks, white part only, cut into
    thick rings
1⅓ cups (200 g/7 oz) diced fetta
400 g (14 oz) firm tomatoes, sliced
5 eggs
1-2 tablespoons sparkling mineral water
cayenne pepper
salt and freshly ground black pepper
1 tablespoon finely chopped fresh parsley

serves 4
preparation 15 minutes
cooking 25 minutes

per serving 1647 kJ (393 calories), 17 g protein,
26 g total fat, 9 g saturated fat, 23 g carbohydrate

1 Peel the potatoes, cut or shave into thin slices and pat dry with paper towel.

2 Heat the oil in a large frying pan and cook the potatoes, peas and leeks for 10 minutes, turning them over occasionally. Stir in half the fetta and place the tomatoes and remaining fetta on top.

3 In a bowl, whisk the eggs with the mineral water, a pinch of cayenne pepper and some salt and black pepper. Stir in the parsley, then pour over the potato mixture and leave to set over low heat for about 10 minutes.

4 As soon as the tortilla has set underneath, slide it onto a plate, invert it back into the pan and fry for another 5 minutes. Serve hot, cut into wedges.

'Bubble and squeak' with poached eggs

1 Melt 25 g (1 oz) butter in a large, heavy-based frying pan (preferably non-stick). Add 1 finely chopped onion and cook for 10 minutes, stirring frequently, until soft. In a large bowl, combine the onion, 2 cups (about 500 g/1 lb) cold mashed potatoes and 1 cup (about 250 g/8 oz) roughly chopped cooked cabbage or other cold cooked vegetables. Add salt and freshly ground black pepper to taste.

2 With lightly floured hands, shape the mixture into four cakes, each about 2 cm (¾ inch) thick. Wipe the pan clean with paper towels, then add 1 tablespoon vegetable oil and heat. Fry the cakes in a large frying pan over moderate heat for about 15 minutes, turning once, until golden and crisp.

3 About 5 minutes before the end of cooking time, prepare the poached eggs. Pour 5 cm (2 inches) of boiling water into a large, wide frying pan. Add 1 tablespoon white vinegar, bring to a boil, then reduce the heat to a bare simmer. Break 4 eggs into a saucer, one at a time, then tip each gently into the water. Cook for 1 minute, then gently spoon a little boiling water over the centre of each egg to cook the yolks. Poach for 2 minutes more, or until done to your liking. Lift out with a spatula, allowing the water to drain. Lay an egg on each bubble and squeak cake, then serve.

Note Bubble and squeak is a British nickname for a hash made from left-over vegetables. The name comes from the sound the vegetables make while being fried.

Potato tortilla with fetta

Potato and mushroom quiche

1 Preheat the oven to 180°C (350°F/gas 4). Cook 750 g (1½ lb) baking (floury) potatoes in a saucepan of boiling water for 15 minutes, or until just tender. Drain, cool slightly, then peel and slice 5 mm (¼ inch) thick.

2 Finely chop 2 French shallots and 2 cloves garlic. Briefly sauté in 2 tablespoons olive oil in a large frying pan over high heat. Add 1 cup (100 g/3½ oz) finely sliced button mushrooms and 100 g (3½ oz) oyster mushrooms, cut into 1 cm (½ inch) thick strips. Sauté for 1 minute, then add 100 ml (3½ fl oz) pure (light/single) cream and cook, stirring, for 2–3 minutes, until the liquid has reduced by half. Stir in 4 tablespoons finely chopped fresh parsley, 1 teaspoon lemon juice, ½ teaspoon grated nutmeg and some salt and freshly ground black pepper. Set aside to cool until lukewarm, then stir in 2 lightly beaten eggs.

3 Layer the potato slices in a buttered 28 cm (11¼ inch) quiche dish. Spread the mushroom mixture over and top with a sheet of oiled foil. Bake for 1 hour, or until the eggs have set. Remove from the oven and allow to stand for 5 minutes, then slice into 4–6 wedges, lift out with a spatula and sprinkle with black pepper.

Potato and pumpkin gratin

Potato and pumpkin gratin

500 g (1 lb) unpeeled small new potatoes, halved
750 g (1½ lb) pumpkin (winter squash), peeled and chopped
½ cup (125 ml/4 fl oz) apple cider
300 ml (10½ fl oz) vegetable stock
1 small sprig fresh rosemary
1 large red onion, halved and thinly sliced
salt and freshly ground black pepper
3 large tomatoes, thickly sliced
leaves from 2 sprigs fresh oregano
2 cups (200 g/7 oz) grated parmesan
1 cup (80 g/2¾ oz) fresh white breadcrumbs

serves 4
preparation 20 minutes
cooking 1 hour 10 minutes

per serving 2100 kJ (502 calories), 31 g protein, 18 g total fat, 11 g saturated fat, 52 g carbohydrate

1 Preheat the oven to 180°C (350°F/gas 4). Cook the potatoes in a saucepan of boiling water for 15 minutes, or until just tender. Drain.

2 Meanwhile, put the pumpkin, cider, stock and rosemary in a large saucepan and bring to a boil. Reduce the heat, partially cover and simmer for 15 minutes. Add the onion and cook for 10 minutes, then discard the rosemary. Season with salt and black pepper.

3 Slice the potatoes and arrange half the slices in a large baking dish. Lay half the tomato slices over the top and scatter with half the oregano leaves. Season again and sprinkle with half the parmesan.

4 Spoon the cooked pumpkin mixture on top, adding all the cooking liquid. Top with the remaining potato, tomato slices and oregano. Mix the remaining parmesan with the breadcrumbs and sprinkle over the vegetables.

5 Bake for 35-40 minutes, or until the topping is crisp and golden brown. Serve hot.

Some more ideas...

* Omit the cider, stock, rosemary and onion. Instead of the pumpkin, use 2¾ cups (250 g/8 oz) sliced mushrooms and a few chopped spring onions (scallions). Layer with the other vegetables in a baking dish and bake for 45 minutes.

* Instead of the pumpkin, you could also use zucchini (courgettes), sliced 3 cm (1¼ inch) thick. Cook them in the cider and stock mixture for 20 minutes only.

Pumpkin

Pumpkins (winter squash) are related to zucchini and come in many types and varying sizes. Buy firm specimens that are heavy for their size, with hard skins. Store whole pumpkins in a cool, dry, airy place, preferably hanging in a net bag. In the right conditions, they will keep for several months. Store cut pieces in the refrigerator for up to 5 days.

Chickpea pie with parmesan and tomato mashed potatoes

1 tablespoon olive oil
2 onions, chopped
2 stalks celery, chopped
1 red capsicum (bell pepper), diced
2 cloves garlic, crushed
2 zucchini (courgettes), sliced
2 x 410 g (14½ oz) cans chickpeas, drained
2 x 410 g (14½ oz) cans chopped tomatoes
3 tablespoons tomato paste (concentrated
    purée)
150 ml (5 fl oz) full-bodied red wine
2 teaspoons dried Italian herb seasoning,
    or dried mixed herbs such as basil, oregano,
    parsley, thyme and sage
salt and freshly ground black pepper

*parmesan and tomato
mashed potatoes*

1 kg (2 lb) baking (floury) potatoes, peeled
    and cut into chunks
4 tablespoons milk
1 tablespoon extra virgin olive oil
1 egg
½ cup (50 g/1¾ oz) grated parmesan
⅓ cup (50 g/1¾ oz) sun-dried tomatoes
    in oil, drained and finely chopped
3 tablespoons chopped fresh basil

serves 6
preparation 35 minutes
cooking 1 hour 10 minutes

---

per serving 1652 kJ (395 calories), 18 g protein,
13 g total fat, 4 g saturated fat, 47 g carbohydrate

1 Heat the olive oil in a large saucepan. Add the onions, celery, capsicum and garlic and sauté over medium heat for 5 minutes. Stir in the zucchini, chickpeas, tomatoes, tomato paste, wine and dried herbs, then season to taste with salt and black pepper.

2 Bring to a boil, then reduce the heat, cover and simmer for 20 minutes, stirring occasionally. Remove the lid, increase the heat slightly and cook for a further 10–15 minutes, stirring occasionally, until the liquid has thickened slightly.

3 Meanwhile, preheat the oven to 200°C (400°F/gas 6) and start preparing the mashed potatoes. Cook the potatoes in a saucepan of boiling water for 15–20 minutes, or until tender. Drain the potatoes well, then return to the pan. Add the milk and extra virgin olive oil and mash until smooth. Beat in the egg, parmesan, sun-dried tomatoes, basil and salt and black pepper to taste, mixing well.

4 Spoon the vegetable mixture into a baking dish. Top with the mashed potatoes, covering the vegetables completely, and decoratively mark the top of the potatoes using a fork. Bake for 25 minutes, or until the topping is nicely browned. Serve hot.

Some more ideas...

* Use canned cannellini beans instead of chickpeas.

* Replace the celery with 2 chopped carrots.

* Add chopped black olives to the mashed potatoes rather than sun-dried tomatoes.

Potato moussaka

Vegetables with cheese crumble

1 Preheat the oven to 200°C (400°F/gas 6). Lightly grease a large baking dish or four individual ovenproof dishes with melted butter. Peel and dice 400 g (14 oz) boiling (waxy) or all-purpose potatoes and 2 carrots and cook together in a large saucepan of boiling salted water for 10 minutes. Reduce to a simmer, add 200 g (7 oz) sliced green beans and cook gently for a further 5 minutes.

2 Meanwhile, rub 25 g (1 oz) diced chilled butter into ¾ cup (90 g/3¼ oz) plain (all-purpose) flour, either using your fingertips or in a food processor. Stir in ¾ cup (90 g/3¼ oz) firmly packed grated mature cheddar. Drain the vegetables and toss them with 2 crushed cloves garlic, 1 tablespoon chopped fresh flat-leaf parsley and freshly ground black pepper to taste. Tip into the prepared dish(es). Pour over ¼ cup (60 ml/2 fl oz) pure (light/single) cream, then cover with the cheese crumble. Bake for 30 minutes (or 20 minutes for individual dishes), or until golden and crisp. Serve immediately.

Potato moussaka

1 kg (2 lb) boiling (waxy) or all-purpose
    potatoes, peeled and sliced into 5 mm
    (¼ inch) rounds
2 tablespoons vegetable oil
2 large onions, finely chopped
150 ml (5 fl oz) vegetable stock or dry
    white wine
700 g (1 lb 9 oz) jar or can tomato passata
    (puréed tomatoes)
1 teaspoon sugar
½ teaspoon freshly grated nutmeg
salt and freshly ground black pepper
1½ tablespoons chopped fresh flat-leaf
    parsley, plus extra to garnish
20 black olives, pitted and chopped
¼ cup (20 g/¾ oz) fresh white breadcrumbs
fresh rosemary, to garnish (optional)

serves 4
preparation 15 minutes
cooking 1 hour

---

per serving *1656 kJ (396 calories), 11 g protein,*
14 g total fat, 2 g saturated fat, 55 g carbohydrate

1 Preheat the oven to 200°C (400°F/gas 6). Cook the potatoes in a large saucepan of lightly salted boiling water for 5 minutes, or until just tender. Drain and set aside.

2 Heat the oil in a deep frying pan and gently cook the onions over a moderately low heat for 5–10 minutes, or until light golden, stirring all the time.

3 Add the stock or wine, passata, sugar and nutmeg to the onions. Season lightly with salt and black pepper, mix well, then cook gently, uncovered, for 15 minutes, stirring from time to time, until the sauce thickens. Stir in the parsley and taste to check the seasoning.

4 Layer half the potatoes in a 2 litre (8 cup/64 fl oz) baking dish (or four individual ovenproof dishes), cover with half the tomato and onion sauce, then scatter over most of the olives, reserving a few for garnish. Repeat with a second layer of potatoes and tomato sauce.

5 Sprinkle the breadcrumbs over the top, then bake for 30 minutes, or until golden and crisp. Pile the reserved olives in the centre of the moussaka, sprinkle with parsley and garnish with rosemary, if you like. Serve hot.

Cook's tips

You could also use sugocasa for this dish.
Sugocasa is similar to tomato passata,
but chunkier and more highly seasoned.
It is sometimes called sugo di pomodoro.
Another option is to use the same weight
of canned chopped tomatoes.

If you prefer, season the moussaka with
chopped rosemary instead of parsley.
Add it with the stock or wine.

Potato crepes with herb curd cheese

600 g (1 lb 5 oz) small baking (floury) potatoes
2 tablespoons plain (all-purpose) flour
100 ml (3½ fl oz) pure (light/single) cream
6 eggs
salt and freshly ground black pepper
freshly grated nutmeg
4 tablespoons butter or ghee
2 tablespoons snipped fresh chives

herb curd cheese

200 g (7 oz) curd cheese
4 tablespoons milk
2–3 tablespoons finely chopped fresh herbs,
    such as snipped chives and basil leaves
100 ml (3½ fl oz) whipping cream

serves 4
preparation 15 minutes + 20 minutes resting
cooking 1 hour

---

per serving *2469 kJ (590 calories), 24 g protein,*
43 g total fat, 25 g saturated fat, 28 g carbohydrate

1 Cook the potatoes in a saucepan of boiling water for 25–30 minutes, or until soft. Drain, allow to steam briefly, then peel and squeeze twice through a potato press into a bowl.

2 Stir the flour and cream into the potato purée, then gradually add the eggs and stir to combine. Season with salt and black pepper and a pinch of nutmeg. Leave to rest for 20 minutes.

3 Meanwhile, prepare the herb curd cheese. In a bowl, stir the curd cheese with the milk until creamy, then season with salt and black pepper. Mix in the herbs. Beat the cream until stiff, then loosely fold into the curd cheese mixture. Refrigerate until ready to serve.

4 Melt some of the butter in a non-stick frying pan over medium heat. Add enough of the potato mixture to just cover the bottom of the pan. Heat for 1–2 minutes, or until golden underneath, then turn and cook for another 1–2 minutes. Remove and keep warm while cooking another 7 crepes, adding more butter to the pan as needed. Spread the warm crepes with the herb curd cheese and fold in half. Sprinkle with chives and serve immediately.

Curd cheese

Curd cheese is similar to cream cheese, but has a lower fat content. It is made by adding a starter (such as rennet, lemon juice or vinegar) to milk. This causes the milk proteins to coagulate and form curds. Curd cheeses include cottage cheese, quark and paneer. They have a pale colour, a light flavour and texture, and a slight acidity.

Potato crepes with herb curd cheese

Potato and pumpkin soufflé

1 Cook 300 g (10½ oz) baking (floury) potatoes in boiling water for 20–30 minutes, or until soft. Drain, peel and squeeze twice through a potato press (potato ricer) into a large bowl, while still hot. In a large saucepan, sauté 1 finely chopped clove garlic in 4 tablespoons olive oil until lightly browned. Add 750 g (1½ lb) chopped pumpkin (winter squash), cover and cook over low heat for 10–15 minutes, or until soft, stirring occasionally. Allow to cool a little, then purée well and add to the potato purée.

2 Melt 2 tablespoons butter in a saucepan, add the potato mixture and cook over low heat for 8–10 minutes, stirring constantly, until all excess liquid has evaporated. Tip into a large bowl and allow to cool a little. Whisk in ½ cup (65 g/2½ oz) finely grated gruyère and 4 tablespoons thick (heavy/double) cream; season with salt, freshly grated black pepper and nutmeg. Whisk in 4 egg yolks, one at a time – the mixture should easily drop off a spoon. Whisk 4 egg whites until very stiff; fold one-quarter into the vegetable mixture to loosen it a little, then carefully fold in the remainder.

3 Preheat the oven to 180°C (350°F/gas 4). Grease 4 individual soufflé dishes with melted butter, brushing the sides thoroughly. Spoon in the soufflé mixture and gently smooth the surface. Place on the lowest shelf in the oven and bake for 20 minutes, or until set, keeping the oven door closed at all times. Serve immediately, with 1–2 tablespoons hollandaise or fresh tomato sauce, if you like.

Note The soufflé mixture can be prepared in advance, covered and kept in the fridge for 1–2 hours, but must be served immediately after baking before it collapses.

Baked hash browns with parmesan

Baked hash browns with parmesan

750 g (1 ½ lb) all-purpose potatoes, unpeeled
2 teaspoons olive oil
¾ teaspoon finely chopped fresh rosemary
¼ teaspoon freshly ground black pepper
3 tablespoons grated parmesan

serves 4
preparation 15 minutes
cooking 25 minutes

per serving *699 kJ (169 calories), 6 g protein, 4 g total fat,*
1 g saturated fat, 25 g carbohydrate

1 Preheat the oven to 240°C (475°F/gas 8) and lightly spray two large baking trays with olive oil spray. Grate the potatoes in a food processor or using a grater and tip into a large bowl. Add the oil, rosemary and black pepper and toss well to coat.

2 Divide the potato mixture into eight portions and spread into four large rounds, each about 5 mm (¼ inch) thick, on each baking tray. Bake for 20 minutes.

3 Preheat the grill (broiler) to high. Remove the hash browns from the oven and carefully turn them over on the baking trays using a spatula. Sprinkle with the parmesan and cook under the grill for 3 minutes, or until the tops are golden brown and the potatoes are cooked through. Serve hot.

Cook's tip

You can cook the potatoes ahead and shape them into rounds as in steps 1 and 2, then refrigerate them for up to 8 hours. When ready to serve, bake them in a preheated oven then grill as in step 3.

Potato and tomato casserole

Preheat the oven to 220°C (425°F/gas 7). Cook 750 g (1 ½ lb) boiling (waxy) potatoes in a saucepan of boiling water for 25–30 minutes, or until soft. Drain, allow to steam briefly, then peel and cut into slices (not too thin). Layer in a greased baking dish with 500 g (1 lb) sliced tomatoes, seasoning the layers with some salt and freshly ground black pepper. Pour 150 ml (5 fl oz) pure (light/single) cream over the top, or 125 g (4 oz) crème fraîche or sour cream mixed with 4–5 tablespoons milk. Sprinkle with 1 finely chopped clove garlic, 1 cup (150 g/5 oz) diced mozzarella and 1 cup (100 g/3½ oz) grated parmesan. Bake for 30 minutes, or until the topping is golden and the cheese has melted.

Mushroom and potato curry

1 small onion, chopped
3 cloves garlic, chopped
2 cm (³/₄ inch) piece fresh ginger,
    peeled and chopped
1 tablespoon olive oil
250 g (8 oz) shiitake mushrooms, quartered
1 teaspoon yellow curry paste
600 g (1 lb 5 oz) unpeeled small new
    potatoes, quartered
1 cup (150 g/5 oz) frozen peas, thawed
²/₃ cup (150 g/5 oz) natural (plain) yogurt

serves 4
preparation 15 minutes
cooking 30 minutes

----

*per serving 920 kJ (220 calories), 9 g protein, 7 g total fat,
2 g saturated fat, 28 g carbohydrate*

1 Put the onion, garlic and ginger in a blender with
3 tablespoons water and purée finely.

2 Heat the oil in a saucepan, add the onion mixture and
sauté for 5 minutes over medium heat, or until the liquid has
evaporated. Stir in the mushrooms and sauté for 5 minutes.

3 Stir in the curry paste, add the potatoes and salt to taste
and mix together thoroughly. Pour in 1 cup (250 ml/8 fl oz)
water, bring to a boil, then cover and simmer over low heat
for 15 minutes, or until the potatoes are soft.

4 Stir in the peas and heat through for 2 minutes.
Remove from the heat, stir in the yogurt and serve.

Mushrooms
Mushrooms belong to the fungi family.
They grow rapidly, becoming darker and
stronger in flavour as they age. Buy firm,
dry mushrooms and store them unwashed
in a paper bag in the fridge for up to 5 days.
When ready to prepare them, trim off any
hard bases of the stalks.

Cook's tip
*There is no substitute for fresh
ginger, so always have some handy.
Ginger is easily frozen; simply peel,
place it in a freezer bag, seal it well,
freeze and use as required. It can be
chopped or grated from frozen.*

Mushroom and potato curry

Sweet potato curry

1 Heat 1 tablespoon vegetable oil in a large frying pan and gently sauté 1 chopped onion and 2 crushed cloves garlic for 4–5 minutes, or until softened. Add 500 g (1 lb) orange sweet potatoes, peeled and cut into chunks, and sauté for 2 minutes, then stir in 1 tablespoon mild curry powder and 1 tablespoon finely chopped fresh ginger and cook for 30 seconds. Stir in a 410 g (14 ½ oz) can chopped tomatoes and 100 ml (3½ fl oz) vegetable stock. Bring to a boil, then reduce the heat, cover and cook gently for 12–15 minutes, until the sweet potatoes are tender.

2 Stir in 1 cup (150 g/5 oz) thawed frozen peas or shelled fresh peas and simmer for 3 minutes. Add 250 g (8 oz) paneer or firm tofu, cut into 1.5 cm (½ inch) cubes, and cook until just heated through. Season to taste with salt and freshly ground black pepper, scatter with 2 tablespoons chopped or whole fresh mint and serve.

Note Paneer is a lightly pressed Indian cheese that is available in Indian grocery stores and some larger supermarkets.

Side dishes

Inexpensive, versatile and easy to cook, potatoes
are the perfect basis for side dishes. This chapter
presents delicious and filling accompaniments for
meat, fish or vegetarian main courses.

Stir-fried sweet potatoes with spinach and spices

3 tablespoons vegetable oil
600 g (1 lb 5 oz) sweet potatoes, peeled
    and diced into 1 cm (½ inch) cubes
2 teaspoons cumin seeds
2 teaspoons grated fresh ginger
½ teaspoon chilli powder
½ teaspoon ground turmeric
1 teaspoon garam masala
3⅓ cups (150 g/5 oz) baby spinach leaves
lemon wedges, to serve

serves 4
preparation 10 minutes
cooking 10 minutes

per serving 1002 kJ (239 calories), 4 g protein,
15 g total fat, 2 g saturated fat, 24 g carbohydrate

1 Heat the oil in a large frying pan or wok over medium heat. Add the sweet potatoes and sauté for 2–3 minutes, or until they start to colour.

2 Add the cumin seeds and stir until they begin to pop, then stir in the ginger, chilli powder and turmeric. Stir-fry for 5 minutes, or until the sweet potato is tender.

3 Add the garam masala and spinach and stir for a minute or two, until the spinach wilts. Season with ¼ teaspoon salt and serve with lemon wedges.

Turmeric
The rhizomes of turmeric, a member of the ginger family, add a vibrant golden colour to dishes such as curries. Turmeric can be used fresh, or dried and ground. If buying it fresh, choose firm, plump, clean rhizomes. Avoid getting the dried powder on your clothing, as it causes stubborn stains.

Potato curry with green beans

3 teaspoons butter
2 tablespoons vegetable oil
2 small green chillies
½ teaspoon cumin seeds
½ teaspoon ground turmeric
¼ teaspoon garam masala
1 clove garlic, crushed
500 g (1 lb) small new boiling (waxy) potatoes,
    cut into thick slices
250 g (8 oz) thin green beans, trimmed and
    cut into 2.5 cm (1 inch) lengths

serves 4
preparation 10 minutes
cooking 20 minutes

per serving *867 kJ (207 calories), 5 g protein,*
13 g total fat, 3 g saturated fat, 19 g carbohydrate

1 Heat the butter and oil in a wide shallow saucepan
or frying pan over high heat. When the mixture starts to
sizzle, stir in the whole green chillies, cumin seeds, turmeric,
garam masala and garlic and stir-fry for 30 seconds.

2 Add the potatoes, season with a little salt and stir until
coated with the butter and oil.

3 Stir in the beans, cover the pan, then reduce the heat
to medium and cook for 15 minutes, stirring occasionally.
The curry is ready when the potatoes are cooked through.

Cook's tip

When chopping chillies, wear
disposable gloves, or wash
your hands thoroughly with
warm soapy water once finished.

Chillies

Chillies vary in intensity from mildly fruity
to blisteringly hot. It is the seeds and white
membranes that contain most of the heat, so
remove either or both if you prefer a milder taste.
Chillies are green or purple when unripe; when
ripe, they may be red, yellow, purple or almost
black. Generally, the smaller the chilli, the hotter
it will be. A remedy for chilli burn on the palate
is milk or yogurt.

Swiss rösti with bacon

750 g (1½ lb) boiling (waxy) potatoes
2 tablespoons vegetable oil
3 slices (strips) rindless bacon, chopped
1 onion, chopped
1 green capsicum (bell pepper), seeded
    and chopped
¼ teaspoon paprika
salt and freshly ground black pepper
fresh flat-leaf parsley sprigs, to garnish

serves 4
preparation 10 minutes + 10 minutes soaking
cooking 35 minutes

per serving *1124 kJ (268 calories), 12 g protein,*
12 g total fat, 2 g saturated fat, 27 g carbohydrate

Cook's tips

Three varieties of boiling (waxy)
potato you could use in this recipe
are Yukon gold, bintje and pink-eye.

Soaking the potatoes in iced water
converts some of the starch to sugar,
which helps the potatoes to brown
faster and absorb less fat. Squeezing
them dry ensures a crisp result.

1 Peel the potatoes and coarsely grate them into a large bowl of iced water. Leave to stand for 10 minutes.

2 Meanwhile, heat 1 tablespoon of the oil in a large frying pan and fry the bacon over medium heat for 5 minutes, or until crisp. Remove with a slotted spoon and set aside in a large bowl.

3 Add the onion and capsicum to the pan and sauté for 5 minutes, or until soft. Add to the bacon.

4 Drain the potatoes, then use your hands to squeeze out as much water as possible. Pat dry and add to the bacon mixture with the paprika. Season to taste with salt and black pepper and mix together well.

5 Add half the remaining oil to the pan and heat. Spread the potato mixture evenly in the pan and cook, without stirring, for 15 minutes, or until golden brown and crisp underneath.

6 Using a spatula, loosen the rösti all around the edge of the pan. Put a large plate over the pan and invert the rösti onto the plate. Heat the remaining oil in the pan, slide the rösti back into the pan and cook for a further 10 minutes, or until golden and crisp on the other side. Cut into wedges and serve hot, garnished with parsley sprigs.

Swiss rösti with bacon

Baked potatoes au gratin

1 Preheat the oven to 200°C (400°F/gas 6) and line a baking tray with baking (parchment) paper. Place 4 large scrubbed baking (floury) potatoes on the baking tray and brush with vegetable oil. Bake for about 1 hour, then allow to cool briefly.

2 Meanwhile, coarsely grate 100 g (3½ oz) cheddar or gouda cheese. To half the cheese, add ½ cup (125 g/4 oz) sour cream, 1 tablespoon snipped fresh chives, salt and freshly ground black pepper to taste and mix well. Cut a 1 cm (½ inch) thick slice off each potato and scoop out the flesh with a tablespoon, leaving a wall about 1 cm (½ inch) thick. Roughly mash the potato flesh in a bowl using a fork, then stir in the cheese mixture. Fill the potatoes with the mixture and sprinkle with the remaining cheese. Bake for a further 15 minutes, or until the cheese has melted. Sprinkle with more snipped fresh chives and serve hot.

Cheesy barbecued potatoes

750 g (1½ lb) boiling (waxy) potatoes, peeled
   and thinly sliced
1 onion, cut into fine rings
50 g (1¾ oz) butter
¾ cup (100 g/3½ oz) grated cheddar,
   emmenthal or Swiss cheese
2 tablespoons finely chopped fresh parsley
2 tablespoons dry white wine
⅓ cup (80 ml/2½ fl oz) chicken stock
salt and freshly ground black pepper

serves 4
preparation 15 minutes
cooking 40 minutes

per serving *1568 kJ (374 calories), 16 g protein,*
21 g total fat, 13 g saturated fat, 28 g carbohydrate

1 Heat a charcoal grill or barbecue hotplate to medium.

2 Spread the potatoes and onions on a large sheet of extra-strength foil, shaping the edges of the foil into a high rim. Top with dots of butter, sprinkle with the cheese and parsley and drizzle with the wine and stock. Season with salt and black pepper and seal tightly with a matching sheet of foil.

3 Cook on the barbecue for 40 minutes, or until the potatoes are tender. Serve hot.

Barbecued potatoes and zucchini

Heat a charcoal grill or barbecue hotplate to medium. Peel and thinly slice
500 g (1 lb) boiling (waxy) potatoes. Slice 2 small zucchini (courgettes).
Cut 4 spring onions (scallions) into 5 cm (2 inch) lengths. Spread the potatoes,
zucchini and spring onions on a large sheet of extra-strength foil and dot with
50 g (1¾ oz) butter. Sprinkle with 2 tablespoons finely chopped fresh parsley
and 1 cup (125 g/4 oz) grated gouda cheese. Drizzle with ½ cup (125 ml/4 fl oz)
chicken stock and 4 tablespoons dry white wine and season with salt and freshly
ground black pepper. Seal tightly with a matching sheet of foil, then cook on the
barbecue for 40 minutes, or until the potatoes are tender. Serve hot.

Cheesy barbecued potatoes

Five ways...

with steamed or boiled potatoes

Use new potatoes, boiling (waxy) or all-purpose types for steaming or boiling. Choose similar-sized potatoes so they cook in the same amount of time. Add the dressing while the potatoes are still warm.

Potatoes with herb dressing

serves	prep	cook
4	10 mins	30 mins

Cook 1 kg (2 lb) unpeeled small boiling (waxy) potatoes in a saucepan of boiling water for 20-25 minutes, or until soft. Drain, refresh under cold water, peel and place in a serving bowl. Whisk together 1¼ cups (300 g/10½ oz) sour cream, ¾ cup (200 g/7 oz) curd cheese, low-fat cream cheese or cottage cheese and ⅓ cup (100 g/3½ oz) natural (plain) yogurt until smooth. Mix in 2 tablespoons lemon juice and 4 chopped hard-boiled eggs. Season to taste with Tabasco sauce and salt and freshly ground black pepper. Mix in 4 tablespoons finely chopped mixed fresh herbs, such as basil, dill, chervil, parsley and chives. Add to the still-warm potatoes in the serving bowl and mix gently but thoroughly.

per serving 2184 kJ (522 calories), 24 g protein, 30 g total fat, 17 g saturated fat, 39 g carbohydrate

Sesame and coriander potatoes

serves	prep	cook
4	20 mins	30 mins

Cook 1 kg (2 lb) unpeeled small new potatoes in a saucepan of boiling water for 20-25 minutes, or until soft. Drain, refresh under cold water and peel. In a bowl, whisk together 1 cup (250 g/8 oz) curd cheese, low-fat cream cheese or cottage cheese, ⅔ cup (150 g/5 oz) natural (plain) yogurt, 2 tablespoons pure (light/single) cream and 2 tablespoons lemon juice until smooth. Add salt and black pepper and stir in 2 chopped spring onions (scallions), 1 tablespoon finely chopped fresh parsley and 1 tablespoon snipped fresh chives. Cover and refrigerate until serving. Melt 4 tablespoons butter in a large frying pan over medium heat. Briefly turn the potatoes in the butter and season with salt. Add 4 tablespoons toasted sesame seeds and 1 tablespoon finely chopped fresh coriander (cilantro) and cook for another 2 minutes, turning the potatoes constantly until covered in a sesame crust. Serve hot with the herbed cheese.

per serving 2167 kJ (518 calories), 20 g protein, 31 g total fat, 17 g saturated fat, 37 g carbohydrate

Potatoes with herb dressing

Caraway potatoes

serves 4 | prep 10 mins | cook 35 mins

Cook 1 kg (2 lb) unpeeled small new potatoes in a saucepan of boiling water for 20–25 minutes, or until soft. Drain, refresh under cold water and peel. Melt 2 tablespoons butter in a large frying pan over low heat until slightly browned. Turn the potatoes in the butter and season with salt and black pepper. Sprinkle with 3 tablespoons caraway seeds and stir in 100 ml (3½ fl oz) pure (light/single) cream, then cover and cook over low heat for about 5 minutes. Turn the potatoes in the cream and simmer for another 3 minutes. Serve hot.

per serving *1482 kJ (354 calories), 8 g protein, 20 g total fat, 12 g saturated fat, 37 g carbohydrate*

Mint potatoes

serves 4 | prep 10 mins | cook 30 mins

Cook 1 kg (2 lb) unpeeled small new potatoes in a saucepan of boiling water for 20–25 minutes, or until soft. Drain, refresh under cold water and peel. Meanwhile, finely chop 80 g (2¾ oz) fresh mint. Heat 3 tablespoons olive oil and 3 tablespoons butter in a large frying pan and briefly turn the potatoes in the mixture. Season with salt and freshly ground black pepper, sprinkle with the mint and cook for an additional 2–3 minutes, turning the potatoes constantly. Serve hot.

per serving *1660 kJ (397 calories), 7 g protein, 26 g total fat, 10 g saturated fat, 34 g carbohydrate*

Potatoes with leeks and curd cheese

serves 4–6 | prep 20 mins | cook 30 mins

Wash 750 g (1½ lb) thin leeks and cut the stalks (white parts only) into 5 cm (2 inch) lengths. Melt 2 tablespoons butter in a wide saucepan and briefly sauté the leeks, then add ½ cup (125 ml/4 fl oz) vegetable stock, a pinch of salt and some grated nutmeg. Cook over low heat for about 30 minutes, stirring occasionally. Mix 2 tablespoons pure (light/single) cream with 1 teaspoon cornflour (cornstarch) and pour over the leeks to thicken the liquid. Meanwhile, cook 1 kg (2 lb) unpeeled small boiling (waxy) potatoes in a saucepan of boiling water for 20–25 minutes, or until soft. Drain, refresh under cold water and peel. In a bowl, combine 1¼ cups (300 g/10½ oz) sour cream, ¾ cup (200 g/7 oz) curd cheese, low-fat cream cheese or cottage cheese and ⅓ cup (100 g/3½ oz) natural (plain) yogurt until smooth. Stir in 2 tablespoons lemon juice, 1 teaspoon dijon mustard and salt and freshly ground black pepper to taste. Mix in 1 cup (30 g/1 oz) finely chopped mixed fresh herbs. Place the potatoes on a serving platter, arrange the dressing next to the potatoes and garnish with fresh herb sprigs. Arrange the leeks next to the potatoes and serve.

per serving *2066 kJ (494 calories), 17 g protein, 30 g total fat, 19 g saturated fat, 38 g carbohydrate*

Potatoes and brussels sprouts with mustard dressing

Potatoes and brussels sprouts with mustard dressing

500 g (1 lb) unpeeled small new potatoes, quartered

300 g (10½ oz) young brussels sprouts, quartered

1 red apple, cored and chopped

2 stalks celery, sliced

3 spring onions (scallions), chopped

mustard dressing

1 tablespoon olive oil

2 tablespoons plain (all-purpose) flour

200 ml (7 fl oz) vegetable stock

1 tablespoon mustard

1 tablespoon horseradish from a jar

½ teaspoon caraway seeds

serves 4

preparation 15 minutes

cooking 20 minutes

------

per serving 848 kJ (203 calories), 7 g protein, 6 g total fat, 1 g saturated fat, 30 g carbohydrate

1 Cook the potatoes in a saucepan of boiling water for 5 minutes, then add the brussels sprouts and cook for a further 5-10 minutes, or until tender but still firm. Drain well and place in a large bowl with the apple, celery and spring onions.

2 To make the dressing, heat the oil in a small saucepan, sprinkle with the flour and cook for about 2 minutes, stirring constantly. Gradually stir in the stock and bring to a boil. Add the mustard, horseradish, caraway seeds and ½ teaspoon salt and simmer over medium heat for about 2 minutes. Pour the hot dressing over the vegetables and gently mix through. Leave for a short while for the dressing to soak in, then serve lukewarm or cold.

Cook's tip

When preparing brussels sprouts, do not completely cut off the small hard stalks or the sprouts will fall apart during cooking.

Creamy potatoes with leeks

Quarter 500 g (1 lb) unpeeled small new potatoes and cook in a saucepan of boiling water for 8 minutes, then add 500 g (1 lb) young leeks, white part only, cut into short lengths. Cook for 5–10 minutes more, or until the potatoes are tender but still firm to the bite. Drain the vegetables well and place in a large bowl. Combine 1 tablespoon plain (all-purpose) flour, 2 tablespoons stock and ½ cup (125 ml/4 fl oz) pure (light/single) cream in a screw-top jar, add salt and black pepper to taste and shake until well combined. Pour over the hot vegetables and stir together well.

Potato, bacon and leeks on rosemary skewers

24 even-sized unpeeled small new potatoes
8 strong, fresh rosemary stalks, each about
   20 cm (8 inches) long
2 tablespoons olive oil
⅓ cup (80 ml/2½ fl oz) balsamic vinegar
1 tablespoon dijon mustard
⅓ cup (80 ml/2½ fl oz) apple juice
4 thick leeks, trimmed
4 slices (strips) rindless bacon

serves 4
preparation 10 minutes + 30 minutes
   marinating
cooking 30 minutes

per serving 2030 kJ (485 calories), 21 g protein,
14 g total fat, 3 g saturated fat, 66 g carbohydrate

1 Cook the potatoes in a saucepan of boiling water for 10 minutes, or until tender, then lift out with a slotted spoon. Return the water to a boil.

2 Meanwhile, strip the leaves from the rosemary stalks, leaving a tuft at the top. Chop enough of the leaves to make 1 tablespoon; place in a large bowl and discard the rest. Add the oil, vinegar, mustard and apple juice and mix together well. Add the hot cooked potatoes and stir to coat them in the oil. Set aside to marinate for 30 minutes.

3 While the potatoes are marinating, cut each leek into eight chunks, each about 2.5 cm (1 inch) long. Place in the saucepan of boiling water, then cover and cook gently for about 8 minutes, or until just tender. Drain well in a colander and set aside.

4 Preheat the grill (broiler) to high. Stretch the bacon slices using the back of a blunt knife, then cut each into four strips. Use a metal skewer to make a hole through the leek pieces, then wrap the bacon pieces around half of them.

5 Drain the potatoes, reserving any left-over marinade, and make a hole in each one. Divide the potatoes and leek pieces (both unwrapped and bacon-wrapped) among the rosemary stalk skewers, threading them on alternately.

6 Place the skewers on the grill tray and cook for about 10 minutes, or until nicely browned, carefully turning the skewers halfway through cooking and brushing them with the reserved marinade. Serve immediately.

Crushed potatoes flavoured with fennel seeds

Crushed potatoes flavoured with fennel seeds

8 unpeeled small baking (floury) potatoes, about 750 g (1½ lb) in total
3 tablespoons garlic-infused olive oil
2 teaspoons fennel seeds
1 teaspoon dried red chilli flakes
1 teaspoon sea salt
1 teaspoon grated lemon zest
1 tablespoon finely chopped fresh parsley

serves 4
preparation 5 minutes
cooking 45 minutes

- -

per serving *1050 kJ (251 calories), 5 g protein,*
14 g total fat, 2 g saturated fat, 26 g carbohydrate

1 Preheat the oven to 240ºC (475ºF/gas 8). Scrub the potatoes and cook in a saucepan of boiling water for 10-15 minutes, or until tender. Drain well and place on a baking tray lined with baking (parchment) paper.

2 Crush each potato using a potato masher. Drizzle with the olive oil and sprinkle with the remaining ingredients. Bake for 30 minutes, or until golden and crunchy.

Florentine potatoes

1 Preheat the oven to 200°C (400°F/gas 6). Cook 8 unpeeled large boiling (waxy) potatoes, about 1.5 kg (3 lb) in total, in a saucepan of boiling water for 15–20 minutes, or until just tender. Drain, refresh under cold water, peel, then cut in half lengthwise. Use a teaspoon to carefully hollow out the halves, leaving a shell about 5 mm (¼ inch) thick. Place the potato flesh in a bowl, finely mash with a fork and set aside. Remove the thicker veins from 500 g (1 lb) spinach and blanch the leaves in boiling water for 1–2 minutes, then drain and squeeze out excess moisture.

2 Melt 1 tablespoon butter in a frying pan. Gently sauté 1 finely chopped onion for 5 minutes, then stir in the spinach and potato flesh. Season with salt, freshly ground black pepper and grated nutmeg and tip into a large bowl. Melt 1 tablespoon butter in a small saucepan, add 2 tablespoons plain (all-purpose) flour and cook, stirring, for 1 minute. Stir in 1 cup (250 ml/8 fl oz) milk and bring to a boil, whisking constantly. Add ⅔ cup (80 g/2¾ oz) grated gouda cheese and stir until melted. Season with more salt, pepper and nutmeg and stir into the spinach mixture.

3 Arrange the potatoes, hollow side up, in a single layer in a well-greased pie dish (pie plate), packing them in tightly. Distribute the spinach mixture over them. Sprinkle with 2 tablespoons breadcrumbs and 2 tablespoons grated parmesan and bake for 20 minutes, or until the topping is golden. Serve hot.

New potatoes with nori

500 g (1 lb) unpeeled small new potatoes
30 g (1 oz) butter
grated zest and juice of $\frac{1}{2}$ small lemon
1 sheet toasted sushi nori, about 20 x 18 cm
   (8 x 7 inches)
salt and freshly ground black pepper
2 tablespoons snipped fresh chives

serves 4
preparation 5 minutes
cooking 15 minutes

----

per serving *590 kJ (141 calories), 3 g protein, 6 g total fat,*
4 g saturated fat, 17 g carbohydrate

1 Cook the potatoes in a saucepan of boiling water for
12 minutes, or until just tender.

2 Reserve 3 tablespoons of the cooking water, then drain the
potatoes and return them to the saucepan with the reserved
water. Add the butter and lemon zest and juice, then toss the
potatoes to coat them with the liquid.

3 Use scissors to snip the sushi nori into fine strips. Sprinkle
the nori over the potatoes and cover the pan. Cook over low
heat for 1-2 minutes, or until the nori has softened. Add salt
and black pepper to taste, sprinkle with the chives and serve.

Cook's tip

*Nori, an edible seaweed, is available in
sheets from Japanese stores and larger
supermarkets. To toast nori, pass the
sheet over the flame of a gas stove
burner, once on each side of the sheet,
or lay the sheet on a grill rack and place
under a preheated grill (broiler) for
a few seconds. The sheet will quickly
darken and give off its aroma – take
care not to overcook and burn it.*

Mix and match

Green beans go well with lemon and potatoes, and can be
added to the dish or used to replace the nori. Snip 200 g
(7 oz) trimmed green beans into short lengths and add
them to the potatoes about halfway through the cooking
time; 4–5 minutes is sufficient for cooking the beans.
Drain and toss with the butter and lemon zest and juice.

New potatoes with nori

New potatoes with asparagus

1 Cook 600 g (1 lb 5 oz) small new potatoes in boiling water for 20–25 minutes, or until soft. Drain and allow to steam briefly. Meanwhile, trim 250 g (8 oz) thin asparagus (or mini asparagus) and blanch the stalks for 2 minutes. Arrange on a warmed platter with the potatoes and season with some salt and freshly ground black pepper. Drizzle with 125 g (4 oz) melted butter and serve.

Note This dish can be served with salmon and omelette rolls. In a bowl, whisk 4 eggs with 2 tablespoons sparkling mineral water, 1 tablespoon finely chopped fresh dill and 50 g (1¾ oz) finely diced smoked salmon. Heat 2 tablespoons butter in a non-stick frying pan and make two omelettes, one at a time, from the egg mixture. Roll up the omelettes and cut into slices. Serve warm or cold.

Patatas bravas

750 g (1½ lb) boiling (waxy) potatoes,
    peeled and cut into wedges
4 cloves garlic, unpeeled
3 tablespoons olive oil
2 tablespoons chopped fresh parsley

sauce

2 tablespoons olive oil
1 onion, finely chopped
2 cloves garlic, crushed
1 teaspoon sweet paprika
½ teaspoon cayenne pepper
410 g (14½ oz) can chopped tomatoes
½ teaspoon sugar
salt and freshly ground black pepper

serves 4
preparation 10 minutes
cooking 40 minutes

----
per serving *1502 kJ (359 calories), 6 g protein,*
23 g total fat, 3 g saturated fat, 31 g carbohydrate

1 Preheat the oven to 200ºC (400ºF/gas 6). Toss the potato wedges and garlic cloves in the oil and place in a single layer on a baking tray lined with baking (parchment) paper. Bake for 35-40 minutes, or until crisp and golden, turning once.

2 While the potatoes are cooking, make the sauce. Heat the oil in a saucepan and sauté the onion and garlic until softened. Add the spices and stir for 1 minute, then add the tomatoes and sugar. Simmer for 20 minutes, or until thickened. Season to taste with salt and black pepper.

3 Season the potatoes with salt. Drizzle the sauce over them, sprinkle with the parsley and serve hot.

Cook's tip

The name of this Spanish dish translates as 'brave potatoes', as the fiery sauce is recommended only for the courageous!

Paprika

Paprika is a bright red chilli powder that is produced by drying and grinding suitable varieties of chilli. There are mildly hot, sweet, and smoked types. Spain and Hungary are the world's largest producers.

Five ways...

with toppings for baked potatoes

Superb comfort food, steaming-hot baked potatoes topped with a variety of fillings also make a filling snack or nutritious light meal. Choose floury potatoes for the best results.

Perfect baked potatoes

Preheat the oven to 200°C (400°F/gas 6). Scrub 4 baking (floury) potatoes, each about 300 g (10 ½ oz), then push a metal skewer through each, or put the potatoes onto a potato roasting rack. (Inserting a metal skewer into the centre of the potatoes is not essential, but it helps to conduct heat through to their centres so they cook more quickly.) Place the potatoes directly on the shelf of the oven and bake for 1 ¼ hours, or until they are tender. Once they are cooked, split open the baked potatoes, holding them with a tea towel (dish towel), then press gently to part the halves, keeping them joined at the base. Pile one of the following toppings onto the potatoes (or simply dollop them with butter or sour cream and a sprinkling of herbs such as snipped chives), and serve immediately.

Asparagus with herb butter

serves 4 | prep 10 mins | cook 25 mins

Put ⅔ cup (150 g/5½ oz) softened butter in a small bowl and stir until smooth. Mix in 1–2 teaspoons mustard and 1 teaspoon lemon juice, season with salt and stir in 2 tablespoons finely chopped fresh herbs. Place on a piece of plastic wrap, shape into a roll and refrigerate until serving. Bring a large pot of salted water to a boil and add 1 tablespoon butter and 1 sugar cube. Cut the woody ends off 1 kg (2 lb 4 oz) white asparagus and peel the stalks. Tie the stalks into bundles with kitchen string and simmer for 20 minutes, or until tender but still firm to the bite. Drain well. (Alternatively, place four bundles of asparagus on separate sheets of foil, top each with 1 tablespoon flaked butter, seal into a parcel and bake with the potatoes for 25 minutes.) Slice the herb butter and arrange over hot baked potatoes with the asparagus. Serve hot.

per serving 2258 kJ (539 calories), 10 g protein, 40 g total fat, 24 g saturated fat, 35 g carbohydrate

Olive and tomato topping, mushroom and zucchini topping, tuna and sweetcorn topping

Mushroom and zucchini topping

serves **4** · prep **10** mins · cook **15** mins

Heat 1 tablespoon olive oil in a non-stick frying pan and sauté 200 g (7 oz) small button mushrooms and 1 sliced zucchini (courgette) for about 15 minutes. Tip into a bowl, including the cooking juices. Stir in 1 tablespoon olive oil, 1 teaspoon vinegar, 1 teaspoon mustard and 2 tablespoons finely chopped fresh parsley. Season with salt and freshly ground black pepper, pile onto hot baked potatoes and serve.

per serving 1299 kJ (287 calories), 8 g protein, 14 g total fat, 2 g saturated fat, 31 g carbohydrate

Olive and tomato topping

serves **4** · prep **15** mins · cook **55** mins

Wrap 1 bulb garlic in foil and bake for 45 minutes with the potatoes. Squeeze the garlic out of the cloves into a bowl. Mix together with 2 tablespoons roughly chopped fresh basil, 1 cup (100 g/3½ oz) diced olives, 1 tablespoon olive oil and 300 g (10½ oz) quartered cherry tomatoes. Pile onto hot potatoes and sprinkle each with 1 tablespoon grated parmesan. Continue baking until the cheese has melted.

per serving 1289 kJ (308 calories), 10 g protein, 13 g total fat, 3 g saturated fat, 38 g carbohydrate

Spinach and cheese topping

serves **4** · prep **20** mins · cook **15** mins

In a bowl, mix together 4 tablespoons grated gouda cheese, 2¼ cups (100 g/3½ oz) baby spinach leaves and ⅔ cup (150 g/5½ oz) sour cream. Season to taste with salt and freshly ground black pepper. Hollow out hot baked potatoes, mash the potato flesh and stir into the cheese and spinach mixture. Pile onto the hollowed-out hot potatoes, sprinkle with 4 tablespoons grated gouda cheese and bake for a final 15 minutes. Serve hot.

per serving 1461 kJ (349 calories), 11 g protein, 20 g total fat, 11 g saturated fat, 32 g carbohydrate

Tuna and sweetcorn

serves **4** · prep **10** mins · cook **2** mins

Put 250 g (8 oz) frozen sweetcorn in a small saucepan of boiling water. Boil for 2 minutes, then drain. Drain and flake a 200 g (7 oz) can tuna in water and add to the sweetcorn. Stir in 2 tablespoons mayonnaise and 2 tablespoons reduced-fat crème fraîche or sour cream. Mix in 2 tablespoons snipped fresh chives or finely chopped spring onions (scallions) and 2 tablespoons chopped fresh parsley, then pile the mixture onto 4 hot baked potatoes.

per serving 1548 kJ (370 calories), 18 g protein, 13 g total fat, 4 g saturated fat, 45 g carbohydrate

Lyon-style potato gratin

béchamel sauce

2 cups (500 ml/16 fl oz) milk

1 small onion or French shallot, peeled and
    studded with cloves

1 bay leaf

a few parsley stalks

6 peppercorns

25 g (1 oz) butter

25 g (1 oz) plain (all-purpose) flour

salt and freshly ground black pepper

750 g (1½ lb) boiling (waxy) potatoes, peeled
    and thinly sliced

4 onions, sliced into fine rings

1 teaspoon sugar

150 ml (5 fl oz) beef or chicken stock

1 tablespoon softened butter, for greasing

serves 4

preparation 30 minutes + 15 minutes infusing

cooking 1¼ hours

_____

per serving *1459 kJ (348 calories), 12 g protein,*
14 g total fat, 9 g saturated fat, 43 g carbohydrate

1 First, make the béchamel sauce. Pour the milk into a small saucepan and add the onion or shallot, bay leaf, parsley stalks and peppercorns. Slowly bring the milk to simmering point then remove from the heat and stir. Cover and leave to infuse for 15–30 minutes, then strain, discarding the solids.

2 Melt the butter in a saucepan. Add the flour and cook over gentle heat for about 2 minutes, stirring constantly with a wooden spoon. Gradually add the infused milk, stirring until the sauce is thick and smooth. Simmer for 20 minutes, stirring occasionally, then add salt and black pepper to taste.

3 Meanwhile, place the potato slices in a bowl, add enough iced water to cover, then set aside.

4 Place the onions in a non-stick frying pan, sprinkle with the sugar and add the stock. Bring to a boil, then cover and simmer over low heat for 20 minutes, or until soft, stirring occasionally. Stir in the béchamel sauce.

5 Preheat the oven to 220°C (425°F/gas 7) and grease a shallow baking dish with the butter. Drain the potatoes and pat dry with paper towel. Layer half the potato slices in the dish, spread half the onion mixture over the top, then repeat the layers with the remaining potatoes and onion mixture. Cover loosely with foil and bake for 30 minutes, then remove the foil and bake for a final 20 minutes, or until golden. Serve hot.

Potato and bacon gratin with cheese

Prepare the potatoes as directed above. Fry 100 g (3½ oz) finely diced lean bacon in 1 tablespoon butter until crisp. Add the onions and sauté briefly. Omit the sugar. Pour in the stock, cover and simmer for 20 minutes. Stir in the béchamel sauce. Layer the potatoes and onions in the prepared dish and bake for 30 minutes. Remove the foil and bake for 10 minutes, then sprinkle with ¾ cup (100 g/3½ oz) grated emmenthal or Swiss cheese and bake for 10 minutes more to melt the cheese.

Lyon-style potato gratin

Twice-baked stuffed sweet potatoes

1 Preheat the oven to 180°C (350°F/gas 4). Pierce each of 2 large orange sweet potatoes (about 750 g in total) twice with the tip of a knife. Place on a baking tray and bake until soft, about 50 minutes. Set aside until cool enough to handle but still very warm. Reduce heat to 160°C (315°F/gas 2–3). Cut potatoes in half lengthwise. Scoop out the flesh and place in a medium bowl, being careful not to tear the skin. Reserve skins.

2 To the potato flesh, add a 225 g (8 oz) can crushed pineapple, 1 tablespoon vegetable oil, 1 tablespoon butter, 1 tablespoon brown sugar, 1 teaspoon grated orange zest and ½ teaspoon salt. Whip with an electric mixer or whisk until slightly fluffy. Place skins on a baking tray and fill with the potato mixture, mounding it a little. Bake for 15 minutes. Sprinkle with pecans and bake for a final 15 minutes.

Note This recipe can be made up to a day ahead. Bake and stuff the potatoes as directed. Place in a shallow dish, cover loosely with plastic wrap and refrigerate. Remove from the refrigerator 30 minutes before baking as directed in the recipe.

Rösti with horseradish

400 g (14 oz) baking (floury) potatoes
1 egg, beaten
3 teaspoons horseradish cream from a jar
6 spring onions (scallions), finely chopped
salt and freshly ground black pepper
3 teaspoons vegetable oil
3 tablespoons crème fraîche or sour cream
chopped fresh parsley or chives to garnish

serves 4
preparation 10 minutes
cooking 8-12 minutes

per serving *775 kJ (185 calories), 5 g protein, 12 g total fat;*
6 g saturated fat, 15 g carbohydrate

1 Peel the potatoes and coarsely grate them into a large bowl of iced water. Leave to stand for 10 minutes. Drain the potatoes, then use your hands to squeeze out as much water as possible. Press dry with a clean tea towel (dish towel) and place in a bowl. Add the egg, horseradish cream, spring onions and salt and black pepper to taste and mix thoroughly.

2 Heat the oil in a large non-stick frying pan over medium heat. Drop eight mounds of the mixture into the pan and press down with the back of the spoon to make potato cakes 5 mm (¼ inch) thick.

3 Fry the rösti for 2-3 minutes on each side, or until firm and golden − you may need to cook the rösti in two batches. Drain well on paper towel and serve hot, topped with crème fraîche and garnished with parsley or chives.

Baking and desserts

The ever-adaptable potato deserves a place even on the dessert menu. The cakes, tortes, dumplings and pancakes in this chapter show the delicious versatility of this vegetable.

Potato bread

400 g (14 oz) baking (floury) potatoes,
    scrubbed and cut into chunks
5 $\frac{2}{3}$ cups (750 g/1 $\frac{1}{2}$ lb) strong flour, plus
    extra for kneading
1 teaspoon salt
7 g ($\frac{1}{6}$ oz) packet dried yeast (2 teaspoons)
1 tablespoon molasses
oil, for greasing

makes 2 small loaves
preparation 25 minutes + 1 hour rising
cooking 1 hour

per serving (8 serves) 1545 kJ (369 calories), 12 g protein,
1 g total fat, 0 g saturated fat, 77 g carbohydrate

Cook's tips

*Using the potato cooking water
in the dough not only increases the
potato flavour, but also retains the
water-soluble vitamins and minerals
that have seeped out into the liquid
during cooking.*

*Adding potato to bread dough greatly
improves the keeping qualities of
the loaf.*

1 Cook the potatoes in a saucepan of boiling water for
15 minutes, or until tender. Drain, reserving 300 ml (10 $\frac{1}{2}$ fl oz)
of the cooking water. When the potatoes are cool enough to
handle, peel them, mash until smooth, then leave to cool.

2 Sift 4 $\frac{3}{4}$ cups (600 g/1 lb 5 oz) of the flour into a large bowl
with the salt. Rub in the mashed potatoes with your fingertips
until well blended, then mix the yeast in well. Stir the molasses
into the reserved potato cooking water, add to the flour mixture
and mix well with your hands. Work in as much of the remaining
flour as needed to give a soft but not sticky dough.

3 Turn out onto a floured surface and knead for 5 minutes,
or until smooth and elastic. Place in a large oiled bowl, cover
with a clean tea towel (dish towel) and leave in a warm place
for 40 minutes, or until well risen.

4 Turn the dough out onto a floured surface. Gently punch
the dough down, then knead for about 3 minutes. Divide in
half and shape each piece into a small loaf. Place in two well-
greased 500 g (1 lb) loaf tins (bar pans), then cover and leave
to rise again for 20 minutes.

5 Meanwhile, preheat the oven to 180°C (350°F/gas 4).
Bake the loaves for 40-45 minutes, or until they are well risen
and brown, and sound hollow when tipped out of their pans
and tapped on the base. Turn out onto a wire rack to cool.
Store in an airtight container for up to 1 week.

Some more ideas...

✳ To make a heartier potato bread, replace half the
flour with wholemeal (whole wheat) flour.

✳ Replace 1 $\frac{2}{3}$ cups (200 g/7 oz) of the flour with rye
flour, and add 1 teaspoon lightly crushed caraway seeds
with the yeast.

Potato bread with rosemary

Cook and mash the potatoes as directed in the recipe opposite. Add 1 teaspoon finely chopped fresh rosemary to the potato dough at the end of step 2, then cover and leave to rise as in step 3. Meanwhile, sauté 1 finely chopped red onion in some olive oil for 5 minutes, then allow to cool. Knead the onion into the dough before shaping the bread loaves as in step 4, then bake as directed.

Potato bread

Potato scones

Potato scones with fetta

Replace the butter with ½ cup (75 g/2½ oz) finely crumbled fetta and knead
it into the flour mixture with 2 tablespoons chopped fresh chives. Finish the dough
as directed in step 3. Instead of the oatmeal, sprinkle the loaf with a mixture of
1 tablespoon plain (all-purpose) flour and a good pinch of sweet paprika.

Potato scones

1¾ cups (220 g/7¾ oz) self-raising flour,
   plus extra for kneading
¼ teaspoon mustard powder (dry mustard)
1½ teaspoons baking powder
¼ teaspoon salt
1½ tablespoons butter, chilled, plus extra
   for greasing
¾ cup (165 g/5¾ oz) cold mashed potatoes
   (with no added milk or butter)
3–5 tablespoons milk
milk or beaten egg, to glaze
2 teaspoons fine oatmeal, to sprinkle

makes 6 scone wedges
preparation 15 minutes
cooking 20 minutes

*per serving 829 kJ (198 calories), 6 g protein, 6 g total fat,
3 g saturated fat, 30 g carbohydrate*

1 Preheat the oven to 220°C (425°F/gas 7). Sift the flour, mustard powder and baking powder into a large bowl and add the salt. Rub in the butter with your fingertips until the mixture resembles fine breadcrumbs.

2 Put the mashed potatoes in another bowl and mix in 3 tablespoons milk. Add to the dry ingredients and stir with a fork, adding another 1–2 tablespoons milk if needed to make a soft dough.

3 Turn the dough out onto a floured surface and knead lightly for a few seconds until smooth, then roll out to a 15 cm (6 inch) round about 2 cm (¾ inch) thick. Place on a greased baking tray. Using a sharp knife, cut the top deeply to mark it into six wedges.

4 Brush with milk or beaten egg, then sprinkle with oatmeal. Bake for 15–20 minutes, or until well risen and golden brown.

5 Transfer to a wire rack and break into wedges. Serve warm or leave to cool. Store in an airtight container for up to 3 days.

Scones and biscuits

Scones are a type of quickbread originating in Scotland but popular throughout Britain and Ireland. They look similar to North American biscuits, but scones are made with cold butter and served, often topped with jam and cream, as a sweet snack with tea and coffee. Biscuits are more often made with shortening and served as a side bread, often for breakfast.

Some more ideas...

✳ You can also make the scones with sweet potato. Peel 1 sweet potato (about 200 g/7 oz), cut into chunks and boil for 15 minutes, or until soft. Drain, allow to steam briefly, then mash finely and use instead of the potato in the recipe above. Replace the mustard powder with ¼ teaspoon grated nutmeg.

✳ If you prefer, make individual scones. Roll the dough out as directed, then use a small cutter dipped in flour to cut out rounds of dough. Press straight down with the cutter; if you twist it, the scones will be ragged or slanted. Brush with milk or beaten egg and bake for 15 minutes, or until risen and golden brown. Serve hot.

Soft potato rolls

500 g (1 lb) unpeeled baking (floury) potatoes
½ cup (125 g/4 oz) sugar
⅔ cup (150 g/5 oz) butter, softened
2½ teaspoons salt
2 eggs
2 x 7 g (⅙ oz) packets dried yeast
　(4 teaspoons)
1⅓ cups (320 ml/11 fl oz) warm water
7 cups (850 g/1 lb 14 oz) plain (all-purpose)
　flour, approximately
oil, for greasing
jam, to serve (optional)

makes 45
preparation 45 minutes + 1½ hours resting
cooking 25 minutes

----

per serving *467 kJ (112 calories), 3 g protein, 3 g total fat,*
2 g saturated fat, 18 g carbohydrate

1　Scrub the potatoes and cook them in a saucepan of boiling water for 25-30 minutes, or until soft. Drain and allow to steam briefly. Peel the potatoes, place in a large bowl and mash finely using a potato masher. Leave to cool.

2　In a large bowl, mix the sugar and ½ cup (125 g/4 oz) butter, then stir in the cooled mashed potato, salt and eggs. Dissolve the yeast in half the warm water and stir into the potato mixture.

3　Add 2⅓ cups (300 g/10½ oz) flour and the remaining warm water and mix well to combine. Add enough of the remaining flour to make a smooth dough. Shape the dough into a ball, but do not knead. Place in an oiled bowl and turn to coat, then cover and leave to rise in a warm place for 1 hour, or until doubled in volume.

4　Grease three round ovenproof dishes with the remaining butter. Divide the dough into thirds and shape 15 little balls from each portion. Arrange five rolls in each dish, then cover and leave to rise in a warm place for another 30 minutes.

5　Preheat the oven to 190°C (375°F/gas 5). Bake the rolls for 20-25 minutes, or until golden. Remove from the oven and cool on wire racks. Serve with jam, if you like.

Yeast

Yeast is a living organism and is very sensitive to temperature. It thrives between 32°C and 46°C (90°F and 115°F) and will die in temperatures above 60°C (140°F). Yeast works by releasing gases when it is combined with liquid. These expand in the oven, causing the bread dough to rise.

Moist potato doughnuts

Moist potato doughnuts

1 Peel 500 g (1 lb) baking (floury) potatoes, chop and cook in a saucepan of boiling water for 15 minutes, or until soft. Pour ½ cup (125 ml/4 fl oz) of the cooking water into a large bowl. Drain off the remaining water, allow the potatoes to steam briefly, then finely mash with a fork. Dissolve 2 x 7 g (⅙ oz) packets (4 teaspoons) dried yeast in the reserved lukewarm potato water, then stir in the mashed potato, 320 ml (11 fl oz) warm milk, ½ cup (125 ml/4 fl oz) vegetable oil, ½ cup (100 g/3½ oz) sugar, 2 eggs and 1 teaspoon salt. Gradually mix in 8 cups (1 kg/2 lb) plain (all-purpose) flour to make a smooth dough. Shape into a ball, place in an oiled bowl and turn to coat. Cover and leave to rise in a warm place for 1 hour, or until doubled in volume. Gently punch the dough down, then cover and leave to rise for another 30 minutes.

2 Roll the dough out on a floured surface to a 1 cm (½ inch) thickness. Cut out rounds using an 8 cm (3¼ inch) cutter, then cut a hole in the centre of each. Heat a generous amount of vegetable oil to 170°C (325°F) in a deep-fryer or large saucepan. Cook the doughnuts in batches until golden, then drain well on paper towel. Mix 1¼ cups (150 g/5 oz) icing (confectioners') sugar with 2–3 tablespoons hot water and brush over the doughnuts.

Crunchy sweet potato rolls

Crunchy sweet potato rolls

2 unpeeled small sweet potatoes, about 350 g
  (12 oz) in total
2 French shallots, peeled and finely sliced
2 ²/₃ cups (350 g/12 oz) plain (all-purpose) flour,
  plus extra for kneading
oil, for greasing
3 tablespoons powdered milk
2 tablespoons soft brown sugar
7 g (¹/₆ oz) sachet dried yeast (2 teaspoons)
1¹/₂ teaspoons salt
¹/₂ cup (125 ml/4 fl oz) warm water
2 tablespoons extra virgin olive oil
3 tablespoons milk

makes 12
preparation 45 minutes + 1³/₄ hours resting
cooking 1 hour

*per serving 712 kJ (170 calories), 5 g protein, 4 g total fat,
1 g saturated fat, 28 g carbohydrate*

1 Cook the sweet potatoes in a saucepan of boiling water for 25-30 minutes, or until soft. Drain and allow to steam briefly. Peel the sweet potatoes, place in a large bowl and mash finely using a potato masher.

2 Stir in the shallots, flour, milk powder, sugar, yeast and salt. Add the water and oil and combine well. Knead the dough thoroughly on a floured surface, adding a little more flour if the dough is too sticky. Place in an oiled bowl and turn to coat. Cover and leave to rise in a warm place for 45 minutes, or until doubled in volume.

3 Thoroughly knead the dough again, then cover and leave to rise for an additional 45 minutes.

4 Line a baking tray with baking (parchment) paper. Divide the dough into 12 even portions and shape them into rolls. Place them on the baking tray, then cover and leave to rise for a final 15 minutes.

5 Preheat the oven to 180°C (350°F/gas 4). Brush the rolls with milk and bake for 30 minutes, or until golden brown. The rolls are ready when they sound slightly hollow when tapped with a knife. Leave to cool on a wire rack for at least 15 minutes before eating. Serve warm or cold.

Sweet potato rolls with sultanas

Cook and mash 2 small sweet potatoes as directed above. Replace the French shallots with 1 heaped tablespoon sultanas (golden raisins). Stir the sultanas into the mashed sweet potatoes, then continue as directed. Serve the rolls with jam.

Potato and almond torte

350 g (12 oz) unpeeled small baking (floury)
    potatoes
butter, for greasing
8 eggs, separated
1 scant cup (200 g/7 oz) sugar
1½ cups (150 g/5 oz) ground almonds
finely grated zest and juice of ½ lemon
2 tablespoons potato starch
icing (confectioners') sugar, for dusting

makes 12 slices
preparation 45 minutes + overnight resting
cooking 1 hour 15 minutes

*per serving 859 kJ (205 calories), 8 g protein,
10 g total fat, 1 g saturated fat, 22 g carbohydrate*

1 Cook the potatoes in a saucepan of boiling water for 20 minutes, or until just soft. Drain, allow to steam briefly, then peel. While the potatoes are still warm, squeeze them through a potato press (see below) into a bowl. Leave to dry, uncovered, in a well-ventilated place overnight.

2 Preheat the oven to 180°C (350°F/gas 4). Grease a 24 cm (9½ inch) springform cake tin (pan). Using electric beaters, whisk the egg yolks and sugar to a thick foam. Stir in the almonds, lemon zest and lemon juice, then gradually add the dried potatoes. Fold in the sifted potato starch.

3 Beat the egg whites until stiff, then fold them into the cake mixture. Spoon the dough into the cake pan, smoothing the surface. Bake on the lowest rack of the oven for 1¼ hours, or until the torte is golden and a skewer inserted into the centre comes out clean.

4 Remove from the oven and leave to cool in the pan for 10 minutes before removing from the pan and cooling on a wire rack. Before serving, dust with icing sugar and cut into 12 slices.

Cook's tip

To stop it from collapsing, this mixture needs to be baked as soon as it is prepared, so ensure the oven is fully preheated and the cake pan greased before the dough is made.

Potato press

If you often cook potato dishes, a potato press (or potato ricer) is a useful gadget. It resembles a large garlic press, and crushes whole, cooked potatoes, extruding them in a light snow. A potato press can be used instead of a potato masher to make mashed potatoes. It is also good for gnocchi. Potato presses are available at kitchenware stores or may be purchased online.

Potato and sultana torte

Potato and sultana torte

1 Cook 250 g (8 oz) baking (floury) potatoes as directed in the recipe opposite, squeeze them through a potato press (potato ricer) into a bowl and leave overnight.

2 Preheat the oven to 200°C (400°F/gas 6). Grease a 24 cm (9½ inch) springform cake tin (pan) and coat it with dry breadcrumbs. In a small bowl, soak ½ cup (60 g/2¼ oz) sultanas (golden raisins) in 4 tablespoons rum for 20 minutes. In another bowl, combine 4 eggs, 1 scant cup (200 g/7 oz) sugar, the zest and juice of ½ lemon and 1 pinch salt. Stir until frothy, then add the potatoes. In another bowl, combine ½ cup (75 g/2½ oz) plain (all-purpose) flour, 1¼ cups (125 g/4 oz) ground almonds, 2 tablespoons potato starch and 1 tablespoon baking powder. Fold into the potato mixture with the drained sultanas. Spoon the dough into the pan, smoothing the surface.

3 Bake on the middle rack of the oven for 1 hour, or until the torte is golden and a skewer inserted into the centre comes out clean. Remove from the oven and leave to cool in the pan for 10 minutes, then remove from the pan and cool on a wire rack. While the torte is still warm, mix together 1⅔ cups (200 g/7 oz) finely sifted icing (confectioners') sugar, 2 tablespoons hot water and 2 tablespoons rum. Pour this icing (frosting) over the warm torte and cut into 12 slices before serving.

Swiss potato and nut cake

Swiss potato and nut cake

butter, for greasing
2 eggs
$\frac{1}{2}$ cup (100 g/3$\frac{1}{2}$ oz) sugar
2 tablespoons water
$\frac{1}{2}$ teaspoon finely grated lemon zest
1 small all-purpose potato (about 50 g/1$\frac{3}{4}$ oz),
    boiled, peeled and finely grated
$\frac{1}{2}$ cup (50 g/1$\frac{3}{4}$ oz) finely ground hazelnuts
$\frac{1}{3}$ cup (50 g/1$\frac{3}{4}$ oz) fine polenta (cornmeal)
2 teaspoons baking powder
1 pinch salt
icing (confectioners') sugar for dusting

makes 8 slices
preparation 15 minutes
baking 45 minutes

per serving 514 kJ (123 calories), 3 g protein, 4 g total fat,
1 g saturated fat, 18 g carbohydrate

1 Preheat the oven to 170°C (325°F/gas 3) and grease a 22 cm (8$\frac{1}{2}$ inch) springform cake tin (pan).

2 Using an electric beater, whisk the eggs, sugar, water and lemon zest for 3-4 minutes, or until pale and foamy. Fold in the potato and ground hazelnuts.

3 In a bowl, mix together the polenta, baking powder and salt, then stir into the egg mixture. Spoon the dough into the cake pan, smoothing the surface.

4 Bake on the lower rack of the oven for 35-45 minutes, or until golden. Remove from the oven and leave to cool briefly, then remove from the pan and cool on a wire rack. Serve dusted with icing sugar.

Storage tip

If you wrap the cooled cake in foil, it will stay fresh for 2-3 days.

Cottage cheese dumplings

1 Soak $\frac{3}{4}$ cup (100 g/3$\frac{1}{2}$ oz) sultanas (golden raisins) in 4 tablespoons rum for 20 minutes, stirring occasionally. Cook 750 g (1$\frac{1}{2}$ lb) baking (floury) potatoes in boiling water for 20 minutes, or until just soft. Drain, allow to steam briefly, then peel. While the potatoes are still warm, squeeze them through a potato press (potato ricer) into a bowl. Allow to cool, then dust with $\frac{2}{3}$ cup (100 g/ 3$\frac{1}{2}$ oz) plain (all-purpose) flour. Mix in 300 g (10$\frac{1}{2}$ oz) cottage cheese or other curd cheese, 3 eggs, 4 tablespoons sugar, 1 pinch salt and $\frac{1}{2}$ teaspoon ground cinnamon. Stir in the grated zest of $\frac{1}{2}$ lemon and the sultanas and rum.

2 Melt some butter in a frying pan over medium heat. Form tablespoonfuls of the mixture into small dumplings. Working in batches, place the dumplings in the hot pan (not too close together) and flatten lightly with a spatula. Fry for 5–7 minutes on both sides, until golden brown. Keep warm until all the dumplings are cooked, then arrange the hot dumplings on a serving platter. Serve sprinkled with 3 tablespoons sugar and 1 teaspoon ground cinnamon.

Potato and cherry torte

250 g (8 oz) unpeeled small baking (floury)
　　potatoes
dry breadcrumbs, for coating
1 tablespoon butter
1 cup (200 g/7 oz) soft brown sugar
3 eggs
½ cup (50 g/1¾ oz) ground hazelnuts
1 tablespoon plain (all-purpose) flour
1 teaspoon baking powder
1 pinch salt

to decorate

1 cup (300 g/10½ oz) cherry jam
1¼ cups (150 g/5 oz) icing (confectioners')
　　sugar
1 teaspoon rosewater
200 g (7 oz) marzipan paste
1½ cups (200 g/7 oz) chopped white
　　chocolate
1 tablespoon white vegetable shortening,
　　such as Crisco or Copha
¼ cup (30 g/1 oz) chopped dark chocolate

makes　16 slices
preparation　45 minutes + overnight resting
cooking　55 minutes

----

per serving　*1242 kJ (297 calories), 4 g protein,*
12 g total fat, 5 g saturated fat, 45 g carbohydrate

Cook's tips

*Slice the torte using a knife that
has been briefly dipped in hot water,
then wiped dry; otherwise, the
chocolate coating might break when
cut. Repeat after cutting each slice.*

----

*Traditionally, this torte uses jam
made from morello cherries (a type
of sour cherry).*

1 Cook the potatoes in a saucepan of boiling water for
20 minutes, or until soft. Drain, allow to steam briefly, then
peel. While the potatoes are still warm, squeeze them through
a potato press into a bowl. Cover and leave overnight.

2 Preheat the oven to 180°C (350°F/gas 4). Grease a
26 cm (10½ inch) springform cake tin (pan) and coat it with
breadcrumbs, tipping out the excess.

3 Add the butter, sugar and eggs to the potatoes and
whisk using electric beaters for 4–5 minutes, or until frothy.
In another bowl, mix together the ground hazelnuts, flour,
baking powder and salt, then stir into the potato mixture.

4 Spoon the dough into the cake pan, smoothing the surface.
Bake for 35 minutes, or until a skewer inserted into the centre
of the torte comes out clean.

5 Remove from the oven and leave to cool briefly, then
remove from the pan and cool on a wire rack. Cut the torte
horizontally into two halves. Spread two-thirds of the cherry
jam on the bottom half, place the other half on top and press
down lightly.

6 Heat the remaining cherry jam in a small saucepan.
Strain it through a sieve, then brush it over the torte.

7 Knead the icing sugar and rosewater into the marzipan
paste. Between two pieces of plastic wrap, roll out the paste to
a circle about 34 cm (13½ inches) across. Remove the top piece
of plastic, then use the bottom piece to place the circle on top
of the cake. Gently press the marzipan cover onto the top and
sides, then cut off the overhanging bits.

8 Melt the white chocolate over a hot water bath, then stir
in the vegetable shortening. Cover the cake with the mixture
and let the coating set. Put the dark chocolate in a freezer bag,
seal well and place in a hot water bath until it has melted. Cut
a small corner off the freezer bag and decorate the torte with
fine lines of dark chocolate. Chill the torte until ready to serve.

Potato and cherry torte

Potato crêpes with mixed berry cream cheese

1 Stir together 1¼ cups (300 g/10½ oz) softened cream cheese, the juice of 1 orange and 4 tablespoons maple syrup, or to taste. Select 300 g (10½ oz) mixed berries, such as blackberries, strawberries and raspberries. Wash only if necessary; dry well. If using strawberries, hull them, then cut the larger ones into quarters and smaller ones in half. Reserve some berries for garnishing, and carefully fold the rest through the cream cheese mixture, using a wooden spoon. Beat 150 ml (5 fl oz) whipping cream until stiff, then gently fold into the berry mixture. Cover with plastic wrap and chill for at least 1 hour.

2 Meanwhile, cook 750 g (1½ lb) unpeeled baking (floury) potatoes in a saucepan of boiling water for 20–30 minutes, or until soft. Drain, allow to steam briefly, then peel. While still warm, squeeze them through a potato press onto a work surface and leave to cool slightly. Mix together 1¼ cups (300 g/10½ oz) ricotta, 3 tablespoons plain (all-purpose) flour, 2 eggs and 1 tablespoon sugar. Press a little hollow into the middle of the mashed potato, add the ricotta mixture and quickly knead until smooth and fluffy. Melt some butter in a frying pan over medium heat. Working in batches, add tablespoonfuls of the potato mixture to the hot pan. Flatten with a spatula into round cakes about 1 cm (½ inch) thick and fry for 5–7 minutes on both sides, until golden brown. Keep warm while cooking the remaining pancakes. Serve hot, with the mixed berry cream cheese on the side, garnished with some reserved berries.

Potato and cherry soufflés

Apricot dumplings

1 Cook 1 kg (2 lb) unpeeled baking (floury) potatoes in a saucepan of boiling water
for 25–30 minutes, or until soft. Drain, peel and, while still warm, squeeze through
a potato press (potato ricer) into a bowl, then leave to cool. Mix in 1⅔ cups (200 g/
7 oz) plain (all-purpose) flour, 2 eggs, 1 pinch salt, ½ teaspoon ground cinnamon
and 2 tablespoons melted butter. Shape the dough into a roll about 5 cm (2 inches)
thick, then cut into 16 slices. Flatten into circles about 10 cm (4 inches) across. Cut
16 small ripe apricots in half and remove the stones. Place 1 sugar cube in 16 of the
halves, then cover with the other halves. Place one apricot on each dough circle and
fold the dough around it. Using wet hands, shape into round dumplings.

2 Bring a large pot of lightly salted water to a boil. Add the dumplings and cook
over low heat for 10–15 minutes, or until they rise to the surface. Remove using
a slotted spoon and drain. Meanwhile, heat ½ cup (125 g/4½ oz) butter in a small
saucepan, add 4 tablespoons dry breadcrumbs and fry until golden. Turn batches
of dumplings in the crumbs, dust with icing (confectioner's) sugar and serve hot.

Potato and cherry soufflés

250 g (8 oz) unpeeled baking (floury) potatoes
melted butter, for greasing
4 teaspoons dry breadcrumbs
scant ½ cup (90 g/3¼ oz) sugar
4 eggs, separated
150 g (5 oz) cherries, pitted and chopped
3 tablespoons sultanas (golden raisins)
1 pinch salt
3 tablespoons icing (confectioners') sugar
100 ml (3½ fl oz) pure (light/single) cream
3 tablespoons kirsch or cherry liqueur

serves 4
preparation 40 minutes
cooking 55 minutes

per serving *1822 kJ (435 calories), 9 g protein,*
15 g total fat, 8 g saturated fat, 58 g carbohydrate

1 Cook the potatoes in a saucepan of boiling water for 20 minutes, or until soft. Drain, allow to steam briefly, then peel. While the potatoes are still warm, squeeze them through a potato press into a bowl, then leave to cool for a while.

2 Meanwhile, preheat the oven to 180°C (350°F/gas 4). Brush four small soufflé dishes (about 10 cm/4 inches in diameter) with the melted butter, then sprinkle each with 1 teaspoon breadcrumbs. Tilt the dishes and rotate them so that the crumbs cling to the insides of the dishes.

3 In a bowl, mix the sugar with 2 egg yolks until frothy, then fold into the potato mash. Stir in the cherries and sultanas.

4 Beat the egg whites with a pinch of salt until stiff. Fold one-quarter of the egg whites into the potato mixture to loosen it a little, then gently fold the remaining egg whites through. Quickly spoon the mixture into the soufflé dishes, smooth the tops and bake for 30–35 minutes, until golden brown.

5 Meanwhile, bring some water to a boil in a large saucepan, then set a metal bowl over the water, ensuring that the base of the bowl does not touch the water. Add the remaining egg yolks to the bowl and whisk until frothy. Gradually add the icing sugar, cream and kirsch and beat until frothy. Set aside.

6 When the soufflés are done, remove them from the oven and invert onto dessert plates. Spread some kirsch sauce around the base and serve the remaining sauce separately.

Cook's tip
If fresh cherries are out of season, use well-drained canned cherries. The syrup from the cherries can replace some or all of the kirsch, if you like.

Index

a

African lamb ragoût with okra 166
aïoli 213
American-style cottage pie 124
anchovy dressing 102
apples 23
  chicken and apple pie 170
  pork and apple salad with hazelnuts 105
apricot dumplings 312
Argentine beef stew 148
artichokes
  potato, artichoke and pancetta salad 96
  warm potato salad with artichokes 97
asparagus 248
  asparagus with herb butter topping 290
  new potatoes with asparagus 286
  potato and asparagus salad 88
  potato tart with asparagus 248
aubergine *see* eggplant
avocados
  potato and avocado salad with prawns 101
  preparing 101

b

bacon
  chicken with potatoes and bacon 188
  liver and bacon casserole with potato crust 152
  mashed potatoes with bacon 128
  potato and bacon gratin with cheese 292
  potato, bacon and leeks on rosemary skewers 282
  potato and bacon salad 95
  potato, bacon and spinach chowder 63
  potato and parmesan soup with bacon 69
  potato soup with bacon gnocchi 69
  Swiss rösti with bacon 274
baked potatoes 17, 28
  baked potato quarters with smoked salmon 32
  baked potatoes au gratin 275
  baked potatoes with caviar 33
  cooking 290
  oven-baked spicy potato wedges 53
  toppings for 290-1
  twice-baked stuffed sweet potatoes 294
banana raita 60
bangers and mash 161

barbecue
  barbecued potato and sausage packet 116
  barbecued potatoes and zucchini 276
  cheesy barbecued potatoes 276
basil 250
beans
  lamb stew with green beans 166
  new potatoes with green beans 286
  potato curry with green beans 273
  sausage and bean casserole with potato and parsnip topping 134
  sausage casserole with green beans 134
  tuna salad with green beans 84
beef
  American-style cottage pie 124
  Argentine beef stew 148
  beef and capsicum hotpot 124
  beef hotpot with small potato dumplings 151
  beef and mushroom hotpot 151
  Belgian potato hotpot 127
  bolognese beef casserole 144
  borsch with beef 76
  Indian beef and potato curry 169
  Japanese potato and meat croquettes 155
  meat and potato turnovers 115
  meatballs with spinach 168
  pan-fried potatoes and beef 173
  pot-au-feu 181
  potato salad with bresaola 83
beetroot 44, 87
  borsch with beef 76
  borsch with mashed potatoes and vegetables 77
  potato and beetroot chips with peanut dip 44
  root vegetable salad with spicy vinaigrette 87
  warm new potato salad with beetroot and pastrami 82
Belgian potato hotpot 127
bell peppers *see* capsicums
blight, potato 13, 15
blue cheese 120
  chicken and blue cheese gratin 120
boiled potatoes 17, 24
  caraway potatoes 279
  chicken and potato hash 182
  potato salad with caramelised carrots 86
  potatoes with herb dressing 278
  potatoes with leeks and curd cheese 279
  sesame and coriander potatoes 278
bolognese beef casserole 144

borsch with beef 76
borsch with mashed potatoes and vegetables 77
bouquet garni 181
breadcrumbs 186
breads
  crunchy sweet potato rolls 305
  potato bread 298
  potato bread with rosemary 299
  soft potato rolls 302
  sweet potato rolls with sultanas 305
bresaola 83
  potato salad with 83
broad beans
  double peeling 253
  pasta with potato, beans and pesto 253
brussels sprouts
  potato and brussels sprout salad 98
  potatoes and brussels sprouts with mustard dressing 281
bubble and squeak with poached eggs 254
Burbank, Luther 15

c

cabbage
  chicken and apple pie 170
  colcannon 170
  fish pie with cabbage and mashed potatoes 205
  Irish stew with savoy cabbage 141
  pot-au-feu 181
  smoked fish hash with savoy cabbage 230
Cajun-style potato salad 92
cake
  Swiss potato and nut 309
  see also torte
capsicums 116
  barbecued potato and sausage packet 116
  beef and capsicum hotpot 124
  potato, celery and capsicum salad 109
cardamom 147
carrots 140
  carrot chutney 60
  potato and carrot patties 40
  potato salad with caramelised carrots 86
  sweet potato, carrot and celeriac patties 41
casseroles
  bolognese beef casserole 144
  braised garlic chicken casserole 143
  fish casserole with pesto potatoes 204
  potato and tomato casserole 265

tomato and chicken casserole 143
see also hotpots
charlottes, potato, with smoked trout 223
cheese
    cheesy barbecued potatoes 276
    cottage cheese dumplings 309
    fish, pea and cheesy potato bake 232
    mashed potatoes with mozzarella 128
    pasta with potato and goat's cheese 252
    potato and bacon gratin with cheese 292
    potato crêpes with mixed berry cream cheese 311
    potato and emmenthal quiche 245
    potato and parmesan soup with bacon 69
    spinach and cheese topping 291
    vegetables with cheese crumble 260
    vegetables with melted brie dressing 247
    see also blue cheese; curd cheese; fetta cheese
cherries
    potato and cherry soufflés 313
    potato and cherry torte 310
chicken
    baked chicken pieces with spicy potatoes 186
    braised garlic chicken casserole 143
    chicken and apple pie 170
    chicken and blue cheese gratin 120
    chicken curry with eggplant 119
    chicken and potato curry 174
    chicken and potato hash 182
    chicken with potatoes and bacon 188
    chicken with potatoes and vegetables 186
    chicken and sweet potato hash 185
    Malaysian chicken curry 174
    pot-au-feu 181
    potato pizza with chicken and rocket 189
    tarragon chicken with creamy vegetables 121
    Thai chicken curry 119
    tomato and chicken casserole 143
chickpea pie with parmesan and tomato mashed potatoes 258
chillies 273
chimichurri pork skewers 146
chips (crisps)
    potato and beetroot chips with peanut dip 44
chips (fries) 17, 26
chives, cutting 84
chorizo
    potato and celeriac purée with seared scallops and chorizo 225
    potato pizza with tuna, chorizo and black olives 203
chuños 10, 11
cilantro 239
clams
    clam and leek chowder 64

coconut prawn and vegetable curry 229
colcannon 170
coriander 239
coriander sauce 239
corn *see* sweetcorn
courgette *see* zucchini
creamy potato and chanterelle soup 71
creamy potato and clam soup 64
creamy potatoes with leeks 281
creole stew 148
crêpes
    potato crêpes with herb curd cheese 262
    potato crêpes with mixed berry cream cheese 311
crisps *see* chips
croquettes
    fish and potato croquettes 217
    Japanese potato and meat croquettes 155
    potato croquettes 155
cucumber
    cucumber sauce 200
    potato and cucumber salad 92
curd cheese 262
    potato crepes with herb curd cheese 262
    potatoes with leeks and curd cheese 279
curry
    chicken curry with eggplant 119
    chicken and potato curry 174
    coconut prawn and vegetable curry 229
    curried vegetable triangles 46
    Indian beef and potato curry 169
    Malaysian chicken curry 174
    mushroom and potato curry 266
    pork korma with potatoes and spinach 147
    potato curry with green beans 273
    sweet potato curry 267
    Thai chicken curry 119
curry paste 230
curry powder 230

d
dips
    radish and yogurt dip 45
    spicy peanut dip 44
    tomato, garlic and basil dip 45
doughnuts 303
Drake, Sir Francis 11
duck breast with mashed potatoes 112
dumplings
    apricot dumplings 312
    beef hotpot with small potato dumplings 151
    cottage cheese dumplings 309
    potato dumplings 25, 154
    potato and semolina dumplings 154

e
eggplant 136
    chicken curry with eggplant 119
    moussaka 136

f
famines 13
fan potatoes 29
fennel 102
    crushed potatoes flavoured with fennel seeds 285
    potato, fennel and zucchini frittata 237
fetta cheese
    fresh sage, rocket and fetta sauce 251
    potato scones with fetta 300
    potato tortilla with fetta 254
fish
    baked fish fillets with gremolata 211
    fish boulangère 228
    fish casserole with pesto potatoes 204
    fish with gremolata crust and saffron mashed potatoes 211
    fish and mushroom pie with mashed potato crust 233
    fish and parsley sauce with mashed potatoes, leek and zucchini 208
    fish, pea and cheesy potato bake 232
    fish pie with cabbage and mashed potatoes 205
    fish soup with spring vegetables 74
    fish and vegetable soup 74
    fisherman's stew 221
    foil-cooked trout with roast potatoes and cucumber sauce 200
    grilled sole with new potatoes 215
    herb-crumbed fish with oven-baked wedges 207
    Indian-style fish 199
    Indian-style salmon fillets 199
    ocean perch with oven potatoes 201
    oily fish 204, 221
    Portuguese-style fish stew 222
    potato charlottes with smoked trout 223
    potato pizza with sardines 202
    smoked fish and potato pie 226
    Thai fish cakes with lime and honey dip 196
    white fish 200, 204, 221
    see also fish cakes; salmon; smoked fish; tuna
fish cakes
    baked salmon fish cakes with parsley sauce 217
    fish and potato croquettes 217
    potato and fish patties with pesto 216
    salmon cakes with creamy tomato and garlic sauce 216
    salt cod fritters 217
fish, cooking 208
fish, storing 221
fisherman's stew 221

Florentine potatoes 285
floury varieties 17, 19, 22
frittata
    frittata with corn and capsicum 236
    potato, fennel and zucchini frittata 237
    potato and spinach frittata 42
frying 26

g

gado gado 80
garlic 143
    braised garlic chicken casserole 143
    garlic mayonnaise 213
    spiced garlic and ginger potatoes 178
    yogurt garlic sauce 185
ginger 266
    mango and ginger salsa 47
    spiced garlic and ginger potatoes 178
    stir-fried potatoes with lamb and ginger
        193
globe artichokes 97
gnocchi
    potato soup with bacon gnocchi 69
    sauces for 250-1
gratin
    baked potatoes au gratin 275
    Lyon-style potato gratin 292
    potato and bacon gratin with cheese
        292
    potato gratin 29
    potato and pumpkin gratin 257
Greek-style braised lamb and potatoes 177

h

ham and potato salad 95
hash
    chicken and sweet potato hash 185
    potato hash with mushrooms 184
    salmon hash with broccoli and peas 231
    smoked fish hash with savoy cabbage
        230
hash browns
    baked hash browns with parmesan 265
    sweet potato hash browns 41
herbs
    herb-crumbed fish with oven-baked
        wedges 207
    herbed mashed potatoes 215
    new potato salad with herb cream 94
    potato wedges with herbs 179
    potatoes with herb dressing 278
hotpots
    beef and capsicum hotpot 124
    beef hotpot with small potato
        dumplings 151
    beef and mushroom hotpot 151
    Belgian potato hotpot 127
    seafood hotpot with saffron and
        vegetables 212
    see also casseroles

i

Idaho potato 15
Indian beef and potato curry 169
Indian-style fish 199
Ireland, famine 13
Irish stew 140
    with savoy cabbage 141

j

jacket potatoes 28
Japanese potato and meat croquettes 155
jerusalem artichokes 21

k

kippers 59
    corn and kipper chowder 59
kumara see sweet potatoes

l

lamb
    African lamb ragoût with okra 166
    Greek-style braised lamb and potatoes
        177
    Irish stew 140
    lamb stew with green beans 166
    roast lamb with zucchini 176
    shepherd's pie 190
    spiced lamb pie with potato topping
        122
    stir-fried potatoes with lamb and ginger
        193
    tex-mex shepherd's pie 158
leeks
    chicken and blue cheese gratin 120
    clam and leek chowder 64
    creamy potatoes with leeks 281
    leek and mustard mashed potatoes 162
    leek and potato topping 170
    pot-au-feu 181
    potato, bacon and leeks on rosemary
        skewers 282
    potato and leek quiche with chilli crust
        244
    potatoes with leeks and curd cheese
        279
    vichyssoise 66
leeks, preparing 162
lemongrass, preparing 196
lentils
    potato and lentil salad 91
    potato and lentil salad with fried onions
        91
    sausage with puy lentils and mashed
        potatoes and pumpkin 165
    spicy lentil dal 60
leprosy 12
light mashed potatoes 129

limes
    juicing 119
    lime and honey dipping sauce 196
liver
    liver and bacon casserole with potato
        crust 152
    liver and mushroom casserole 153
    preparing/cooking 152
Lyon-style potato gratin 292

m

Malaysian chicken curry 174
mango and ginger salsa 47
mango, preparing 47
manioc 21
marinades 139
mashed potatoes 17, 25
    American-style cottage pie 124
    bangers and mash 161
    borsch with mashed potatoes and
        vegetables 77
    chickpea pie with parmesan and tomato
        mashed potatoes 258
    duck breast with mashed potatoes 112
    fish casserole with pesto potatoes 204
    fish with gremolata crust and saffron
        mashed potatoes 211
    fish and mushroom pie with mashed
        potato crust 233
    fish and parsley sauce with mashed
        potatoes, leek and zucchini 208
    fish pie with cabbage and mashed
        potatoes 205
    herbed mashed potatoes 215
    light mashed potatoes 129
    mashed potatoes with bacon 128
    mashed potatoes with mozzarella 128
    pepper steak with mashed potatoes
        and leeks 162
    sausage and bean casserole with
        potato and parsnip topping 134
    sausage casserole with green beans 134
    sausage with puy lentils and mashed
        potatoes and pumpkin 165
    seared pork fillet with cumquats and
        mashed potatoes 112
    shepherd's pie 190
    spiced lamb pie with potato topping
        122
    spicy pork and bacon pie with potato
        topping 123
    tex-mex shepherd's pie 158
meat
    Japanese potato and meat croquettes
        155
    meat and potato turnovers 115
    meatballs with spinach 168
    see also beef; lamb; pork; veal
meat, marinating 139
moist potato doughnuts 303
Moroccan sweet potato soup 56
moussaka 136
    potato moussaka 261

mushrooms 266
 beef and mushroom hotpot 151
 creamy potato and chanterelle soup 71
 fish and mushroom pie with mashed potato crust 233
 liver and mushroom casserole 153
 mushroom and potato curry 266
 mushroom and zucchini topping 291
 potato hash with mushrooms 184
 potato and mushroom quiche 256
 spinach, sweet potato and shiitake salad 106
mustard dressing 281

n

new potatoes 17, 23, 133
 Cajun-style potato salad 92
 fish, pea and cheesy potato bake 232
 Greek-style braised lamb and potatoes 177
 grilled sole with new potatoes 215
 Indian-style fish 199
 new potato salad with herb cream 94
 new potatoes with asparagus 286
 new potatoes with lemon and rosemary 179
 new potatoes with nori 286
 pan-fried potatoes and beef 173
 pork and pear salad with pecans 105
 roast new potatoes with thyme 178
 seafood hotpot with saffron and vegetables 212
 warm new potato salad with beetroot and pastrami 82
 warm potato salad with artichokes 97
new potatoes, cleaning 24
nori 286
 new potatoes with 286
nuts
 pork and apple salad with hazelnuts 105
 pork and pear salad with pecans 105
 potato and beetroot chips with peanut dip 44
 Swiss potato and nut cake 309

o

okra, African lamb ragoût with 166
old potatoes 17
olive and tomato topping 291
onions
 pan-grilled steak and potatoes 130
 potato and lentil salad with fried onions 91
 potato and onion soup topped with garlic prawns 66
 potato salad with spring onions 95
organic potatoes 23
oven-baked spicy potato wedges 53

p

pan-fried potatoes 26
pan-fried potatoes and beef 173
pan-fried potatoes with veal 131
pan-grilled steak and potatoes 130
pancakes, potato 27
 see also crêpes
paprika 289
parmesan, grating 69
parsnip and potato topping 190
pasta with potato and goat's cheese 252
pastries
 curried vegetable triangles 46
 meat and potato turnovers 115
 potato and zucchini turnovers 115
 spicy filo triangles 47
patatas bravas 289
patties
 potato and carrot patties 40
 potato patties with smoked salmon 40
 potato and sage patties 53
 potato and spinach cakes 39
 potato and zucchini patties 41
 sweet potato, carrot and celeriac patties 41
 vegetable patties with coriander sauce 239
peanut sauce 80
pepper steak with mashed potatoes and leeks 162
pies
 American-style cottage pie 124
 chicken and apple pie 170
 potato pie with tomatoes and olives 244
 seafood pie with potato pastry 218
 shepherd's pie 190
 smoked fish and potato pie 226
 spiced lamb pie with potato topping 122
 spicy pork and bacon pie with potato topping 123
 tex-mex shepherd's pie 158
 venison and mushroom pie with sweet potato topping 157
pizzas
 potato pizza with chicken and rocket 189
 potato pizza with sardines 202
 potato pizza with tuna, chorizo and black olives 203
pizzas, cooking 189
pork
 chimichurri pork skewers 146
 pork and apple salad with hazelnuts 105
 pork korma with potatoes and spinach 147
 pork and pear salad with pecans 105
 seared pork fillet with cumquats and mashed potatoes 112
 spicy pork and bacon pie with potato topping 123

Portuguese-style fish stew 222
pot-au-feu 181
potato press (ricer) 306
potato salads, best varieties for 17
potatoes
 botany 12, 14
 breeding 15
 freeze-dried 11
 history 10–11, 12
 nutrients 14
 peeling 133
 selecting 22
 skins 133
 storage 23
 types 17
 and vitamin C 56
prawns
 coconut prawn and vegetable curry 229
 potato and avocado salad with prawns 101
 potato and onion soup topped with garlic prawns 66
puffs, potato 155
pumpkin 257
 potato and pumpkin gratin 257
 potato and pumpkin soufflé 263
 sausage with puy lentils and mashed potatoes and pumpkin 165
puy lentils 165

q

quality checks 22
quiches
 potato and emmenthal quiche 245
 potato and leek quiche with chilli crust 244
 potato and mushroom quiche 256

r

radicchio, potato salad with 109
radish and yogurt dip 45
raita 169
ravioli
 folded potato ravioli 241
 ravioli with potato filling 240
risotto 48
 sweet potato risotto with crisp sage 48
roast potatoes 17, 28
 foil-cooked trout with roast potatoes and cucumber sauce 200
 new potatoes with lemon and rosemary 179
 ocean perch with oven potatoes 201
 potato wedges with herbs 179
 roast new potatoes with thyme 178
 roast root vegetables 179
 roasted potato salad with cumin and yogurt dressing 36

roast potatoes *continued*
    spiced garlic and ginger potatoes 178
    vegetables with melted brie dressing
        247
root vegetables
    roast root vegetables 179
    roasted vegetable crumble 243
    root vegetable salad with spicy
        vinaigrette 87
rösti 27
    potato rösti 27
    rösti with horseradish 295
    Swiss rösti with bacon 274
russet burbank 15
Russian potato salad 88
rutabagas *see* swedes

S

saffron 212
salad leaves, refreshing 36
salad potatoes 17
salads
    Cajun-style potato salad 92
    gado gado 80
    new potato salad with herb cream 94
    pork and apple salad with hazelnuts 105
    pork and pear salad with pecans 105
    potato, artichoke and pancetta salad
        96
    potato and asparagus salad 88
    potato and avocado salad with prawns
        101
    potato and bacon salad 95
    potato and brussels sprout salad 98
    potato, celery and capsicum salad 109
    potato and cucumber salad 92
    potato and ham salad 95
    potato and lentil salad 91
    potato and lentil salad with fried onions
        91
    potato salad with bresaola 83
    potato salad with caramelised carrots
        86
    potato salad with radicchio 109
    potato salad with spring onions 95
    potato and tuna salad 84
    potato and turkey salad with mustard
        dressing 94
    roasted potato salad with cumin and
        yogurt dressing 36
    root vegetable salad with spicy
        vinaigrette 87
    Russian potato salad 88
    salad niçoise 102
    spinach, sweet potato and shiitake
        salad 106
    sweet potato salad with mushrooms 106
    tuna salad with green beans 84
    warm new potato salad with beetroot
        and pastrami 82
    warm potato salad with artichokes 97
    warm potato and spring vegetable
        salad 98

salmon 32
    baked potato quarters with smoked
        salmon 32
    baked salmon fillets with gremolata 211
    baked salmon fish cakes with parsley
        sauce 217
    Indian-style salmon fillets 199
    potato patties with smoked salmon 40
    salmon cakes with creamy tomato and
        garlic sauce 216
    salmon hash with broccoli and peas 231
salt cod fritters 217
sardines, potato pizza with 202
sauces
    coriander sauce 239
    cucumber sauce 200
    mustard dressing 281
    peanut sauce 80
    spicy hot sauce 289
    tomato pesto sauce 253
    yogurt garlic sauce 185
sauces for gnocchi
    blue cheese and walnut sauce 251
    fresh sage, rocket and fetta sauce 251
    grilled vegetable sauce 251
    thyme and cheese sauce 250
    tomato and basil sauce 250
sausage with puy lentils and mashed
    potatoes and pumpkin 165
sausages
    bangers and mash 161
    barbecued potato and sausage packet
        116
    potato and sausage soup 63
    sausage and bean casserole with
        potato and parsnip topping 134
    sausage casserole with green beans
        134
    sausage with puy lentils and mashed
        potatoes and pumpkin 165
scallops 225
    potato and celeriac purée with seared
        scallops and chorizo 225
scones 301
    potato scones 301
    potato scones with fetta 300
scurvy 12
seafood
    potato and celeriac purée with seared
        scallops and chorizo 225
    seafood hotpot with saffron and
        vegetables 212
    seafood pie with potato pastry 218
    see also fish; prawns
sesame and coriander potatoes 278
shepherd's pie 190
    tex-mex 158
skewers
    chimichurri pork skewers 146
    potato, bacon and leeks on rosemary
        skewers 282
smoked fish 226
    smoked fish hash with savoy cabbage
        230
    smoked fish and potato pie 226

soft potato rolls 302
Solanaceae family 12, 14
solanine 12, 14, 22
sole, grilled, with new potatoes 215
soufflés
    potato and cherry soufflés 313
    potato and pumpkin soufflé 263
    potato soufflés with parmesan and
        pancetta 39
soup
    borsch with beef 76
    chunky vegetable soup 56
    clam and leek chowder 64
    corn and kipper chowder 59
    creamy potato and chanterelle soup 71
    creamy potato and clam soup 64
    creamy sweetcorn and potato soup 70
    fish soup with spring vegetables 74
    fish and vegetable soup 74
    Moroccan sweet potato soup 56
    potato, bacon and spinach chowder 63
    potato and chervil soup 72
    potato and onion soup topped with
        garlic prawns 66
    potato and parmesan soup with bacon
        69
    potato and sausage soup 63
    potato soup with bacon gnocchi 69
    potato soup with watercress 73
    spicy lentil dal 60
    vichyssoise 66
Spanish tortilla, layered 35
spice-glazed mashed sweet potatoes 129
spiced garlic and ginger potatoes 178
spiced lamb pie with potato topping 122
spicy filo triangles 47
spicy lentil dal 60
spicy peanut dip 44
spicy pork and bacon pie with potato
    topping 123
spicy potato wedges, oven-baked 53
spicy potatoes with baked chicken pieces
    186
spicy vinaigrette 87
spinach 42
    coconut prawn and vegetable curry 229
    Florentine potatoes 285
    meatballs with spinach 168
    pork korma with potatoes and spinach
        147
    potato, bacon and spinach chowder 63
    potato and spinach cakes 39
    potato and spinach frittata 42
    spinach and cheese topping 291
    spinach, sweet potato and shiitake
        salad 106
    stir-fried sweet potatoes with spinach
        and spices 270
    veal schnitzel with spinach, potatoes
        and herbs 133
steak
    grilled steak with glazed potatoes 139
    pan-grilled steak and potatoes 130
    pepper steak with mashed potatoes
        and leeks 162

steaming, potatoes in their jackets 24
stews see casseroles; hotpots
stir-fried potatoes with lamb and ginger 193
stir-fried sweet potatoes with spinach and spices 270
storage 23
sugocasa 261
swedes, and vitamin C 56
sweet potatoes 11, 12, 21
    African lamb ragoût with okra 166
    chicken and sweet potato hash 185
    crunchy sweet potato rolls 305
    fish and vegetable soup 74
    mashed sweet potatoes with maple and orange glaze 129
    Moroccan sweet potato soup 56
    potato hash with mushrooms 184
    roasted vegetable crumble 243
    scones 301
    spice-glazed mashed sweet potatoes 129
    spinach, sweet potato and shiitake salad 106
    sweet potato, carrot and celeriac patties 41
    sweet potato curry 267
    sweet potato hash browns 41
    sweet potato risotto with crisp sage 48
    sweet potato rolls with sultanas 305
    sweet potato salad with mushrooms 106
    twice-baked stuffed sweet potatoes 294
    venison and mushroom pie with sweet potato topping 157
sweetcorn
    chicken and sweet potato hash 185
    corn and kipper chowder 59
    creamy sweetcorn and potato soup 70
    frittata with corn and capsicum 236
    tuna and sweetcorn topping 291
Swiss potato and nut cake 309
Swiss rösti with bacon 274

t
tarragon chicken with creamy vegetables 121
tex-mex shepherd's pie 158
Thai chicken curry 119
Thai fish cakes with lime and honey dip 196
tomatoes
    chickpea pie with parmesan and tomato mashed potatoes 258
    olive and tomato topping 291
    potato moussaka 261
    potato and tomato casserole 265
    tomato and chicken casserole 143
    tomato, garlic and basil dip 45
    tomato pesto sauce 253
torte
    potato and almond torte 306
    potato and cherry torte 310
    potato and sultana torte 307

tortillas 35
    layered Spanish tortilla 35
    potato and asparagus tortilla 51
    potato tortilla with fetta 254
    potato and zucchini tortilla 50
Toulouse sausages 165
trout
    foil-cooked trout with roast potatoes and cucumber sauce 200
    potato charlottes with smoked trout 223
tubers 12, 14, 21
tuna
    potato pizza with tuna, chorizo and black olives 203
    potato and tuna casserole 219
    potato and tuna salad 84
    salad niçoise 102
    tuna salad with green beans 84
    tuna and sweetcorn topping 291
turkey and potato salad with mustard dressing 94
turmeric 270

V
varieties
    all-purpose 20
    floury 17, 19, 22
    waxy 17, 18, 22
veal
    pan-fried potatoes with veal 131
    veal schnitzel with spinach, potatoes and herbs 133
vegetarian
    baked hash browns with parmesan 265
    bubble and squeak with poached eggs 254
    chickpea pie with parmesan and tomato mashed potatoes 258
    chunky vegetable soup 56
    mushroom and potato curry 266
    pasta with potato, beans and pesto 253
    pasta with potato and goat's cheese 252
    potato crêpes with herb curd cheese 262
    potato, fennel and zucchini frittata 237
    potato and leek quiche with chilli crust 244
    potato moussaka 261
    potato pie with tomatoes and olives 244
    potato and pumpkin gratin 257
    potato and pumpkin soufflé 263
    potato tart with asparagus 248
    potato and tomato casserole 265
    ravioli with potato filling 240
    roasted vegetable crumble 243
    sweet potato curry 267
    vegetable patties with coriander sauce 239
    vegetables with cheese crumble 260
    vegetables with melted brie dressing 247

venison and mushroom pie with sweet potato topping 157
vichyssoise 66
vitamin C 56

W
walnuts 12
watercress 73
    potato soup with 73
waxy varieties 17, 18, 22
wedges
    herb-crumbed fish with oven-baked wedges 207
    oven-baked spicy potato wedges 53
    potato wedges with herbs 179
winter squash see pumpkin

y
yams 21
yeast 302
yogurt garlic sauce 185

Z
zucchini 50
    barbecued potatoes and zucchini 276
    mushroom and zucchini topping 291
    potato and zucchini patties 41
    potato and zucchini tortilla 50
    potato and zucchini turnovers 115
    roast lamb with zucchini 176

Notes on the recipes

Terminology For readers in South Africa, the following are substitutions and alternative terms:

capsicum	sweet pepper
cumquat	kumquat
eggplant	aubergine, brinjal
oregano	origanum
shiitake mushrooms, fresh	rehydrated dried shiitake mushrooms
wholemeal	wholewheat
zucchini	courgette, baby marrow

Weights and measurements All cup and spoon measurements are level unless stated otherwise.
✳ Australian metric cup and spoon measurements have been used throughout; 1 cup equals 250 ml, 1 tablespoon equals 20 ml and 1 teaspoon equals 5 ml. Imperial cup and spoon measures are smaller – 1 cup is 235 ml (8 fl oz) and 1 tablespoon is 15 ml ($\frac{1}{2}$ fl oz) – so if using these measures, some adjustments may need to be made. For example, 1 metric cup = 1 imperial cup + 1 tablespoon, and 1 metric tablespoon = 1 imperial tablespoon + 1 teaspoon. ✳ A small variation in the weight or volume of most ingredients is unlikely to adversely affect a recipe. The exceptions are yeast, baking powder and bicarbonate of soda (baking soda); for these ingredients, adjust the recipe accordingly.

✳ Use either metric or imperial measurements; do not mix the two systems. ✳ Can sizes vary between countries and manufacturers; if the stated size is unavailable, use the nearest equivalent.

Ingredients All fruits and vegetables are medium sized unless the recipe says otherwise. ✳ You should peel any fruits and vegetables (such as apples, bananas, oranges, carrots, garlic, onions, parsnips, potatoes, pumpkin and sweet potatoes) that would normally be peeled before cooking. If they aren't meant to be peeled, the recipe will say so. ✳ All eggs are large. ✳ Pasta is dried unless it says otherwise. ✳ Nuts are raw and unsalted unless it says otherwise. ✳ Dairy foods (such as milk, cream, sour cream and yogurt) are full fat unless it says otherwise. Using a low-fat dairy product in a recipe written for a full-fat product may give a different result.

Oven temperatures These recipes have been written for regular ovens; if you have a convection (fan-forced) oven, reduce the temperature by 20°C (35°F).

Special dietary concerns Certain people (pregnant women, elderly people, or those with compromised immune systems) are advised to avoid some foods, including but not limited to raw eggs, soft cheese, shellfish and raw cured fish. If in doubt, consult your health practitioner.

Book code GR 1376/IC
Product code 041 3851